Architectural Guide
Almaty

Architectural Guide
Almaty

Edda Schlager

001 E

091 E

070 D

062 D 054 D 076 D 038 C 051 C

037 C

081 D

063 D

097 E

033 C

099 E

ҚАЗАҚ ССР ҒЫЛЫМ АКАДЕМИЯСЫ
АКАДЕМИЯ НАУК КАЗАХСКОЙ ССР

097 E

063 D

054 D

078 D

059 D

054 D

053 D

095 E

066 D

061 D

Kcell

098 E

078 D

057 D

058 D

065 D

ОТАНЫМЫЗ — БІР, МЕМЛЕКЕТІМІЗ — БІР, ХАЛҚЫМЫЗ — БІР!

082 D

112 E

090 D

098 E

092 E

103 E

076 D

093 E

082 D

Contents

Through Four Neighbourhoods in Almost Two Decades: How I Became an Almatinka

Edda Schlager

When I came to Almaty, Nazarbayev Avenue was still called 'Furmanova', there was a petrol station on the corner with Al-Farabi Avenue, and Nurly-Tau was just being built. There were still *marshrutkas* (minivans operating as small buses) and trams ran on Frunze Street. Ramstor was *the* place to go for western groceries; Mega Centre, Dostyk Plaza, and Mart Mall had not yet even been built. To go online, you had to scratch a number code off a plastic card and then surf the internet very slowly via modem using your prepaid data volume. There was no Coffeedelia, no Marrone Rosso, no Daridjani. Instead, the smell of the Rakhat Chocolate Factory wafted over the neighbourhood at the Green Bazaar; the *barakholka* (flea market) on Severnoye

Koltso was the place to stock up on everything you needed, from clothes to potting soil to carpets. I carried my 35mm films to a photo shop on ulitsa Pravdy opposite Narkhoz University and picked them up developed a few days later. You would flag down a taxi from the side of the road – there was no ordering by app – even at 3 am for a trip to the airport. The junction of Al-Farabi Avenue and Navoi Street was a roundabout, and Al-Farabi could be crossed on foot; the First President's Park did not yet exist. The presidential residence, though, was still standing, as were the Alatau Cinema, Zhetisu Hotel, and Baikonur Cinema in Orbita. The exchange rate of the tenge to the US dollar was 1:130, and I knew practically nothing about Kazakhstan.

Arrival in Samal

Almaty was an unknown organism to me, whose language I did not understand and which could spit me out at any moment if I didn't keep up. 'Ostanovka bar ma?' – 'Anyone for the next stop?' – the conductor on the bus would shout in a mixture of Kazakh and Russian over the heads of the packed passengers in their damp, steaming jackets. The fare of 25 tenge would already have been handed to the conductor earlier

Rakhat, a traditional chocolate factory, has been producing confectionery since 1942.

with the help of the same grim-faced passengers, and the change came back the same way. And even when I arrived at my stop, I sometimes kept on going because I was afraid of shouting 'Yest!' too loudly or because I didn't know how to ask people to make room for me to get off. In the first few days my Almaty was a dark, low, cloudy Almaty, an early February Almaty, with smog in the air, but seemingly far less bad than today in my memory. There was slippery slush on the streets, and sometimes I walked from the Green Bazaar to the Palace of Pioneers despite the icy cold, because, as an introvert, I wasn't strong enough to cope with the strenuous situation on the bus.

Deutsche Allgemeine Zeitung, where I was doing the internship for which I had come to Kazakhstan, had its office in the Green Bazaar. This newspaper has since 1966 been the organ of Russian-Germans in Kazakhstan – the descendants of those exiled from the Volga and Crimea to the steppes when Stalin deported them to the farthest reaches of the Soviet Union from

Ramstor in Samal in 2006

Letter boxes in an apartment building

the end of the 1930s forwards to prevent them collaborating with the Germans. Opposite the Palace of Pioneers, I stayed with a Russian-German woman in her 50s who shared her three-room flat in a nine-storey prefabricated block from the 1980s with her daughter, dog, and cat, a student, and me.

The flat was small and cramped – in the kitchen there was a table with the obligatory oilcloth tablecloth and tiny stools without backrests; you could hardly turn around – and I only found out later that this area was considered upmarket. Anyone who owned a flat here in Samal was not badly off, well off, or middle-class. Still, my landlady was unhappy and always in a bad mood; the economic upheavals of perestroika, which had just

been more or less overcome, were still fresh in her mind. After a few weeks, she suggested – without giving me any option of saying 'no' – that I look for a new place to live. At the time I had already experienced my first – noticeable but harmless – earthquake and had timidly explored the area around the National Museum, Republic Square, Panfilov Park, and the Arbat, visited the even more inhospitable Astana, and learnt to speak a little – *chut-chut* – in Russian.

Friendships in Taugul

In Taugul I stayed with friends of friends, who rented me their apartment in a prefabricated building at an affordable price, including a family connection since

Tram depot with retired vehicles, some originally from Germany, in 2005

2005

2006

View looking south east from the very same point at the intersection of Navoi and Ryskulbekova streets in the Taugul micro-district

2007

2008

2011

2024

Commemorative plaque for the Soviet functionary Gibadulla Myrzagaliev, a former minister who lived on Tulebayev Street from 1973 until his death in 2000

they always preferred to shower there on Sundays rather than in their small, one-storey, stove-heated house that their parents had built a few minutes' walk from the apartment. I shared many interests with this family of geographers who had travelled Europe. They helped

me with the foreign language and all the other practicalities of being a foreigner in an unfamiliar place – and they became my friends. Sitting in the front row of the Navoi with a view of the mountains, I saw the *chastny sektor* ('private sector') opposite being demolished, Almaty growing upwards – and the mountains disappearing behind new buildings. The sword of Damocles which was the threat of their house being demolished also hung over my friends. But then the financial crisis saved them. They still live in their little house today, and their now grown-up son and his own family have moved into my former flat next door.

During my time in Taugul, I felt more and more at home in Almaty. I explained to other expats who lived in the centre or in large houses with gardens south of Al-Farabi Avenue and felt sorry for me when they heard that I had to travel from one of the distant Soviet dormitory districts to meetings in the city centre that it was no more than 15 minutes by bus to the opera or Kasteyev Gallery. This was true – if there were no traffic jams on Dzhandosova and Timiryazeva. But there were more and more of them, especially when there was construction work going on somewhere.

By now I was working as a freelance journalist, had travelled to all the neighbouring countries of Central Asia, and really appreciated coming 'home' when I returned to Almaty. Now I was explaining to

Panfilov Street, the most popular boulevard in Almaty after the Arbat

taxi drivers who themselves had come to Almaty from Taraz or Kyzylorda only a few months earlier how best to get from A to B and what shortcuts to take to avoid traffic jams. I could jump back and forth between old and new street names with virtuosity: Mira and Zheltoksan, Lenina and Dostyk, Kalinina and Kabanbai Batyra.

On to Golden Square

Then I moved on to Golden Square – the historical centre of Almaty, built from the 1930s to the 1970s and stretching from Zheltoksan Street to Zenkov Street and from Gogol to Satpayev. Tulebayeva, where the legendary film *The Needle* starring Viktor Tsoi was shot in the late 1980s and where a monument to Tsoi now stands, became my home neighbourhood.

The broken traffic light, which emitted a constantly changing but annoyingly regular signal on warm spring nights, getting closer and then farther away, and which at first kept me awake, turned out not to be the result of a technical defect but the mating call of the Eurasian scops owl, which is at home in Almaty's lush green spaces and parks. The call of the little owl – whose Russian name *splyushka* comes from the fact that it sounds like it's calling 'splyu, splyu' ('I'm sleeping, I'm sleeping') – became my sound of the city, like the cheeky call of the ever-present flocks of mynas, the Afghan starlings.

During the Soviet era the spacious flats on Tulebayeva were mainly occupied by officials, scientists from the nearby Academy of Sciences, artists, writers, and other intellectuals; this was a neighbourhood of short distances and small, meticulously kept parks. A few blocks away was the house of Dinmukhamed Kunayev, First Secretary of the Communist Party of Kazakhstan until 1986 and the country's political leader. The house is now a museum. Almost every building here has a plaque commemorating a prominent Soviet figure who lived in it.

Despite the authoritarian political situation in Kazakhstan, the long presidency of Nursultan Nazarbayev, which made Kazakhstan's population as a whole weary and increasingly dissatisfied, and the frequent changes of Almaty's mayor, always

Nedelka Fountain in spring, before the water is turned on. The fountain was built in 1972 and its seven arches are symbols of the days of the week.

appointed by the president and always a pawn in Kazakhstan's overall balance of power, the quality of life in Almaty improved; the city became a centre of attraction for many who moved here from rural areas. Streets were widened; new apartment blocks were built. But there were also more restaurants, digital apps made life more convenient, and buses ran on natural gas and became more punctual.

In 2017 Panfilov Street, along which the old government district was built in the 1930s and which was one of the centre's smaller thoroughfares, was transformed into a pedestrian zone from Kabanbai Batyr Street to Zhibel Zholy Street. Together with other projects for reorganising the pedestrian infrastructure of Timiryazev Street, Zhibek Zholy Street, and Dostyk Avenue, this cost the city 6.3 billion tenge, about $20 million at the time. The authorities were heavily criticised. However, the new promenade on Panfilov Street has been welcomed by the city's residents and visitors.

The new system of one-way streets in the centre of Almaty was established after initial protests. There were now fewer parking spaces, and they had to be paid for. Electric scooters replaced bicycles. The tram disappeared. And I moved again, to a four-storey *khrushchevka*, where I felt relatively safe during the recurring small earthquakes to which I had almost become accustomed. *Khrushchevkas*, prefabricated buildings built in the 1960s and 1970s on the orders of Nikita Khrushchev, the then Soviet leader, to provide quick and cheap housing, were supposed to be earthquake-proof.

At Nedelka in the heart of the city

If I had to name my favourite place to live in Almaty, it would be here: near Nedelka Fountain and the little park by the opera house. This area combines buildings from all eras of Almaty's urban development in just a few hectares: next to the opera are some of the city's few remaining Constructivist buildings – the first House of Government, the old General Post Office (now: Hotel Almaty), a reminder of how small the city once was if this modest but elegantly built hotel was the city's top address; and, of course, here too we find Stolichny Tsentr (Capital Centre), despised by many for destroying the historical cityscape but which has itself become part of the city's architectural history.

It was here that I experienced the most recent upheavals in Kazakh history, events which preoccupied me as a journalist but also as a person: Nazarbayev's resignation in 2019 and his strategic move of appointing Kassym-Jomart Tokayev as his successor in a bid to keep the reins in his own hands. The small hope cherished by many that Kazakhstan might become more democratic after all is now generally regarded in Kazakhstan as having been in vain. With the change of president, a new *akim* (head of local government) took over the city's destiny, and a new chief architect was appointed.

In January 2022 the government was almost overthrown. Across Kazakhstan 238 people died in the bloody riots and security crackdown; around 4000 were injured and 9000 arrested. I was in Germany at the time, constantly on the phone, trying to reach friends in Kazakhstan and

to understand the power struggle between the forces surrounding the old ex-president and his successor. When I returned to Almaty, where the clashes between demonstrators, rioters, and security forces had been the most violent, people were still paralysed by what had happened a few days after Tokayev had regained control,. Everyone wanted to talk about their experiences during the days of chaos.

The buildings on Republic Square were badly damaged by fire and gunfire, including the *akimat*, the presidential residence, and office buildings on the square's north edge. Over the next few months, the *akimat* was rebuilt; it reopened a year later. The office buildings were repainted. The presidential residence was demolished – a political decision. Since the events of 'Bloody January', Nazarbayev, the formerly all-powerful president, and his family have been stripped of many privileges and political posts. The capital, which was renamed 'Nur-Sultan' in Nazarbayev's honour after his resignation in 2019, was given back the name of 'Astana'. But the former president is still present in Almaty. His handprint on the Golden Man stele in Republic Square is still touched by tourists and wedding couples. The First President's Park has not been renamed, and Nazarbayev Avenue is to keep its name. The discontent of the Kazakh people has not diminished. But soon after January 2022, Almaty returned to its usual rhythm. More and more people from all over Kazakhstan are moving into the city's growing suburbs. The cranes on construction sites around city never stop, and new massive residential high-rises are being built. At Golden Square the more affluent enjoy the city's relaxed lifestyle.

Almaty in my luggage

Although my time in Almaty has come to an end, I still feel at home there. Every trip back is a return to friends, to the familiar, to an environment where I feel like a fish in water. Here I have become an *almatinka*, a citizen of Almaty who prefers this vibrant, chaotic, relaxed city not only to – sorry, Astana – the capital but also to any other city in Central Asia.

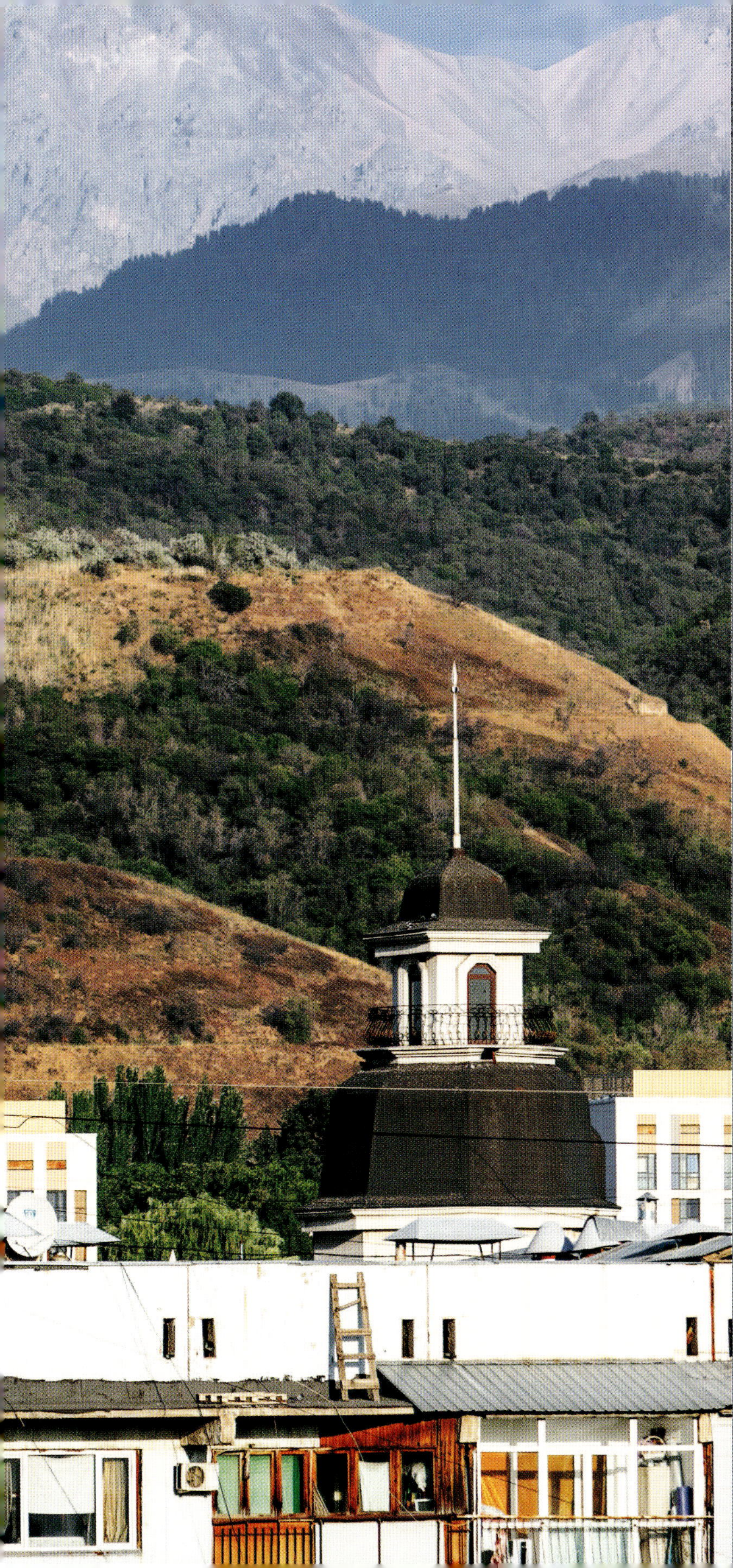

Abai Avenue, looking west, mid 1960s

Alma-Ata, 1968

From Military Fortress to Polycentric City: 170 Years of Urban Planning in Almaty

Edda Schlager

Although the first settlements at the foot of the northernmost spurs of the Tien Shan, a fertile region with favourable climatic conditions, date back to the Bronze Age, Almaty is a young city only about 170 years old. For centuries horse-riding peoples, such as the Saka and Scythians, as well as nomadic shepherds, populated the steppes to the north of present-day Almaty and the green hills to the south, which quickly rise to the high mountains. The first archaeological finds in and around Almaty date from the twelfth to eighth centuries BC. The remains of a settlement of Saks from the sixth to third centuries BC were found near Terenkara Stream, north east of Almaty, between the old and new roads to Chilik. The inhabitants raised livestock, practised crafts, and built permanent dwellings for humans and animals. In spring and summer they moved around the countryside with their herds of cattle, returning to these winter quarters in autumn.

On the remains of history

Before the Middle Ages numerous settlements had already been established in the region of present-day Almaty. Remains of these settlements – irrigation systems, clay ovens, and everyday objects, such as ceramic vessels – have been found in the city's micro-district of Gorny Gigant, on the east bank of the River Esentai (formerly: Vesnovka), at the confluence of the Esentai and Malaya Almatinka rivers near the village of Otegen Batyr (until 1999: Energetichesky), north of Almaty, and in the area of the Botanical Garden.

This region was on a northern branch of the Silk Road, which ran along the north edge of the Alatau mountain range, virtually along the route traced by today's A2 motorway, from the Kazakh-Uzbek border near Tashkent via Shymkent, Taraz, and Almaty to Khorgos on the Kazakh-Chinese border. The region owes its economic and cultural boom to this ancient trade route. When the Turkish-Islamic Kara-Khanids ruled southern Central Asia from 942 to 1212, rapidly growing cities were built here. Roads were paved – as was later discovered in Talgar; aqueducts were built; and baths were constructed. The name 'Almatu', which denoted a cluster of settlements in the area of the modern city of Almaty and appeared on coins and in Arabic and Chinese records, is also documented for the first time in this period.

Mongol and Timurid campaigns in the thirteenth and fourteenth centuries destroyed these towns and settlements, and in the seventeenth and eighteenth centuries the Dzungar cavalry prevented urban development. Throughout all these warlike raids and conquests the Semirechye region between the Ili and Tentek rivers was inhabited by nomadic and semi-nomadic tribes, the ancestors of today's Kazakhs.

Petroglyphs from the Bronze Age at Tamgaly near Almaty are early signs of people living in this region.

Almaty: Etapy urbanisatsiy, 2008

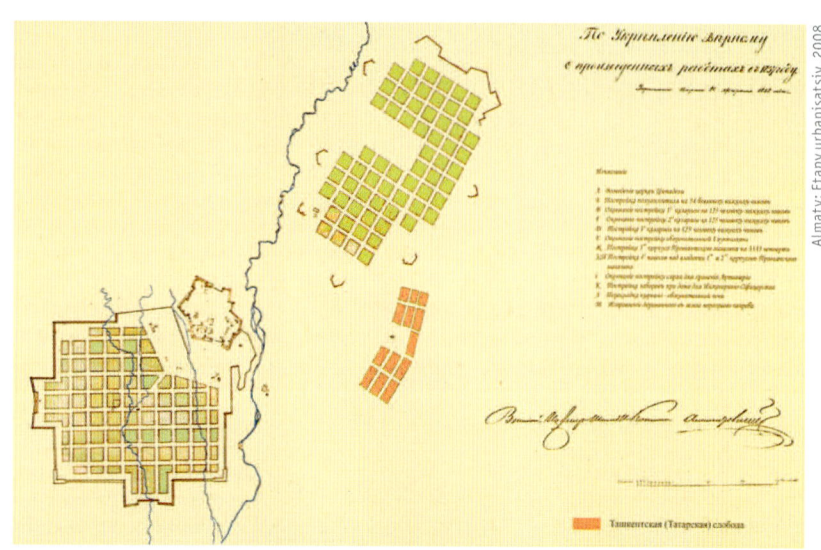

Plan of Vernoye Fortress (centre left), Bolshaya (bottom left)
and Malaya Stanitsa (top right), and the Tatarskaya slobodka (orange), around 1858

Plan of Verny in 1884 by Zhukovsky. Russian State Historical Archive (RGIA), f. 1293,
op. 168. Semirechenskaya oblast. D.Z.

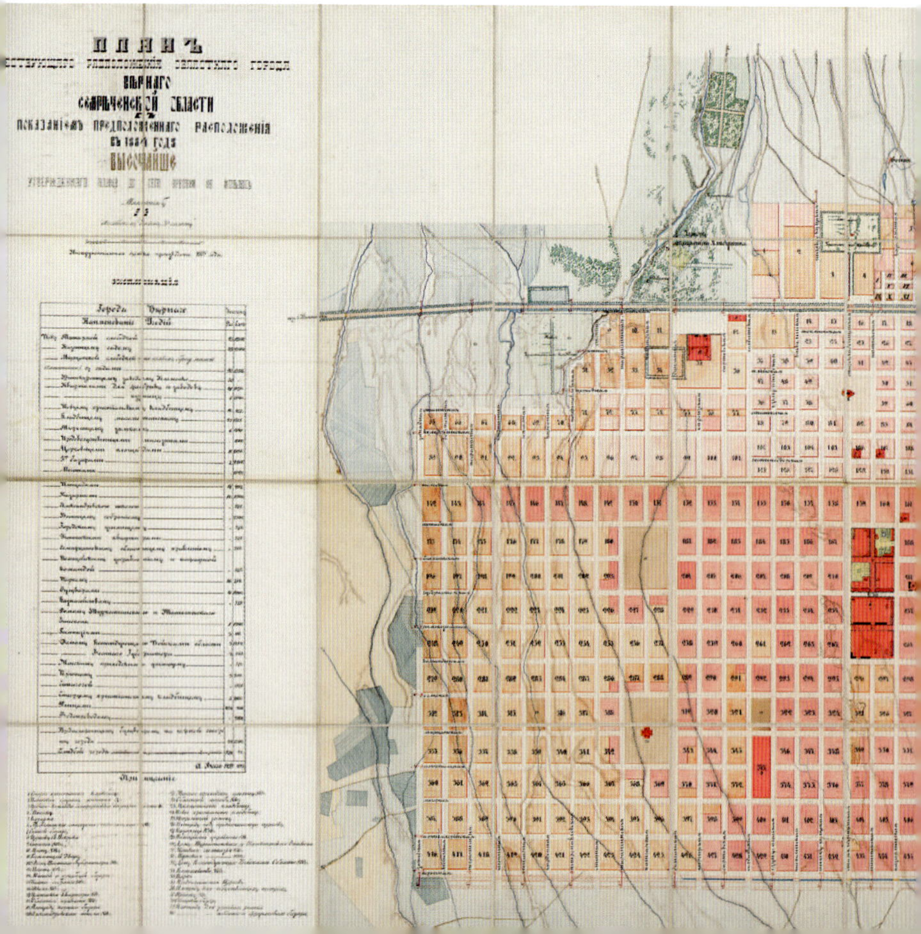

A fortress for the Russian Empire

The development of the city of Almaty as we know it today is closely linked to the Russian Empire. In the nineteenth century the empire began to expand into Central Asia. To secure the new territories against the southern Kokand Khanate and the Dzungars, the Russian military built Zailiyskoye Fortress on the left bank of the Malaya Almatinka River in 1854. In 1855 the fortress was renamed 'Vernoye' and the village of Bolshaya Stanitsa was founded, bordering the military complex to the south west. Its rectangular network of streets still dominates the centre of Almaty today. Siberian Cossack families and Russian peasants settled here.

The head of the military post, Major Mikhail Peremyshelsky, wrote as follows to the Governor General of West Siberia, describing the founding of the fortress: 'Having examined the settlements and the valley between them, we found farmland crisscrossed by irrigation ditches, pastures, and hay meadows, all far better than the areas near Issyk and Talgar,

so we proposed this place as the site of the future settlement.' According to Peremyshelsky, there was enough building material nearby for the construction of the fortress, and good timber and granite in the mountains. Today nothing remains of the fortress itself. But there is a memorial column where the structure once stood, between Tatibekov and Copernicus streets.

The first development plan was drawn up in the mid-1850s but was never officially confirmed due to the frequently changing and disputed administrative responsibilities for the town of Verny. This first plan extended the village of Bolshaya Stanitsa and continued the structure of 100-to-250-metre-long blocks of houses that make the city centre so pleasant for pedestrians today. To the east of Bolshaya Stanitsa, Tatarskaya (or Tashkentskaya) Slobodka was founded in 1857; this is a district that attracted merchants from Semipalatinsk (now Oskemen), Kazan, and the Tobolsk, Tyumen, and Turkestan regions, as well as Kazakh nomads. And in 1861 settlers founded the

The house of the bishop in Pervogildeyskaya (now Zenkov) Street.
View looking north east, before 1887

village of Malaya Stanitsa, north east of the fortress on the right, east, bank of the Malaya Almatinka. In 1867 the new, fast-growing town, which became the administrative centre of the newly formed Semirechye oblast, was named 'Verny'.

That year, the Russian architect Pavel Zenkov, a native of Tobolsk, answering the call of the military governor of Semirechye Oblast (Region), moved to Verny with his family, including his then four-year-old son, Andrey, who would also go on to make his mark on the town as an architect. From then on, Pavel Zenkov, as a regional architect, devoted himself to town planning and developing a master plan, together with the military engineer Nikolay Krishtanovsky.

Under his aegis St Sophia's Church was moved from Bolshaya Stanitsa to the new Malaya Stanitsa and renamed 'Kazan Cathedral' (004), and the house of the landscape gardener Eduard Baum at 68a Amangeldy Street was built in 1880. When Verny came under civil administration in 1877, Zenkov was elected its first mayor by the city assembly, a post he held until 1888.

Earthquakes destroy the town

On 8 June (28 May by the Julian calendar, whose use was rescinded by the Bolsheviks in 1918) 1887, at about half past four in the morning, the city was shaken by a violent earthquake. In the newspaper

The governor's house on the corner of Gubernatorskaya and Kolpakskaya streets (now Kazybek bi Street and Dostyk Avenue), before 1887. The main façade faces north.

Merchants' houses on Pervogildeyskaya (now Zenkov) Street. View looking south east from the junction with Torgovaya Street (today: Zhibek Zholy Street), before 1887

Turkestanskie Vedomosti, Nikolay Karazin, an eyewitness, recalled: 'The first tremors were soon followed by others, even stronger and more prolonged, which shook the ground so violently that it was almost impossible to stand on one's feet, all accompanied by an underground rumbling. This was combined with the rumbling and crashing of collapsing buildings and the roaring of animals that had broken loose and were rushing wildly in different directions.' The city was shrouded in thick clouds of dust and appeared to have been levelled, Karazin said. 'Half-dressed residents crossed themselves in the middle of the street, waiting in horror for their deaths.' More than 300 people died, and more than 1700 buildings,

mostly of brick but also including about 800 wooden structures, were completely destroyed. Almost the entire town lay in ruins. What remained was almost exclusively wooden houses. One house near the junction of then Gubernatorskaya (later: Sovetskaya, today Kazybek bi) Street and then Saratovskaya (later: Uzbekskaya Street; today: Seyfullin Avenue) was spared (014). It belonged to Ivan Lutmanov, the town's deputy mayor, who left it to his boss, Zenkov, after the earthquake.

This earthquake, which had an estimated magnitude of 7.3 on the Richter scale, was not the only one to almost completely destroy the city. Just two years later, another earthquake of the same magnitude struck,

The governor's house south of the governor's garden (now: 28 Panfilov Guardsmen Park) on 28 May 1887, after an earthquake nearly completely destroyed Verny

К. БОГДАНОВИЧЪ, И. КАРКЪ, Д. МУШКЕТОВЪ. Земл. 1910 г. въ сѣверн. цѣпяхъ Тянъ-Шаня.

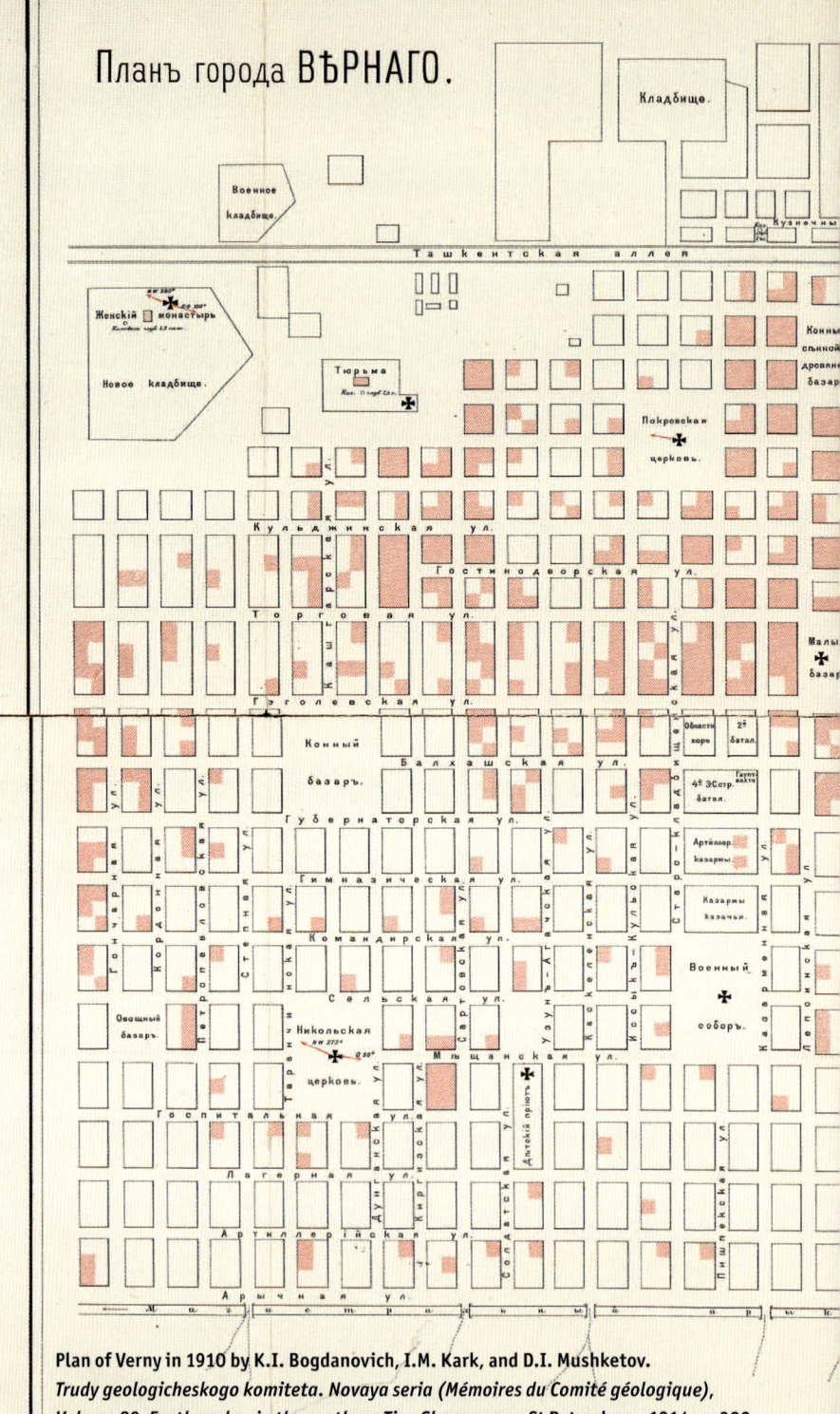

Планъ города ВѢРНАГО.

Plan of Verny in 1910 by K.I. Bogdanovich, I.M. Kark, and D.I. Mushketov.
Trudy geologicheskogo komiteta. Novaya seria (Mémoires du Comité géologique),
Volume 89. *Earthquakes in the northern Tien Shan ranges,* St Petersburg, 1914, p. 302

Табл. II.

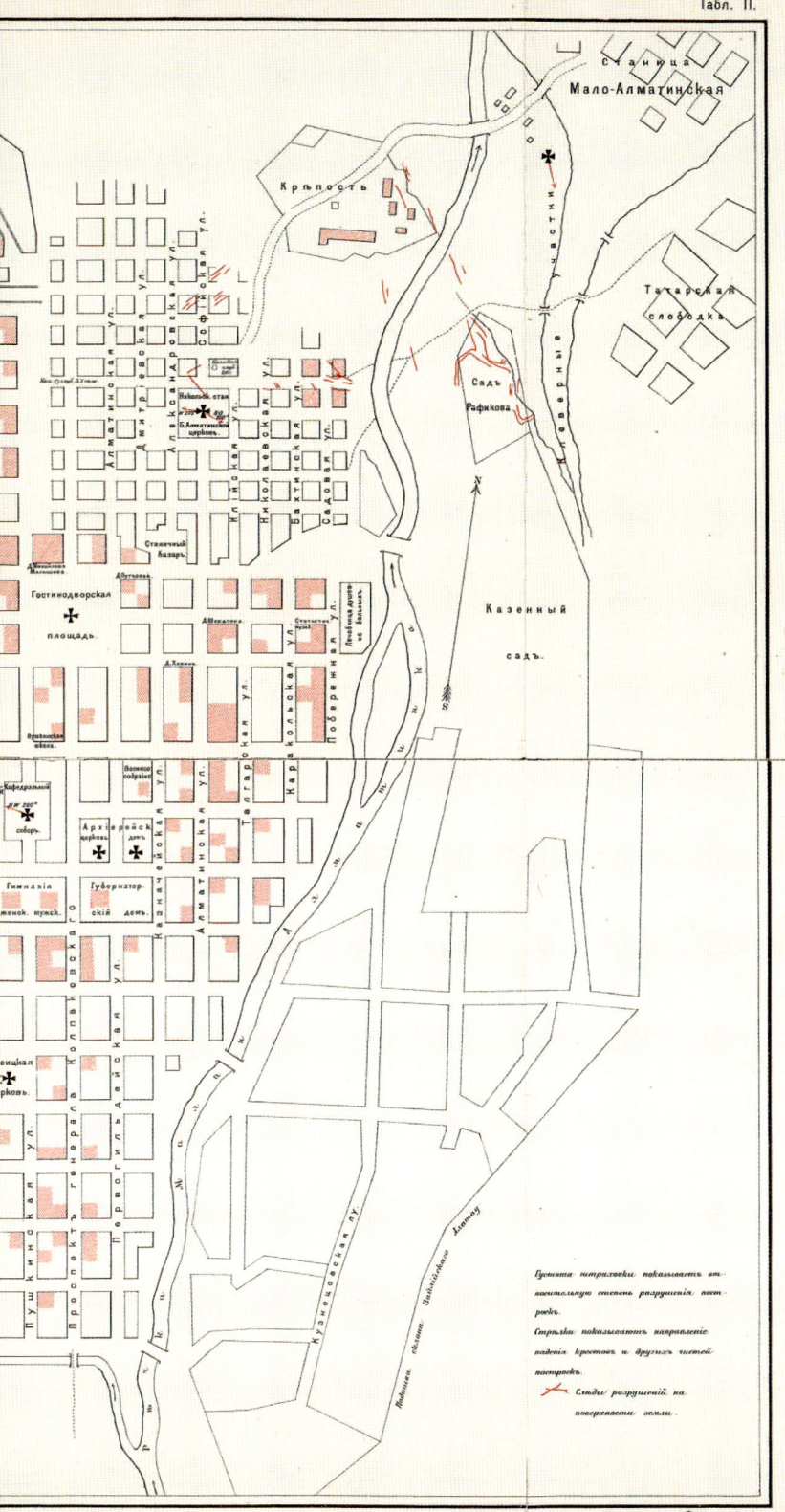

Крѣпость

Татарская
слободка

Садъ
Рафикова

Казенный

садъ.

Гостинодворская

площадь.

Кафедральный

соборъ.

Архіерейскій
церковь. домъ.

Гимназія
женск. мужск.

Губернатор-
скій домъ.

Гусента штриховки показываетъ от-
носительную степень разрушенія построекъ.

Стрѣлки показываютъ направленіе
паденія крестовъ и другихъ частей
построекъ.

Слѣды разрушеній на
поверхности земли.

Kapalskaya Street (today: Kunayev Street), looking north, 1910

although its epicentre was further away in Chilik, causing less destruction in Verny. However, on 3 January 1911 (22 December 1910 under the Julian calendar), the Kemin earthquake, with its epicentre in the Chon-Kemin valley in present-day Kyrgyzstan and a magnitude of around eight on the Richter scale, shook the entire region. In Verny more than 450 people died and more than 770 buildings were destroyed.

Earthquake-resistant construction based on experience

After the earthquakes of the 1880s, people began to build earthquake-proof structures, at least for important buildings. Andrey Zenkov was one of the pioneers of this approach. The Ascension Cathedral (001), one of the buildings he

designed, withstood the great earthquake of 1911. He later recalled: 'With its grandiose height, the cathedral was a flexible structure. The bell tower swayed like the top of a tall tree and behaved like a bendable beam.'

In 1913 the Russian Geographical Society wrote of Verny in one of its publications: 'The streets are wide and well laid out, but they are not kept clean and are covered with a thick layer of dust that rises with every movement of carriages and even pedestrians. In autumn the dust turns into unbearable mud.'

Soviet takeover and designation as capital

According to the first comprehensive census taken in the Russian Empire, the city

A house completely destroyed by the earthquake of 22 December 1910

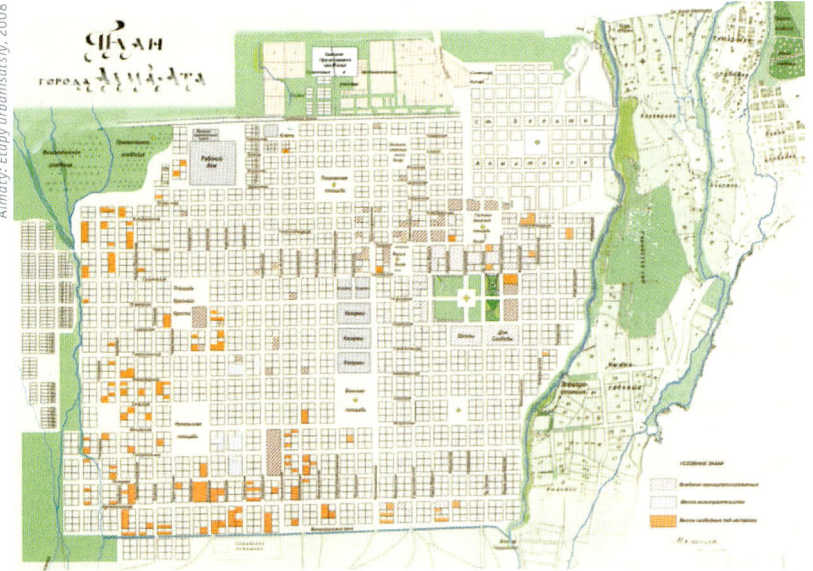

Almaty: Etapy urbanisatsiy, 2008

Plan of the young capital Alma-Ata in 1936

had 22,700 inhabitants in 1897. By 1915 this figure had risen to 36,600. However, Verny was considered backward and provincial. During the Soviet era the city received a huge boost. After the revolution of 25 October (7 November under the Gregorian calendar) 1917, Soviet power was established not only in Russia but also in the more remote regions of the former empire of the tsars. For many merchants, landowners, and members of the former regime in Verny, this meant expropriation and the loss of their property. For example, the Gabdulvalievs' mansion (017) was nationalised and used by the new Soviet authorities.

Even before the founding of the Soviet Union in 1922, Verny and the Semirechye region had become part of the Turkestan Autonomous Soviet Republic (TASSR). After several territorial transfers, this was renamed 'the Kazakh Autonomous Socialist Soviet Republic (KASSR)' in 1925 and 'the Kazakh Socialist Soviet Republic (KSSR)' in 1935. The latter lasted until the collapse of the Soviet Union in 1991, when Kazakhstan became independent.

Verny was renamed in 1921. The new name was a reversion to a variant of the medieval 'Almatu'. Whether this had anything to do with 'alma', the Turkic word for apple, is not entirely clear. However, the Soviet authorities created the artificial word 'Alma-Ata', based on Kazakh and usually translated as 'father of apples'. In 1929 Alma-Ata became the capital of the KASSR, replacing Kyzylorda, and was connected to the Turkestan-Siberian Railway (Turksib) with the construction of Almaty-1 Station (075), which led to a veritable building boom.

The first Soviet master plan (1937)

In 1937 the architects Anatoly Repkin and Yosef Gurevich drew up the city's first Soviet 'general plan'. As understood by the Soviets, a general plan (*generalny plan* or *genplan* in Russian) corresponds to a master plan. However, whereas in many countries the master plan is an informal planning instrument for urban development that must be incorporated into zoning plans, development plans, and municipal statutes through legally prescribed procedures, in the former Soviet Union the general plan was a binding legal document that was passed into law. In many former Soviet republics, including Kazakhstan, this is still the case today.

This first legally binding master plan for the city of Alma-Ata provided for a significant expansion of the pre-revolutionary road network. At the time the city's limits ran roughly along the Bolshaya Almatinka River, which comes from the Almarasan Valley, in the west, the

Alma-Ata, 1968

The area around the Central Stadium in the 1960s. View looking south east

Malaya Almatinka in the east, Tashkentsky (now: Raiymbek) Avenue in the north, and Timiryazev Street in the south. In the 1930s the Government District with the first House of Government (020) and

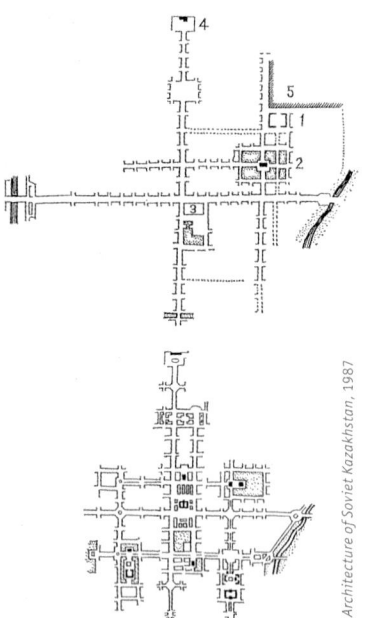

Architecture of Soviet Kazakhstan, 1987

Layouts of the central district planning development

1 Bazaar
2 Ascension Cathedral and city garden
3 Square
4 Almaty-2 Station
5 Bolshaya Stanitsa

numerous other government buildings was built between today's Panfilov Street and what used to be Vokzalnaya Street (today: Abylai-Khan Avenue), which ran south from Almaty-2 Station (032) to Arychnaya Street with the main canal (Magistralny Aryk), today's Abai Avenue. Earthquake-resistant construction became mandatory for administrative and public buildings; experience at the turn of the century had raised awareness of this issue, and technology had improved considerably. Brick and reinforced-concrete buildings of up to four storeys were permitted, as well as six- and seven-storey buildings on main roads. The wide avenues and green spaces that still characterise the city centre today were not merely ornamental but provided protection from collapsing buildings and a means of escape in the event of disaster. The extensive green belts along the rivers and canals also played an important role in protecting the city centre from mud slides, such as the one that hit the city in 1921.

Post-war years and the second master plan (1950)

In the post-war years, around 1950, the city's second master plan was drawn up by Lengiprogor (Leningrad State Institute of Urban Planning) and the architects D.D. Baragin, I.I. Byelotserkovsky, and

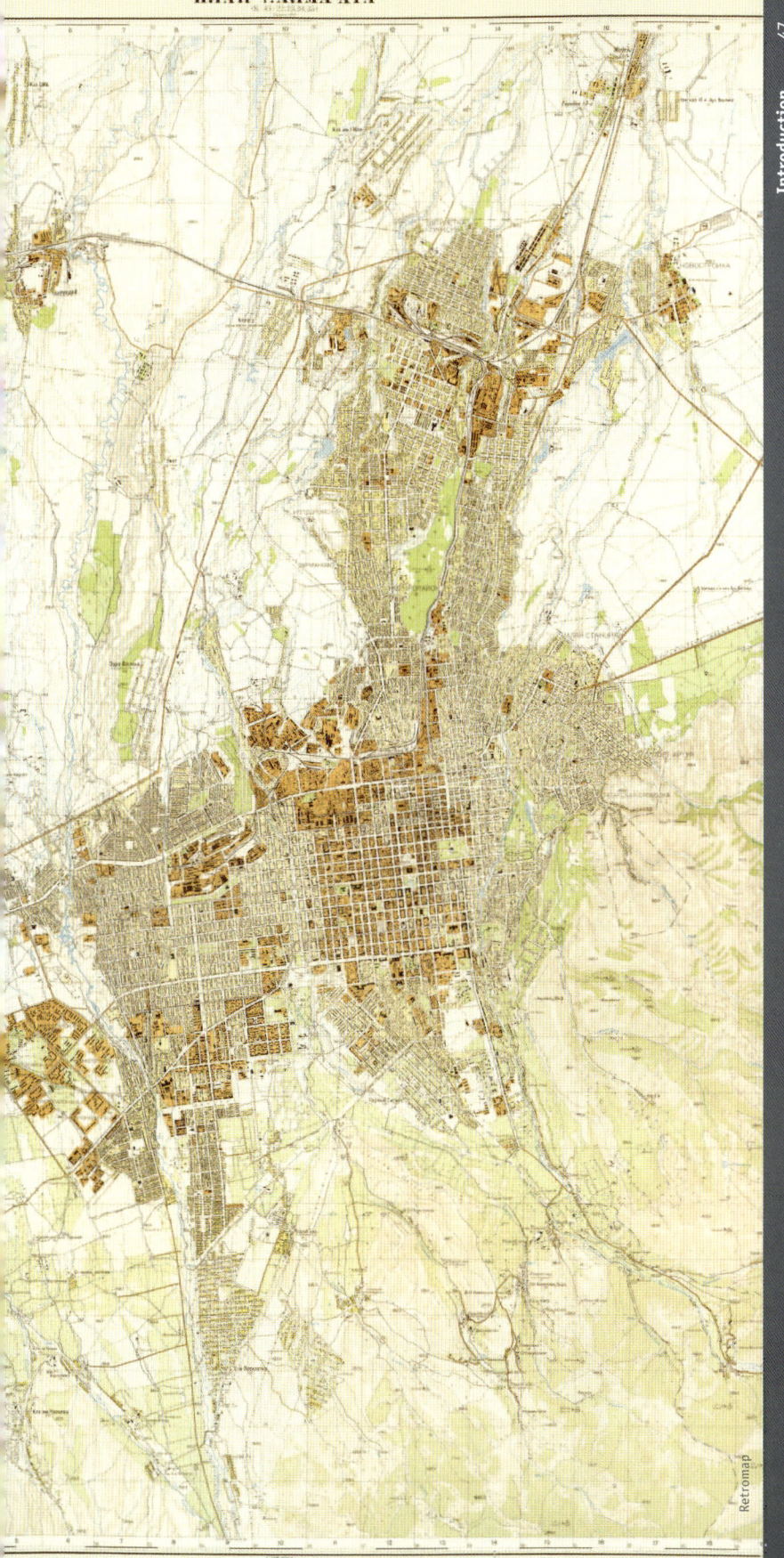

ГЕНЕРАЛЬНЫЙ ШТАБ

ПЛАН г. АЛМА-АТА

Retromap

1:25 000

Alma-Ata, 1968

View looking south to north on Abylai Khan (then Kommunistichesky) Avenue in 1967, with the building of the Central Committee of the Communist Party of the Kazakh SSR (037)

L.K. Vertousov. This provided for the development of other main roads. For example, Uzbek Street (now: Seyfullin Avenue) was to be extended to Almaty-1 Station (075). The Kargalinisk Tract (now: Dzhandosov Street), running diagonally from the centre to the south west, was to link the new micro-districts being built in the south west to the central part of the city. In addition, bypass roads were built to the east and north, connecting to the motorway to Talgar.

Rapid growth and the third master plan (1963)

With the population growing rapidly and housing being built in new micro-districts,

Sándor Bojár

Abai Square in 1968 with the Palace of the Republic (053) under construction

a third master plan was needed in 1963. Once again, Lengiprogor was in charge, along with the leading urban planners G.A. Bobovich and Toleu Basenov, both of whom had also made their mark on the city as architects and authors of numerous building designs. The focus was on development of new urban areas in the west, preservation and reconstruction of building fabric in older districts, and exploration of the potential for future development of urban areas in the east.

The third master plan divided the city into four planning districts. Three of these were main construction areas located south of Tashkentsky (now: Raiymbek) Avenue: Central District, east of the Vesnovka (now: Esentai) River; Exhibition District, named after Atakent Exhibition Centre, between Bolshaya Almatinka and Vesnovka rivers; and Western District, west of the Bolshaya Almatinka. The fourth district, north of Tashkentsky Avenue, categorised as an area of high seismic risk, was planned as an area of low-density housing.

Reality overtakes planning

The third master plan was based on a 25-year planning horizon. It foresaw that Alma-Ata would have 750,000 inhabitants by the end of the 1980s. In 1969, however, the actual population was already just under 700,000. In 1967 Almatygiprogor State Institute of Urban Planning was established to plan and implement urban development measures. Shortly afterwards, the institute began work on another master plan. Among other things, this focused on

Architecture and urban development, 1998

Master plan of Alma-Ata, covering the period from 1978 to 1990, by Almatygiprogor

the city's main transport axes, including Seyfullin and Abai avenues, as well as Raiymbek Avenue with a new connection to the airport.

Lenin (now Dostyk) Avenue was developed in the years that followed. The iconic ensemble of the Palace of the Republic (053) and Hotel Kazakhstan (054) on Abai Square at the intersection of Lenin and Abai Avenues was created. Freed from the constraints of efficiency and cost-cutting, Soviet Modernism integrated Kazakh national forms and technology and particularly excelled in design of public spaces. Alma-Ata was given a Soviet-Central Asian face of its own but always in keeping with the guidelines from Moscow that applied throughout the Soviet Union at the time.

Peak of Soviet urban planning; the fourth master plan (1978)

Almatygiprogor drafted the city's fourth master plan, which was adopted in 1978 and oversaw development until 1990 under the direction of Adambek Kapanov, V.S. Gershberg, V.B. Ignatyev, S.E. Isanbayeva, and others. The urban challenges faced by the growing metropolis were immense. They included the functional zoning of the city into residential, industrial, commercial, educational, and public areas and the need to create additional space for large new residential

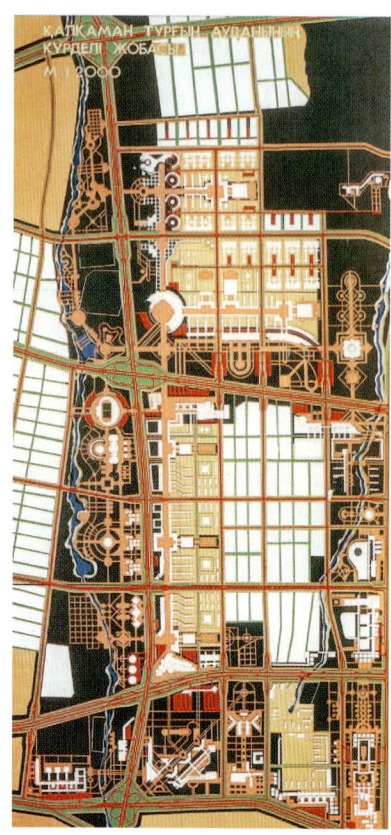

Detailed planning of Kalkaman District in the city's west, by Almatygenplan

districts, as well as complex supply systems for water, sewage, gas, and refuse collection, and a transport concept consisting of public transport and management of increasing private traffic (admittedly a

Architecture and urban development, 1998

Aksai-4, one of the then newer residential areas west of the city, early 1990s

Architecture and urban development, 1998

Nursultan Nazarbayev, the former president seen here on an election poster in 2015, defined the country's search for identity until 2019 and influenced architecture and urban planning with his desire for simplistic, national symbolism.

mere breeze when seen from today's perspective). Environmental problems, such as noise and poor air quality, were also addressed. Soviet urban planners had much work to do in developing their plans from previous years. On many occasions, reality threatened to overtake these plans.

The end of the Soviet Union; the fifth master plan (1989)

At the end of the 1980s Almatagenplan, a new urban planning institute whose remit was restricted to urban planning and its implementation, drew up the city's fifth master plan. Adopted in 1989, it called for further development in a radial-ring road pattern with bypasses at all the city's edges, a compact settlement structure, and integration of neighbouring settlements into the city. Covering the period to 2010, the plan introduced an approach that involved planning individual urban areas in more detail than had previously been the case (necessary due to the growing size of the urban area and the increase in the number of city districts). The new urban districts included the settlements of Kalkaman in the west and Pervomaisk and Burundai in the north; these were incorporated into micro-districts. By the end of the 1980s Alma-Ata was home to

around one million people and there were signs of major political upheaval in the Soviet Union. But no one could have imagined how far-reaching they would be. On 16 December 1991 the Kazakh SSR declared its independence and became the Republic of Kazakhstan.

The fall and rise of the construction industry

In the years that followed, the country struggled with the economic decoupling of the former Soviet republics and experienced a severe economic crisis. Many professionals, including architects, urban planners, and civil engineers, left. Former state institutions for urban planning and construction were privatised or closed down. There were simply no more state construction contracts, neither for housing nor for social or industrial facilities. After the first few years of shock, it was mainly the profiteers of the new, young Kazakhstan who started building again. They built single-family dwellings on plots bought at ridiculously low prices in what are now the best parts of the city – for example, south of Al-Farabi Avenue, where until then agriculture and fruit growing had predominated. To this day old-timers in Almaty regret the large-scale annihilation of the apple orchards in the foothills on the city's

The construction boom in the 2000s, before the financial crisis, saw many older neighbourhoods fall victim to demolition.

southern edge. The construction of commercial buildings, banks, offices, and hotels, financed mainly by private investors, slowly began again. Bazis Group, still one of the most powerful players in local construction industry, was founded in 1991 by Aleksandr Byelovich after he left his job as an engineer at the Almaty House Building Combine (ADK). Today he is a billionaire and one of the country's richest.

The end of Almaty's status as capital; the sixth master plan (2002)

Kazakhstan's search for a political identity – initiated by Nursultan Nazarbayev, the country's president until 2019 – led to symbolic decisions. Freedom from the legacy of the Soviet Union and the development of a modern Kazakh national conscience were top priorities. In 1993 Alma-Ata was renamed again, becoming Almaty, a version adapted to the Kazakh language. Aqmola, the former provincial town of Tselinograd in the north of the country, became Kazakhstan's capital in 1997 before being renamed 'Astana' in 1998. The vast, flat steppes around it offered plenty of space to build a new vision of a capital city undisturbed by potential earthquakes and mud slides. Astana's location in the country's geographical centre was also a political hint.

At the end of the 1990s, as Kazakhstan began to stabilise economically, the Centre for Urban Planning Projects, founded in 1995 by former state urban planners, drew up the first development plan for Almaty, taking into account the new economic, demographic, and administrative conditions. The city's sixth development plan came into force in 2002, with a planning horizon of 20 years.

New dynamics in Kazakhstan's construction sector

Over the past two decades Almaty's cityscape has undergone massive transformation. Along Al-Farabi Avenue, south of Rozybakiyev and Gagarin streets, Seyfullin Avenue, and along Abai Avenue, Tole bi Street, and Raiymbek Avenue, entire seas of houses have sprung up, with 15- or 20-storey high-rises blocking the view of the mountains. Many people in the immediate neighbourhood do not like the densification and infill development, but the authorities say it is necessary in order to create more living space. Are these houses earthquake-proof? Even if they are on paper, can they withstand a major quake? In many places traffic, pollution, and the supply and disposal situation have been unsatisfactory for a population which has exceeded two million since the mid-2010s.

Poorly maintained *aryks* (aqueducts), open channels on the roadside, and the sealing of drainage areas lead to heavily flooded roads when it rains.

During the Soviet era construction in Almaty was governed by state regulations, compliance with which was strictly monitored. In newly independent Kazakhstan too there were building and development regulations and new legislation governing construction and urban planning, which was adapted and internationalised after often lengthy reform projects. However, in the end these regulations were often changed in the interests of developers – for example, by creating opportunities to build higher up or on land in historical surroundings, regardless of architectural style.

The dark side of power; the seventh master plan (2023)

But even these guidelines were easily flouted – and still are. Nepotism, favouritism, and corruption do not stop at the construction sector in Kazakhstan. Almaskhan Akhmedzhanov, the head of Almaty's Department of Urban Planning and Development, was arrested in summer 2023 after three years in office. He is accused of corruption and abuse of power in the allocation of land and building permits in the interests of particular construction companies.

Almaskhan Akhmedzhanov headed Almaty's Department of Urban Planning and Development from 2019 to 2023 before being arrested and charged with corruption.

Specific economic development envisaged for Almaty's polycentres outlined in the seventh master plan for the period from 2023 to 2040, by Almatygenplan

1 North: removal of industries and markets with redevelopment of vacated areas and
   new areas for recreation and landscaping, with a well-developed services sector
2 East Gate: logistics hub, exhibition and entertainment centre in the airport area
3 Historical centre: tourism with a well-developed services sector
4 West: large industrial companies and transport and logistics hub
5 South west: mini industrial parks, trade, logistics

Akhmedzhanov gave an interview to the author of this book the year before he was arrested. During his tenure the Almatygenplan and Almatygiprogor planning institutes completed the seventh general plan, which was finally adopted in May 2023. More than 20 years passed between the last two general plans – a long time for a city as dynamic as Almaty. Akhmedzhanov explained in 2022 what the difficulties had been: 'In the last six or seven years alone Almaty's area has almost tripled. In 2002 the city was 21,700 hectares. Today it is 70,000 hectares. We started making adjustments to the old master plan around 2013. But then a few tens of thousands of hectares were added here and there, and of course we couldn't plan for an area that on paper was only half the size of the actual city.' The risk of earthquakes would have posed

an additional challenge as hazard zones for the new urban areas would have had to be determined first.

New goal of polycentrism

Originally, the new master plan was to run until 2030. Now, however, it is scheduled to cover the period to 2040. Akhmedzhanov commented: 'Yes, we have adjusted it so that we don't fall behind again. For example, we have lowered the target for construction of housing and now set the number that is needed, taking into account urban development projects. The city is currently growing by about 60,000 people a year.'

In 2022 Akhmedzhanov also explained the new concept of the polycentric city that Almaty is now being developed into: 'The *akim* has ordered that the city should have several centres in the future, so people will need to travel less. We want to have the main public facilities where people live, so they don't have to use cars or public transport. The United Nations also envisages such polycentric agglomerations for the cities of the future,' said Akhmedzhanov. 'We already had this concept in Almaty. In the Soviet Union microdistricts were developed as independent sub-centres with all necessary facilities, such as schools, hospitals, and shopping and leisure facilities. Now we are recreating that paradigm.'

The new general plan has been widely criticised by the public: the secondary concepts for development, transport, and ecology are said to lack coherence; the public was not sufficiently involved in drawing up the plan; and there was a general lack of transparency.

Modernisation using old methods?

Nurlan Kamitov is critical not of the new master plan explicitly but of the development of urban planning and architecture in Kazakhstan in general. The architect founded his architecture and design firm INK Architects in 2003. The company develops its own projects, such as the President's Park residential complex (114), and designs projects for major developers, such as the 4You residential complex (113) for BI Group.

'In independent Kazakhstan the school of urban planning and architecture is still the same as it was 50 or 60 years ago,' says Kamitov. 'At the universities they teach practically the same, now outdated, building regulations as they did back then.' Kamitov, who trained in Kazakhstan but also works abroad, wants to build in a modern way. 'I want Almaty to be the most modern city in Central Asia. And not only in Central Asia, but beyond.' But old regulations and standards are holding him and other younger architects back: 'We want to build something new and beautiful. But developing new technologies in accordance with Soviet rules doesn't work. All you end up with is a Lada car once again!'

Kamitov is enthusiastic about modern architecture and urban planning in Barcelona and Miami, for instance, and recommends looking abroad for inspiration. The next five to seven years are crucial for Almaty, he says. 'We must first understand what is holding us back, what is at the heart of the problem of largely unimaginative urban planning. We need to adapt, copy the rules of other cities, modernise our own, invent new ones, and bring it all together, taking into account current and future trends.'

Architect Nurlan Kamitov wants a modern local approach to urban planning and architecture.

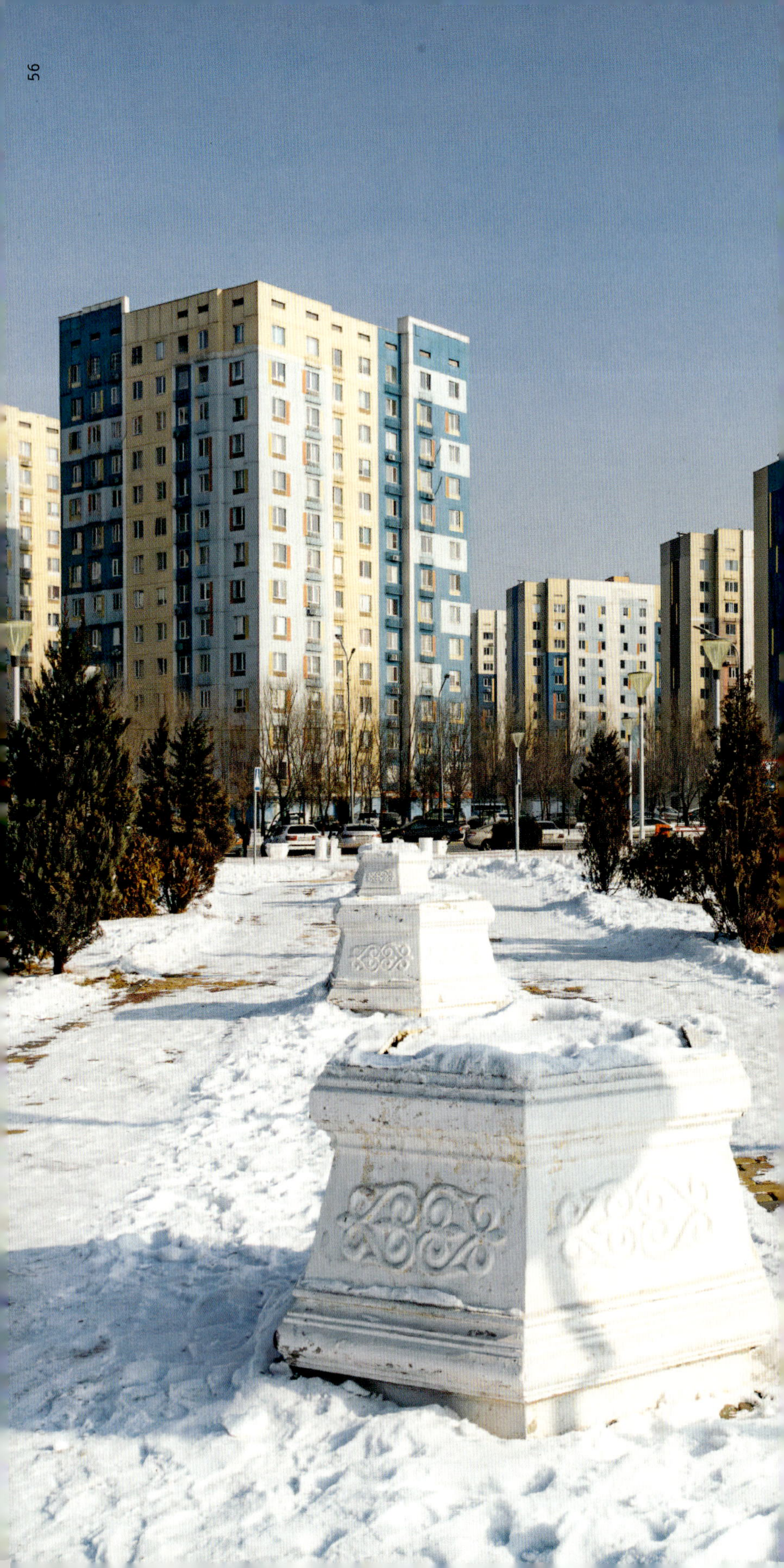

Akbulak micro-district in the north west of Alatau district
is one of the new neighbourhoods built in the 2010s and 2020s.

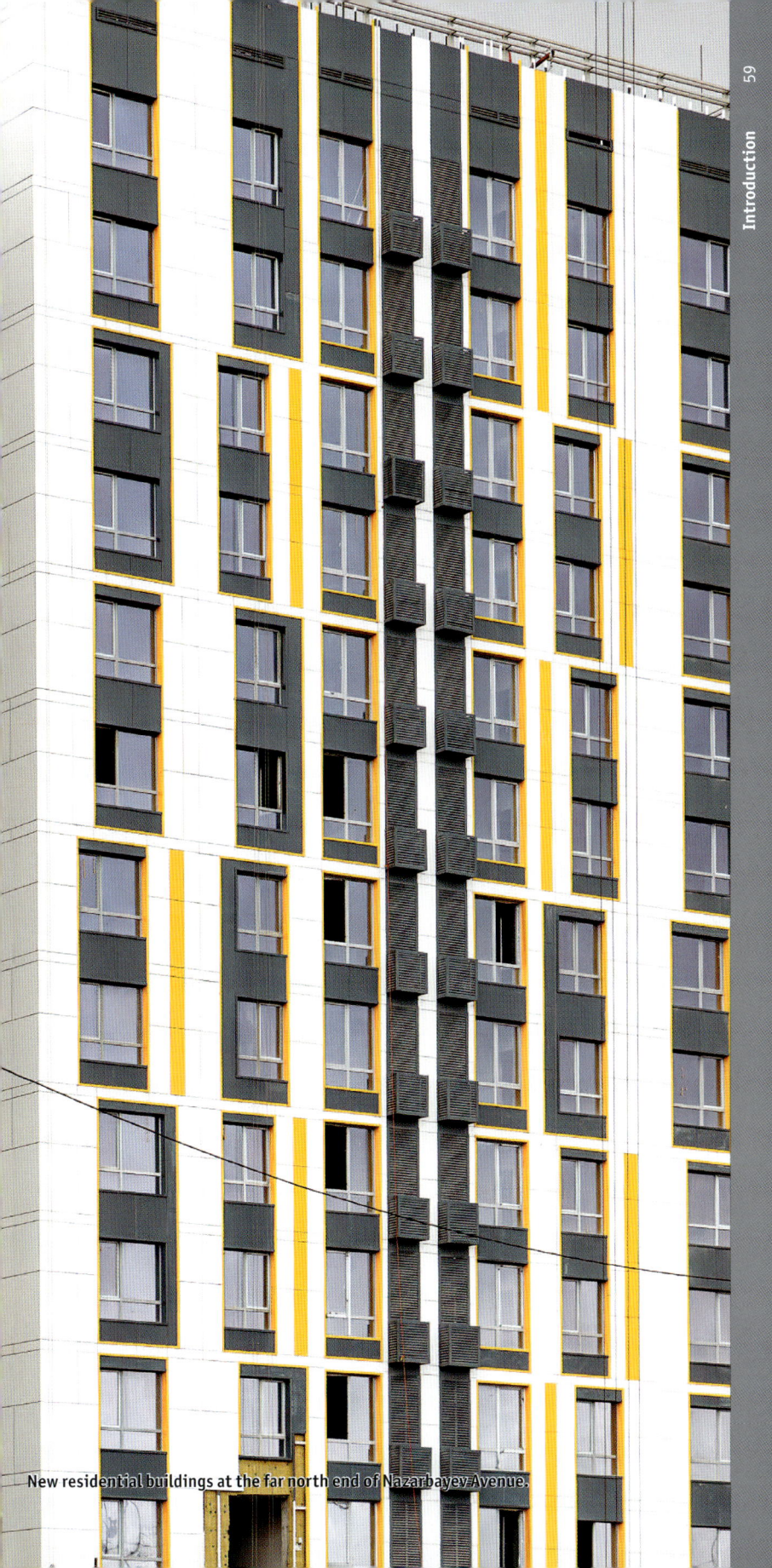

New residential buildings at the far north end of Nazarbayev Avenue.

'Architects Today Are Essentially the Servants of Property Developers.'

Architect Aidyn Akbai on the development of Almaty's modern cityscape.
Interview by Svetlana Romashkina

Aidyn Akbai is a member of Almaty's recently reconstituted City Planning Council, fought to preserve the old airport building (096), and took part in the public review of the city's master plan adopted in 2023. He speaks about the work of the City Planning Council, comfortable building heights, and the status of architects in Kazakhstan.

Aidyn Akbai

The City Planning Council was established in 2022 with a remit to improve the efficiency of decision-making in the implementation of urban planning policy and to ensure sustainable and balanced development of the city. On average, how many projects are rejected by the council?

I can't tell you the exact percentage. The *akim* said 70 per cent, which sounds about right. The projects that are rejected are those that do not comply with the detailed planning plan (*plan detailnoy planirovki* or PDP) – for example, by violating requirements in terms of density or quality of architecture.

Have you complained that the council sometimes only gets handed unfinished projects to discuss drafts?

My personal impression is that they want to use the City Planning Council as a body that approves everything. There have been cases where clients and designers have submitted projects with violations. I think it is a question of the level of design, the level of the client, and the attitude towards the project.

Almaty is an eternal construction site, especially when it comes to residential buildings.

Should Almatygenplan [the state institute responsible for coordinating Almaty's urban planning policy] somehow check projects before they come to you for discussion? Should they assess the quality of the projects? For example, should they say to the clients: here you have crossed a red line; here the density is too high; here you've broken the regulations on number of storeys? So that the City Planning Council doesn't have to deal with these technical issues?

They've started to do that, and Almatygenplan itself is already rejecting a lot of projects. But sometimes the client insists on taking his project to the City Planning Council, which is his right. And everything is discussed there. The members of the City Planning Council always justify their decision with reference to the regulations.

What changes need to be made in the work of the City Planning Council to make it more effective?

The City Planning Council is less than a year old, so some things are still being analysed and changed. The only thing I can say is that there are a lot of projects at a City Planning Council meeting, because it's a big city and it's difficult to look at everything at the same time.

Do you receive the documents for a project in advance, or do you only see them at the meeting itself?

You know, there is a preliminary reading. Sometimes additional documents, such as mock-ups, are presented at the City Planning Council meeting itself. I hope that the City Planning Council has been set up in such a way as not to dictate but recommend. We have gathered relevant experts because only they will be able to make recommendations, find mistakes, and make an argued case. Developers and investors understand that when experts make comments, there is good reason for them to do so. Above all, everyone avoids tastefulness – like it or not, there is discussion based on arguments.

One criticism of the City Planning Council is that there are architects on it who are connected to construction companies. If a project is being considered by an architect who is a member of the City Planning Council, does he or she withdraw?

Yes. And he or she doesn't take part in the vote, I think that, on the contrary, very close attention is paid to such cases, to make sure there is no lobbying. It's a great opportunity for me to improve the city, a responsibility and an honour to be entrusted with such an opportunity. This is serious volunteer work. Some projects have to be double-checked: you have to do your own calculations, read the building codes and regulations, argue, refer to laws. This is work that requires real expertise.

You've been in the building industry for many years. Do you feel that something is changing in the approach to design and construction?

I've always been a bit abstract about this. There is a well-known formula for creating an architectural masterpiece: the first thing is the location of the future building; the second is how knowledgeable the client is; the third is having a talented architect; and the fourth is the construction. I have been working in Kazakhstan since the late 1990s, and I can see that there have always been many talented architects in Kazakhstan, and the percentage of educated clients is increasing. For example, you no longer have to convince anyone that you need a car-free courtyard, that it is necessary to create an inclusive environment. Of course, due to inertia some people still do not take this into account, but the approach has changed a lot. I think clients themselves are interested in selling their property, and only a comfortable environment will attract them. The only thing is that there is still a big problem with density. There are still violations of density; developers and architects make their projects very high, but this is permitted by the building code itself. The code was passed, as far as I remember, in 2008; before that, the permitted density was lower. It seems to me that we should go back to what we had before and pass legislation preventing the construction of so-called *cheloveiniki*, human anthills – whole neighbourhoods of densely packed high-rise apartment blocks. For example, when we consider a project at a meeting of the City Planning

Council, we can see that the density is high, but it is still legal and under the law we cannot reduce it; we can only make recommendations and suggestions. One of the functions of the City Planning Council is to educate: this is a dialogue with clients, with designers. If I may, I'd like to raise a very serious issue. I try to tell people that all our problems with creating a comfortable environment, with people's houses, are due to the fact that we do not grant architects the status they need. Architects have no authority, no influence: architects today are essentially the servants of developers. They cannot recommend competent architectural solutions and cannot defend or insist on them. This is exactly what the City Planning Council is trying to correct; there is a lot of work going on with designers. I think the only way to solve these problems is to raise the status of the architect.

How can we do that?

Firstly, by changing copyright law. Right now, for example, in our copyright law, the architect only owns the idea; he has a non-property right. And the project that is developed belongs to the firm. So, for example, if the author of the project has developed it, then the law firm can fire the architect and, in the construction phase, hire a more accommodating specialist who will sign everything. The second thing is the use of the building. Our façades are compromised; balconies and historical buildings are rebuilt. In the west, by contrast, the architect's rights extend throughout the period of the building's use. If someone wants to glaze a balcony, for example, they have to apply to the author of the project. There the architect's responsibility is greater, and so is the payment for his work. Just compare: everyone has been abroad, has seen beautiful things, but no one understands how they were made, how they were designed, what budgets the architects there had to work with. For example, the design of the most beautiful buildings costs 15 per cent of the construction and installation work. In our country, meanwhile, the cost of design has already fallen to one per cent. In Soviet times it was three per cent for standard construction and 15 for unique construction. So we are even violating the Soviet norm. And we architects lost our Soviet status when Khrushchev's infamous decree on architectural excesses came out and architecture was relegated to the level of just another component in a project. How will you design now? We have low-voltage engineers who are paid more than an architect. Every year, officials report what they have saved on construction through design. But as any manager will tell you, you can't cut corners on design. If we skimp on it, we get poor-quality buildings. The third thing is design time. All over the world, design takes a reasonable amount of time. For example, a five-storey building takes a year to design, but in our country it takes one to two months. How can you produce a decent project under such conditions? That is why we end up with such a terrible, uncomfortable environment. We need to change the law. They're currently working on a design code for the city, and I'm participating in its development, but they don't listen to me. We can't say that our laws are bad; it's just that even the ones we have are not enforced. We have a regulation that defines design conditions, but it is not taken into account. There are rules for calculating design and survey work, but they are not taken into account either. As a result, in tenders, with the existing discount systems, the amount allocated to design

is reduced even further. Naturally, specialists will not stay in the profession if they are underpaid. And the general level of our specialists sinks as a result. We are always reacting to tactical problems: a building has been badly designed, or a historical building has been poorly restored, or a densely built residential complex has been started, but the main problem is the status of the architect. If we solve this problem, it will be much easier and, for example, at the City Planning Council we will not have to spend time checking the project and its compliance with building regulations but will discuss its architectural appearance and value.

In our country it is customary to appoint architects from other countries for large projects in private and public construction. Is it necessary to give priority to Kazakh architects in order for them to develop? Or is it just that our projects are inferior?

It is a vicious circle. Scientific and technical documentation for such projects is developed separately, and research is carried out. This costs money and requires experience. Objectively speaking, we will not be able to do an EXPO project to the same standard with our one per cent of the budget allocated to design. And since that's the case, we turn to foreign

Architectural experiments in Almaty

Nur Alem, which was built at the centre of Expo 2017 in Kazakhstan's capital Astana, is the world's largest spherical building. It has a diameter of 80 metres and is 100 metres high. It was designed by Adrian Smith and Gordon Gill Architects from Chicago.

specialists. That means that a lot of money ends up going abroad. As a result, they get more experience and more money, and we are left without development. I often call for sectoral protection, based on a famous saying, which I have reworded as follows: 'If you don't want to feed your own architects, you will feed other people's architects.' And that's the situation we have.

So maybe we should change our approach to designing public buildings?

We can legislate for such restrictions. For example, there is support for local producers. We can also restrict the participation of foreign architects. Yes, of course, we can organise international competitions, but we are not competitors. And now this is pointless. One of the tools for developing architecture and changing its image is architectural competitions. They have a multiplier effect – above all, on tourism. Landmark buildings will appear; the city will become more attractive; there'll be more tourists. Tourism will lead to improvements in the economy. There are many aspects that can be influenced by architectural competitions. At the same time, our rules do not include the need to hold an architectural competition for a building of

particular importance. Any building, even if it is private but more than 2000 square metres large, is already significant, is big; everyone will notice it, and it is already necessary to hold an architectural competition, for a fee, openly, among local architects. That way, we will begin to develop, and there will be better-quality solutions. In a competitive environment the best works always win. Almaty already has height limits. In some places it is possible to build up to nine storeys high, in others up to 12. How will this affect the construction business now? There is an opinion that it will no longer be so profitable for construction companies to build: the number of square metres will be reduced, and this will lead to higher prices for projects. These regulations on the number of storeys solve a lot of problems, especially uneven economic activity. Of course, everyone tries to build in the city centre, and there is not much land there. In order to be profitable, [developers] start building higher, and this is where attempts are made to break the law, to increase density, to build anthills. The city's panorama has already been spoiled; there is already too much traffic load; etc. Almaty is big, and in order for it to develop evenly, we need to shift the emphasis.

Al-Farabi Avenue, one of the busiest and most important roads in Almaty

How can this be done? What are the possibilities?

We have a lot of vacant land that can be successfully developed, and we can earn money on construction. In this way we will relieve the centre and there will be polycentres. In addition to the economic aspect you mentioned, there is also comfort. The most comfortable number of storeys is five to seven. We have set ourselves the goal that all development in Almaty should be between five and seven storeys high and only the most unique buildings in prominent positions, at the intersection of highways, should be tower-type buildings. There should be few of them, and they should be scattered around the city so they do not spoil the panorama but, on the contrary, embellish it. And the fact that they have now limited the number of storeys above Abay Avenue is the first stage.

Now it seems to me this should be done throughout the city. Business is flexible; I think it will find a way to make money in all conditions. The main thing is to introduce the right regulations so that they improve the city. On top of all this, we ask that the principle of mixed development be applied in housing, that there be active ground floors, that houses with façades facing the main streets should have shops, etc. We need to get away from the Soviet practice of having separate housing and separate shops in a neighbourhood: the more mixed, the better the economic development. In Almaty's Almalinsk District in Soviet times there were a lot of office and administrative buildings, while in the Aksai microdistrict in Auezov District they built a lot of housing. And you can see from the dynamics that economic activity is high in Almalinsk District, while Auezov District has the highest population density – so there's pendulum migration during the day.

In the past various settlements were annexed to Almaty, and new districts were created. How can they be integrated into the city?

The master plan for the city was adopted in 1978. At that time a large area was annexed to Almaty, but they did not change the road network, which had been developed for collective farms, to an urban system; there were reasons for that. In fact, all subsequent general plans were reprints of the 1978 general plan. Finally, after 45 years, building lines and a network of roads suitable for a megalopolis have been included in the general plan. This will provide a framework for the city's development and will also help solve the problem of uneven economic activity. Multiple centres will be developed, and dispersed population densities will appear. The new master plan has a revolutionary breakthrough principle. Yes, there are still many problems, but we will finally solve the first and main problem.

Will the city be densified in the future? Everyone now has a negative attitude towards densification, due to past experience, which has not been very good.

Nothing can be done about that; densification has taken on negative connotations. It is allowed, but what we have had is not densification or infill development but violations of the density regulations. For example, in Soviet times, when there were gaps between buildings, they would build infill. That was densification or 'spot development', and it fitted in perfectly and there was nothing wrong with it – that's just normal practice all over the world. I hope that with time we will explain to people that these are the correct terms and that it is normal. But hyper-density needs to be tackled, and that's what we're doing. Keeping street blocks to a height of between five and seven storeys will alleviate the problem of hyper-density in the future. The problem we have is that in Soviet times they liked to make large open spaces. Over time people forget that this is necessary standardised open space and say, 'Let's put a building there', and end up with overcrowding. That's why I'm proposing dispersed, uniform development, which will eliminate the possibility of subsequent over-densification.

Let's talk about 'renovation' [renewal or replacement of areas of Soviet housing]. Don't you feel we have gone the way of Moscow and will have problems in the future? When we demolish two-to-four-storey buildings and build anthills in their place?

The way you put that is wrong. Of course, renovation in our country has negative connotations because of negative experiences in other countries. But with the right planning it is possible to improve the urban environment. If we legally reduce the standard density, it will be impossible to build human settlements even with renovation.

Have you seen the project for the renovation of the block at the junction of Shevchenko, Manas, Zhambyla, and Baizakov streets? The project on the Almatygenplan website shows high-rise buildings in place of two-storey ones.

I think they're still working on this. What they proposed was rejected, and the client redesigned the project. That's what I was talking about. They have kept to the density allowed by the regulations, and here we can only hope that the developers will somehow reconsider the economic model.

Between Satpayev Street, Abai Avenue, and Baitursynov and Masanchi streets. This is one of those neighbourhoods of Stalin-era brick buildings that are unlikely to be renovated but will probably sooner or later have to make way for luxury apartment blocks.

High-rises with a Kazakh national tinge and the Dostyk Plaza shopping centre on Dostyk Avenue

Won't renovation in the future involve old neighbourhoods being completely demolished and new ones springing up in their place, which will mean that historical Almaty will be lost?

Our city is always young. On average, everything here is torn down and rebuilt every 50 years. This is because we do not have a culture of maintaining buildings. Buildings built 20 years ago are already falling apart, and in another 20 years they will be unusable and there will be talk of demolishing them. This is extremely unprofitable. All over the world, demolition and rebuilding means double the cost and double the damage to the environment. It is proper building maintenance that must be established, and this is the solution to the problems. If the buildings on Shevchenko Street had been renovated in time, they would have become elite houses – this was potentially an elite neighbourhood. And, by the way, in the previous master plan many neighbourhoods were identified for demolition, and, knowing this, people do not invest in their housing, do not repair it. We have private houses that were served demolition notices in the 80s.

Maybe it makes sense to keep some of the areas of small, single-family houses? For example, in Almaty-1?

To give you an idea of the scale, Almaty today occupies the same area of land as Seoul. Seoul has 12 million people, and in 10–15 years we will have four million at most. We do not need to build skyscrapers everywhere; we will develop this area for another 100 years. It is difficult from an economic point of view to buy out the single-family dwellings, and they should be allowed to live normally. By the way, we don't have an owners' association for the areas of singe-family dwellings; there's no unified design code, nothing at all: these are abandoned neighbourhoods, the city's dark zones. It is necessary to build the city evenly and calmly, to work out clear rules of the game for everyone, and this requires a lot of work.

When new houses are built in Almaty, they are very similar to those in Astana.

Serdeli micro-district on the north-west outskirts, which were only recently incorporated into Almaty's territory.

Perhaps it is a problem of world architecture that all façades are now similar. But how can Almaty keep its identity?

Yes, it is a global problem. I recently came out of Almatygenplan on Abai Avenue / Zharokov Street and found myself thinking that I was in Astana. It was so similar: those construction signs, the lack of a design code. But here is the answer: if you want to change all this, change the status of architects. Then they will have opportunities for creativity. But now they have neither money nor time to go looking for creative ideas, to work on matters of style. And if foreigners are always being hired, then what style can we talk about? They will bring their cities with them: London, Seoul, etc. One of the main tasks is to create Almaty's own building codes and regulations, which will describe all these things. But all this needs money and is work not for one person but for the whole architectural community. And if all architects are to do this, there is again the question of status. This cannot be done on enthusiasm alone. By the way, the new general plan was almost entirely based on enthusiasm. Out of habit, everyone started cursing the general plan, and I think that is wrong. I try to tell everyone that the

Aidin Akbai

Aidin Akbai wanted to incorporate the historical airport building into the new terminal (096), but the old building has been demolished and will be rebuilt. Design study.

new general plan is a great success for the city; it contains many important things. Of course, the implementation period is very long. But how many years have we wasted! So many years are needed to fix everything. At least 30–40.

I want to talk about architectural monuments. We are expecting the reconstruction of the Circus (057), Auezov Theatre (059), and the Academy of Science (033). Judging by the demolition of the airport building, people are discussing things, getting involved, but such cases create an impression of learned helplessness.

We have to take an active part ourselves. Today I went to the the city's cultural administration to express my concerns about the theatre and the circus. I went there to tell them about the law on historical monuments, but it turned out that they know everything themselves. They are trying to restore the city's buildings, but there are buildings for which they are not responsible since they are republican monuments. People there know that the monuments should be preserved, although my first impression was that nobody knows anything. But today I was convinced that the administration is on our side in the defence of monuments.

Now we have to communicate this to the clients and the organisations that operate the buildings.

When we participated in the hearings on the airport, I noticed that citizens themselves do not consider these buildings as monuments. Unfortunately, this is ignorance and lack of awareness. It is not their fault; we need more educational work, we need to create an emotional attachment of residents to these things. All this needs to be created. It is complex, multifaceted work. First of all, we have to respect the laws. Everything is written in them, but they are often forgotten, and then there are misinterpretations. For example, in the case of Auezov Theatre, it was said that everything would be replaced, all the materials, and the existing appearance would be recreated, but in fact only the frame will remain. So, it turns out that the historical building is just a concrete frame? We just have to keep our hands on the situation. My position is that it is not necessary to create a conflict but to engage in dialogue and discussion – because in a conflict you automatically defend yourself, and all your energy goes into accusation and defence. If you ask people to work together and talk to each other, it seems to me that things will go differently.

Sometimes there are doubts about the competence of people who make decisions and reconstruct monuments.

The legislation contains the term 'public hearings', but so far all hearings have been held at the end, when all decisions have already been taken, when resources have already been spent on design, and some work may even have begun. And here comes a person who makes an argument that, unfortunately, the clients have not thought of. And then there's conflict because the resources have been spent and something has to be done. So, public hearings should be held at the very beginning. And the public should not be involved in reviewing a project but in formulating the design task. And if the design task takes into account all requirements, then the design and construction will proceed automatically and there will be no conflicts. The second thing I am asking for is that after raising the status of the architect, the term 'client' should be broadened. There should be more than one client, but also the public. We should also allow a decent amount of time for pre-design work. This

Residential building in the centre of Almaty

means research, public hearings, architectural competitions, feasibility studies. We pay almost no attention to this. Many mistakes can be corrected at the pre-design stage.

The skyline of the densely built-up capital Astana

Let's talk about Astana. It is often criticised for the *cheloveiniki*, the lack of a pleasant urban environment, and much more. Can anything be done about that?

Yes: increase the density. The streets there are too wide, and you can literally add whole blocks to give people more space. For example, one of the suggestions that was made, and I'm glad I'm not the only one to think of it, was that the space underneath the Light Rail Transit (LRT) be given over to commerce, so that there's some activity there that at least pays for itself. Otherwise, we have a huge empty alleyway again, with the LRT running in isolation above it, and who will take the tram if there are no people there? That's why it's economically unviable, because there are no people there. Increasing density will increase comfort and bring streets closer to the human scale. Again, reduce the number of storeys: not high-rises, but buildings of five to seven storeys. Then you'll get these cascades. The current tall buildings will be at the back, and in front of them there will be another line of buildings of five to seven storeys.

But Astana is a city of micro-district development as opposed to development consisting of city blocks.

In our micro-districts we can redesign the plan for neighbourhood development, for example by adding buildings. You can do the same in Astana.

But still, Almaty's micro-districts are very cosy and quiet. There's no over-densification, there are wide yards, and often you can't see the neighbouring houses. People don't want this to be destroyed.

The landscaping makes them look cosy, but they are cut off from the city. There's nothing there in terms of economic activity; you get terrible traffic jams forming around them and you can't drive through the neighbourhoods. You have to avoid creating isolated areas in a city. The master plan reflects that there is no one there during the day, and that is already bad – people spend a lot of time travelling.

Because of the problems with water, isn't there a feeling that Astana is reaching its peak and there aren't enough resources?

No, there are not enough resources because the infrastructure was not built in time. But Almaty and Astana are developing fast; they are vacuum cleaners sucking everything out of the regions. There is a need for economic development throughout the republic, the small towns should be developed so that people stop leaving. How does development occur in our country now? When they want to develop a place, they move the administrative centre there: Astana, Turkestan, Taldykorgan, Konaev. I think this is inefficient. In our country only administrative blocks become cities. At the same time, there's no proper scientific research into architecture and urban planning because there's no money for it. What has prevented us from having a street grid in the city for 45 years? Inertia in everything. We are not responding to climate change at all, and that's been known for a long time. I read the reports in 2005, and I knew that we were going to have all the rainfall concentrated in one period, the spring, and that the summer and autumn would be dry. Every year we traditionally scream about the *aryk* system when the city drowns, cars float, and everyone starts demanding that the water be diverted. We should be thinking not about diverting water but about accumulating it. And by using not just the rivers but reservoirs too. I believe that 20–30 per cent of the area of all parks should be used for ponds, and water should be accumulated there. In this way we will increase the city's water table. We tend to have open façades, but we need to plant trees everywhere as much as possible. Shops should attract shade, not heat. We can lower the temperature in the city, for example by painting the roofs white. When climate change hits us in full force, we will implement and redesign all this quickly. I think it's going to happen soon.

The interview was first published by the independent Kazakh online news media Vlast.kz in June 2023. This is a translation from the Russian, slightly shortened and edited with the kind permission of Vlast.kz.

Almaty's modern skyline in front of the Alatau mountain range

Satbayev Technical University, built in 1988. The use of a façade curtain as a shading element is a Central Asian solution for protection against the hot climate.

Advertisement for a beauty salon on a Soviet façade

Architecture in Almaty and Questions of Identity

Khalima Truspekova. Edited by Edda Schlager

The importance of Almaty for the cultural development of Kazakhstan is enormous, especially for the 'westernisation' of the population. Even at the time of its foundation, the city presented a mixed picture of nationalities: in addition to Russian and Slavic immigrants, Tatars and Dungans from China were actively developing the region. Russia's policy of opening up the peripheral regions of its empire led to a veritable boom in migration. During the development of Verny, a territorial segregation by nationality was created by variously shaped *slobodas*, i.e. neighbourhoods inhabited by Tatars, Dungans, and Ukrainians – but the city, as a place of common trade and exchange of information, was also always a place of cultural contacts, bringing the various ethnic groups together into a common society.

Stylistically, the architecture of Verny, as Almaty was called when it was founded at the end of the nineteenth century, was initially associated with the 'Russian Empire' style. And since the traditional form of dwelling in Central Asia was an enclosed interior, Russian architecture was completely new to the local population. European architecture came to Verny, but in a version that was disrupted by the Russian interpretation of these architectural traditions. In addition to the well-known architect Pavel Zenkov, a native of the Tobolsk Governorate in western Siberia, the French architect Paul Gourdet was also active and very successful here. He was the city's leading architect from 1883 to 1903.

The late nineteenth and early twentieth centuries were a time when the cultural achievements of Europe penetrated this part of the oriental world. And it was in what is now Kazakhstan that the national traditions of the native eastern peoples were westernised to a greater extent than in any other Central Asian country. Larger urban settlements had already changed the region's appearance. But the dwellings of most ethnic Kazakhs presented a very different picture. Of course, the nomads were familiar with the architectural traditions of Russian architecture, if only through the examples of Omsk, Tomsk, and Orenburg. They were also familiar with the traditions of wooden architecture – from time immemorial, as graves from the Saken period attest.

Nevertheless, this period marked a major change in the traditional culture of the Kazakhs, as the entire territory of the Semirechye region was transformed. Yurts, mobile dwellings, are perfect from a structural and aesthetic point of view. However, the Kazakhs also had permanent houses for wintering. At the turn of the twentieth century, these were extremely modest. Most were designed for the sake of the *kora* (stable, barn), while the actual living space tended to be small and 'hidden' in the depths of the enclosure.

Given that urban space was limited, such a system was important for the Kazakhs: they could no longer lead the lifestyle of true nomads, but they still remained cattle herders and shepherds. This was not the case for the sedentary Kazakhs, of whom there were many in the southern regions of the country.

The changes in the architectural appearance of Verny were first and foremost a massive intervention in the consciousness of the local population. The naturalist Albert von Regel noted in his diary in 1876 that the town was 'well furnished, with very European houses...' However, he made this observation before the catastrophic earthquakes, including that of 1887, which destroyed most of the city's stone buildings. After several earthquakes, Verny's architectural appearance became more modest, with a larger proportion of wooden buildings. However, full use was made of the rich tradition of decorative carving (cornices, window

Pavel Leibin

The Voenny (Military) Cathedral in 1910, between today's Panfilov Street, Abylai Khan Avenue, and Karasai Batyr and Bogenbai Batyr streets

sills), which gave buildings an elegant and attractive appearance.

It is difficult to speak of national characteristics in the stylistic approach to architectural forms, as no attempt was made to integrate oriental traditions. Nevertheless, such characteristics were present, albeit mainly in details in the decoration and construction of religious buildings. There was no prohibition on the use of stylistic principles from different regions of the world in the construction of mosques, madrasas, and other buildings for the Muslim population. Islamic architecture in Central Asia is usually classified as Persian in style. However, the Chinese architectural

tradition was also present in the construction of mosques in Kyrgyzstan and Kazakhstan, such as Zharkent Mosque in eastern Kazakhstan. Construction of these buildings was initiated by the Muslim population of Verny, by Tatars, Dungans, and Uyghurs. As far as we can see from surviving photographs, the Tatar mosque in Verny was built to the same pattern as all the other buildings.

Elements of Tatar culture were present in the decorative ornamentation of the architecture, even when it was designed and built by a non-Tatar such as Paul Gourdet, who was known for borrowing from Art Nouveau with a Russian 'accent'. An example of this is the trading house of the

Argunov

A postcard of 1929 showing the Tatar Mosque on Lepsinskaya Street (Nazarbayev Avenue)

Turkestanskiy albom, 1872

The *shanyrak*, the roof crown of a Kazakh yurt, was used as a decorative feature in Almaty's Stalin-era architecture: a photograph from the late nineteenth century (above) and decoration on the building of the People's Commissariat of Finance (below; 043).

merchant Iskhak Gabdulvaliev, now Kyzyl-Tan (005). This period is notable for the fact that the nomads, unlike the rest of the population, had to adapt to this new environment. Although they were familiar with the partly oriental cityscape, it was organised in a strictly linear way and with comparatively more openness.

The next period in the city's architectural history is associated with the Soviet era. Renamed 'Alma-Ata' in 1921 and appointed the new capital in place of Kyzyl-Orda in 1929, the city experienced an upswing and major changes, including construction and reconstruction, from the second half of the 1930s forwards. Its new status of capital drove the city's development. From this point onwards, a large army of Russian-Soviet architects transformed Central Asia.

On the one hand, this brought an invasion of new architectural trends, such as Constructivism and Functionalism; on the other, there was a return to tradition. Examples of Constructivism in Kazakhstan are the first House of Government (020) by Moisey Ginzburg, now the Academy of

Arts, and the General Post Office (021) building by Georgy Gerasimov. This period was relatively short but marked by avant-garde changes in architecture, in which Russian-Soviet architects played a leading role. The internationalism of the new avant-garde architecture of the early twentieth century set it apart from national cultural identity. The latter, however, soon returned to centre stage.

At the end of the 1930s the political situation in the USSR changed, confronting architects and the country's intelligentsia with new tasks: a return to national traditions, i.e. the use of old cultural codes to counteract freedom of creative thought, which the authorities regarded as dangerous. In this context questions of national identity were actively discussed in all forms of art but at the same time subjected to strict censorship. Based on the postulate of so-called 'Socialist Realism', the state apparatus sought total control over all forms of existence. At the same time it set out to showcase what had been achieved by this country, bent on building a 'bright communist future'. Many civil, public, administrative, and cultural buildings were erected as monumental complexes. Neoclassicism was the style best suited to achieve these goals.

This style had already been resurrected a number of times by totalitarian regimes whose rulers wished to glorify their actions, as had been the case in the French and Russian empires. From the late 1930s forwards, the same trend took over Soviet architecture in an incarnation known as the 'Stalin Empire' style after Joseph Stalin, general secretary of the Communist Party of the Soviet Union from 1922 to 1952 and the most powerful dictator of the Soviet era. Traces of this style can still be seen in the architecture of Almaty today.

One of the attractions of this stylistic phenomenon in architecture is its linear clarity and establishment of a hierarchy of principal and secondary components in an 'ensemble' of buildings. Spaces of this kind are easy to navigate and are perceived organically by comparison with the complex labyrinths of a medieval city's streets – something that Georges-Eugène Haussmann applied to the reconstruction of nineteenth-century Paris.

Neoclassicism became one of the defining features of post-war construction in the Soviet Union. Alma-Ata's appearance began to resemble that of European cities. Numerous architectural ensembles were created, although almost all projects were realised with significant changes to the designs. For example, the Academy of Sciences (033) ended up surrounded by an entire complex of buildings.

National authenticity was one of the main characteristics of Soviet architecture of this period. The emphasis on national character came to the fore at this time but also sank under the burden of expediency, fashionable trends, and ideological convictions. In this respect, Aleksey Shchusev's design for the Academy of Sciences building deserves close attention.

Abai Opera House (031), which opened in 1941

In his first version Shchusev used a portal-dome form taken from Central Asian architecture, in which the corners are accentuated by slender vertical columns typical of oriental buildings. In the final version, however, he gave his design forms that met the requirements of Stalinist monumentalism. The result is a grand ceremonial building with a fountain complex and a monument to the Kazakh scientist Shoqan Valikhanov which blends organically into its surroundings but clearly dominates them.

National features in the figurative interpretation of the Academy of Sciences building are literally 'interwoven' with its Classical architectural structure. The geometry typical of Central Asian architecture is reduced to strict simplicity and extreme linearity. The main façade is accentuated by elements of oriental architecture: a portal with a flat niche in the form of a round pointed arch and ornamental decorations. Everything is austere and majestic. The overall architectural appearance is not rich in 'decorative extravagance'. Traditional Kazakh ornamentation is used in a very organic way, without any obvious excess – at the top of the cornices, on the capitals of the pilasters, and in the surrounds of the window openings.

The solemnity of the façades finds its logical continuation in the architecture of the interiors: the main lobby displays the same solemn and monumental forms. Neoclassical buildings with their gables, colonnaded porticoes, and rich cornices decorated Alma-Ata's cityscape. They dominate the urban space and are recognised by the population.

The period from the 1950s forwards saw the creation of the city's principal works of public and cultural architecture. These included the Central Stadium (074), Auezov Theatre (059), Old Square (now: Astana Square) with the monumental

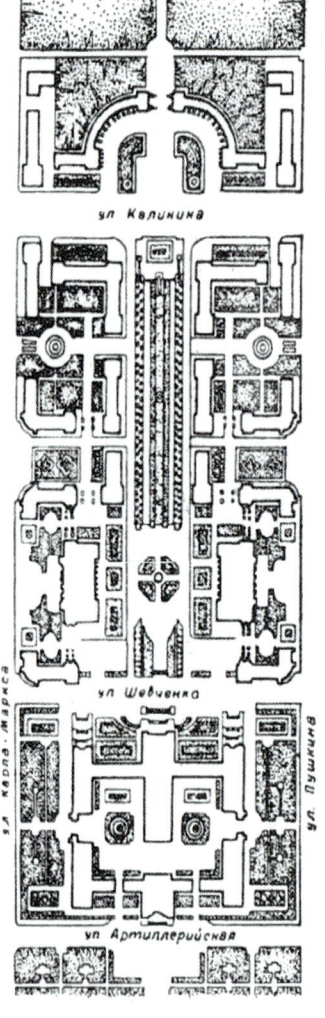

Arkhitektura goroda Almaty, 1953

ул Калинина

ул Шевченко

ул Пушкина

ул Карла-Маркса

ул Артиллерийская

One of the Neoclassical designs for the ensemble around the Academy of Sciences (033), inspired by the splendour of nineteenth-century European cities. Not realised

Kazakh ornaments interwoven with the Soviet star at the Academy of Sciences

architecture of the second Government Building, and many other buildings. This architecture was perceived by the population as an achievement of socialism; as people watched, Alma-Ata was transformed from a provincial town (Verny) into a real capital.

From this point on, the final westernisation of the city took place, and a period of assimilation began for the original inhabitants of the immediate and wider region. Architecture in the style of the ancient Classical order was increasingly seen as proof of man's great deeds as the creator of 'future communism'.

Landscape architecture was used to adapt the urban landscape to the needs of the population. The gardens and parks that already existed in Verny were seen by the city's inhabitants as a fundamental and beneficial feature. All the architectural ensembles built between the 1940s and 1960s were designed with landscape architecture in mind. A cultural space was created which incorporated the traditions of the Muslim principle of environmental perception, i.e. the aesthetic value of oriental gardens. Not only do such spaces provide a pleasant microclimate and high recreational value, but they also reflect the divine order of the world given to man in paradise. Despite the active eradication of all forms of religious thought by the Soviet authorities, important ideas and concepts remained in the minds of Muslim communities, especially as all religious festivals were for a long time celebrated unofficially.

In Islam paradise is associated with a garden – *jannat* in Arabic, *zhumak* in Kazakh: the Garden of Eden, from which the first man was expelled. Compositional design in Islamic architecture is based on the Muslim interpretation of the symbol of paradise with its abundance of water and gardens.

The genetic codes of the consciousness of Almaty's inhabitants, rooted in the religious teachings of Islam, also created conditions for the existing architectural-spatial cityscape with its squares, gardens, parks, and fountains to be perceived as paradisiacal. The hierarchical combination of principal and secondary buildings seemed to this consciousness a harmonious whole.

This period in the history of the country and city could be described as key to Kazakhs' awareness of their integration into the new urban environment. City dwellers were proud of their shady, comfortable, and sunny city. The term 'asphalt Kazakhs' emerged, meaning ethnic Kazakhs who assimilated with the asphalt cities built by the Russians and with the latter's values. Differences between representatives of different ethnic groups disappeared. The younger generation grew up in this space and considered it 'their own world'; each had his or her own place of worship, where young and old could happily meet.

It was no coincidence that the ancient system of order that formed the basis of Classical architecture formed an organic link that was rapidly accepted by the city's population. Stylistically, the Greco-Roman architectural experience is rooted in the semantics of the altarpieces of antiquity and has been preserved at a deep genetic level – in the subconscious, in the memory of all the peoples of Eurasia; it is 'familiar' to them. Its recognition as a harmonious form is also made possible by the entire history of the development of this architectural system, which has been 'tried and tested' over the course of almost three millennia. Above all, however, it is appropriate for human beings.

There have already been opportunities for harmonisation, and the development of the Classical order is almost at the same level as the laconic precision of Kazakh national ornamental design, whose forms have been perfected through centuries of collective practice by the artistic intuition of the Kazakh people. The same can be observed in the case of Classical architecture. As soon as Classical buildings appeared in the space of a city, they were recognised as 'beautiful buildings that please the eye'. The situation was to change subsequently, as other architectural styles were introduced. There would be more criticism from the citizens. However, the Soviet planning system also led to distortions since it concentrated not only public administration and business but also cultural institutions in the city centre and confined cultural and leisure activities for the population to the outskirts of the city. The development of construction in Almaty from the 1960s to the 1980s is closely linked to Dinmukhamed Kunayev, the political leader of the Kazakh SSR from the early 1960s to 1986. This period also saw the construction of large,

Nazarbayev Avenue and Satpayev Street, east of Republic Square, built 1977–1980

Powerful, brutalist forms for government buildings. The Regional Committee of the Communist Party (Obkom) building (062), built in 1986

often grandiose buildings, but with a new stylistic interpretation.

With the words 'We must build faster, cheaper, and better!' Nikita Khrushchev, successor to Joseph Stalin (who died in 1953) and First Secretary of the Communist Party of the Soviet Union from 1953 to 1964, initiated, starting in 1955, one of the most radical changes in architectural history.

The Soviet state policy documents 'On Measures for Further Industrialisation, Quality Improvement, and Cost Reduction in Construction', 'On the Development of the Production of Prefabricated Reinforced-Concrete Elements and Structures for Construction', and 'On the Elimination of Superfluous Design and Construction', adopted in 1954 and 1955, led to a review of all architectural and planning issues involved in architectural design and planning. The principle of functionalism was retained, and the plasticity of the architecture that was designed was largely determined by innovations in construction technology. In general, the development of large-scale construction technologies created conditions for completely new design possibilities in architecture.

One of the most vivid examples of the new technical possibilities is today's Palace of the Republic, known in the Soviet era as 'Lenin's Palace' (053).

A huge 10,000-square-metre roof slab rests on eight reinforced-concrete pylons and is supported by a reinforced-concrete frame on independent columns – a technological masterpiece. Thus in late-Soviet architecture the quest for 'authenticity' and 'uniqueness' of compositional design was realised with the help of technology.

The architecture of the late Soviet period in Almaty has an oriental / Central Asian flavour, although the synthesis and layering of different cultures can still be seen in many buildings. During this period architecture was more in keeping with the spirit of oriental culture itself. In fact, in the Soviet period attempts to incorporate national forms into architecture almost always emphasised the principles of iconic architecture, the form of the yurt, and ornamentation.

Large domed structures were first created in the vast Eurasian steppes of present-day Kazakhstan. Portal and dome façades also come from the depths of the oriental religious architectural tradition. They reappeared in Kazakh architecture in the 1970s and 1980s.

However, the 'primary sources' are only a starting point for their reinterpretation and transformation into a new figurative expression. For example, the use of classical stalactites to decorate the façade of the ASK-2 Television Studio Centre (061).

The Palace of the Republic (053), the Koktobe complex with the TV tower (076), Hotel Kazakhstan (054), and Medeo Ice Stadium (077) are thus architectural icons of Almaty, places of recreation, and obligatory destinations for visitors. Despite its many outstanding buildings, the cityscape is not always attractive or aesthetically consistent. Large distances and emptiness are not only not perceived positively but also stand in the way of organic coherence of the whole. The 'changing of the guard' and paradigm shift in many cases led to a lack of logical coherence in architectural solutions, especially in the new districts. In this sense the established central streets tended to offer a more complete and coherent picture.

The notion of so-called 'sanitary standards' is an important postulate in construction, but excessive gaps between the principal architectural landmarks and the links connecting them cannot help but irritate perception. This phenomenon was characteristic of Soviet architecture, especially when new urban districts were being linked. Alma-Ata gradually grew beyond its borders, and suburbs with unimpressive one-storey buildings were incorporated into the city.

In the late Soviet period the Soviet economy was in increasingly poor shape. Nevertheless, this period was extremely productive in the capital of the Kazakh Soviet Republic, thanks to its leader, Kunayev: buildings were constructed that still characterise the city's appearance

The Palace of the Republic (053) following reconstruction

Traditional Kazakh ornaments on the façade of a prefabricated residential building,

on a carpet,

on the façade of a late Soviet building,

as a wall mosaic in the metro,

on a carpet,

and on another carpet

today; they include the Central State Museum (089), the Regional Committee of the Communist Party building (062), and Alatau Sanatorium (083).

Of course, the critical view of Soviet and global Modernist and Postmodernist architecture should also be mentioned here. At the beginning of the twentieth century new materials and construction methods had led to new solutions in urban planning; the tectonics of architectural form were realised using a fundamentally different basis. There were new needs and a new sense of harmony. At the same time we know that it has always been difficult for architects and planners to predict how a form will 'behave' in space at the level of idea and design once it has been built. Especially as the sheer scale of urban living spaces has multiplied worldwide, in contrast to all previous architectural standards.

Modern architecture also reflects national character, albeit often in a cheap-looking way.

All this is also characteristic of the current situation, as Kazakhstan's independence has ushered in a new phase of urban development – the busiest period of construction in Almaty's history, involving both local architects and foreign companies. The cityscape is changing rapidly and is increasingly dominated by the high-tech style of glass and metal, especially in the south of the city along Al-Farabi Avenue.

The population has apparently had enough of the drab grey of concrete, and there is a renewed interest in the refined aesthetics of façades, especially of residential buildings. The facelessness of Soviet-era prefabricated buildings no longer meets society's heightened aesthetic requirements, even if it has to be admitted that these buildings were a solution to the major social problems of the time.

The dominant style is now Neomodernism with its eclecticism and diverse borrowings from the arsenal of world architectural history. We see this manifested in the abundance of buildings in different styles – from Neo-Renaissance, Neoclassicism, and Neo-Baroque to references to ancient Egyptian architecture.

Such omnivorousness seems to be in keeping with the spirit of postmodernism in contemporary culture. But architectural design today offers the most incredible compositional solutions, which require courage and acceptance from clients and the public alike.

The presence of the world's leading schools of architecture in Almaty, as well as in today's capital, Astana, is remarkable for the way the current possibilities of modern architectural practice are explored to create a stylistic polyphony. Local architects alone would probably have been unable to bridge the gap so quickly because Soviet professionals simply did not have the opportunity to see all the new trends with their own eyes, let alone apply them themselves. In Kazakhstan there is also a very serious problem of quality of construction.

The changes that are taking place before our eyes are often in complete contradiction to the previous experience of spatial organisation of the cityscape. New, large-scale connections between buildings and between entire ensembles of buildings are being created. Projects built in Verny or during the Soviet era are

One of the very first shopping malls in the city: Mega Centre on Rozybakiyev Street

being destroyed or shamefully concealed by so-called 'reconstruction'. Concepts of architectural composition such as 'mass', 'texture', and 'space' have been given new parameters. The appearance of today's skyscrapers, for example, is very different from the 'moderate' building practices of the past. Nevertheless, comfort of urban environment has been an important parameter for contemporary architecture in Almaty since the early 2000s.

Against the backdrop of this dynamic urban redevelopment, the population itself has also changed dynamically. The younger generation prefers comfort above all else, while nostalgia continues to haunt the minds of old-timers, for whom the new scale of the city is itself alien. It is difficult to speak of adaptation at this point as the new glass and reinforced-concrete buildings have not yet been visually accepted by everyone. But buildings that possess stylistic unity, such as Esentai Park (092), are already perceived as an identity-forming part of the cityscape.

The internationality of Almaty's modern architecture is also seen as part of the challenge of our times, when futuristic buildings built with the latest technologies can bring glory to both country and city. However, ultra-modern buildings require huge investment, which cannot always be afforded. Large shopping and entertainment complexes have expanded their influence on the city, with masses of people flocking to Esentai Mall, Mega Centre, or elsewhere for cultural leisure rather than ordinary shopping. The sophisticated aesthetics and comfort of these shopping centres, which cannot be compared to the Soviet traditions of commerce and gastronomy, are enthusiastically accepted.

People are being changed by their urban surroundings, becoming more demanding and demanding more comfort. Today's people are different from yesterday's. In recent decades technology has created a deeply interconnected world, with all the advantages and disadvantages that that implies. The architecture of Almaty is undergoing a dynamic transformation. In the reshaping of human consciousness, especially that of former nomads, surrounding urban space has played an important accompanying role, alongside more violent change. The adaptation phase was over by the middle of the twentieth century, when westernisation of the country began in earnest. Nomads in the recent past, Kazakhs have fully integrated into the new cultural environment and are now bearers of a new mentality that carries the nomadic codes of consciousness only at a genetic level.

Literature

Abrasilova, G. S., 'The Phenomenon of the Garden in the Spatial Culture of the East Khabarshy', *Scientific Journal* (Almaty: KazGASA, 2010), No. 1/35.

Azimov, I. M., Kuspangaliev, B. U., *History of the Architecture of Kazakhstan* (Almaty, 2016).

Dutsev, M. V., *The Modern City as a Space of Dialogue* (NIITIAG).

Gulyanitsky, N. F., *The History of Architecture, Vol. 1. Architecture of Civil and Industrial Buildings (in 5 volumes)* (Moscow: Stroyizdat, 1978).

Ikonnikov, A. V., *Space and Form in Architecture and Urban Planning* (Moscow: Comkniga, 2006).

Ikonnikov, A. V., *Utopian Thinking and Architecture. Social, World Outlook and Ideological Tendencies in the Development of Architecture* (Moscow: Arch, 2004).

Lynch, K., *The Image of the City* (Moscow: Mir, 1974).

Panova, L. P., *Systemicity of Architectural Environment* (Kharkov, 2010).

Ryabushin, A. V., *Architecture of the Turn of the Millennium* (Moscow: XXI century, 2005).

Ryabushin, A. V., *New Horizons of Architectural Creativity, 1970–1980s* (Moscow: Stroyizdat, 1990).

Modern Architecture of the World, Issue No. 2, 2012.

Volchak, Y. P., Ivanova, E. K., Katsnelson, R. A., *Constructions and Form in Soviet Architecture* (Moscow, 1988).

This article was first published in a longer version in The Central Asian Journal of Art Studies 3 (03), *2016.*

Reinterpreted stalactites at ASK-2 Television Studio Centre (061), built in 1983

ARCH
CODE
ALMATY

Shopping bags with architectural motifs popular in Almaty

Construction site fences with historical views of the city are very popular in Almaty

'We Need to Preserve Collective Memory.'

Architects Anel Moldakhmetova and Adil Azhiyev on Almaty's identity
and the fight to preserve historical buildings.
Interview by Edda Schlager

The architects Anel Moldakhmetova and Adil Azhiyev are founding members of ArchcCode Almaty. Established in 2015, ArchcCode Almaty is an initiative dedicated to the preservation and acceptance of historical architecture in Almaty. The initiative currently advises the Almaty city administration on architecture and urban planning.

What is ArchCode?

Moldakhmetova: The project was originally conceived as a research project on the architectural identity of the city. One of the triggers for its creation was the demolition of the house at 115 Zheltoksan Street, which was originally supposed to be an architectural monument but had this status withheld. We protested against the demolition and conducted surveys among the residents of the house to find out why it should stay. I found that people couldn't explain why the building was important to them.

They said it was valuable but couldn't say why. All these protests were very unproductive – the building was demolished at the end of 2015 – because they were not thought through strategically: we had no arguments for preserving the house. And then we thought about how we could prevent further demolitions in advance, not reactively, but preventively. We started documenting historical buildings on a map to get an overview of the city's architectural heritage. We also wanted to find tools for increasing participation by the public so that they could assert their rights, interact better with the state, and plan more effectively and strategically.

How would you describe the city of Almaty?

Azhiyev: The urban road network here is very dense, and the street blocks are relatively small, like in Europe, for example between Zheltoksan Street and Ablai Khan Avenue. This road network was

Anel Moldakhmetova and Adil Azhiyev, founding members of ArchcCode Almaty

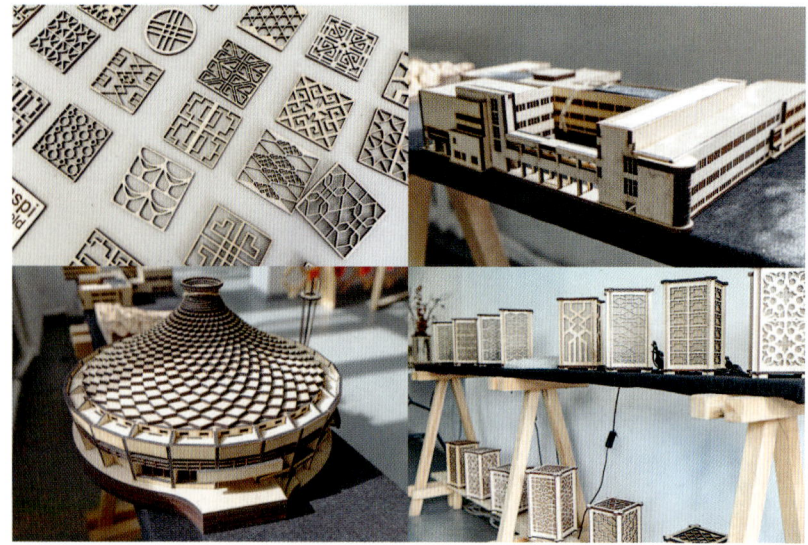

Models of the First House of Government (020) and the Circus (057), as well as traditional ornaments used in Kazakh architecture as decoration in interior design

laid out when this was Verny, long before the Soviet era. But there are also examples of more chaotic development in districts with a lot of private development, in the Malaya and Bolshoya Stanitsa districts. This is what Almaty developed from. And then there is the street network which goes back to Soviet urban planners and how Le Corbusier recommended free-standing buildings. This is the case, for example, in the west of the city, in the newer districts, where the grid is wider. These are *mikrorayons*, micro-districts; they include a degree of functional separation, with schools, kindergartens, shops, and administrative buildings. Typically constructed of prefabricated panels, these districts are all built on this principle, with very large distances between the streets, in which everything is laid out but which you can't drive through. There are few commercial buildings, as these are mainly residential areas. People used to sleep there and mostly work in nearby industrial plants, such as the Almaty Prefabricated-house-building Plant or the cotton combine, both of which no longer exist.

What is Almaty's identity?

Azhiyev: Almaty was designed early on as a Soviet republican capital, with

Façade curtains of concrete and metal – a typical local element of Soviet Modernism

large central buildings for state institutions and parks around them. The centre of the city was built around Baiseitov Street. After the capital was moved from Kyzylorda to Alma-Ata in 1929, this became the central axis. The building of the first House of Government, designed by Moisey Ginzburg and completed in 1931 (020), stands on the middle of this axis. It now houses the Academy of Arts.

The much larger building of what is now the Kazakh-British Technical University (037), which was built in the Stalinist style as a new government building before 1957, is also located on this axis. And in the late Soviet era, under Leonid Brezhnev, another new architectural centre was created, now called Republic Square (058), with several administrative buildings and the seat of government. This is today's *akimat*, although it burned down in January 2022 and has since been rebuilt. Brezhnev also created a prestigious infrastructure around the square, including parks and the Central State Museum (089).

In Almaty you will also, of course, find design elements such as small courtyards for shade and façade curtains to protect against the hot climate (often built from standardised elements that made Soviet construction quick and cheap). There are similar elements in many cities in Central Asia; they may differ in some decorative aspects, in the materials, but mostly they are made of reinforced concrete or metal because these were materials that were easily available at the time.

Moldakhmetova: There are several examples in Almaty that reflect the identity of the city very well. For example, Arman Cinema (052), which was designed by Alexander Korzhempo to look like a glacier coming down from the mountains. This is a very visual allegory – an allusion to the mountainous landscape that surrounds the city.

The cinema is also metaphorically linked to the cosmos. There is this monumental wall relief on the west side with several references to space, to technological achievements. Space is important to Kazakhstan as the Kazakh Soviet Republic with its Baikonur Cosmodrome played an important role in the exploration of space. Mountains, glaciers, and space are important aspects of the country's identity. The mural also echoes ornaments on the other sides of the cinema and the crown. They are all related to the 50th anniversary of the October Revolution, as the cinema was built in 1968. There are astronauts, revolutionaries, tractors forging new territory, and grain. But there are also references to the Kazakh language.

This is one of the distinctive things about Almaty's architecture even if it undoubtedly derived from the Soviet Union. Dinmukhamed Kunayev, the ethnic Kazakh head of the Kazakh SSR, had a very strong influence on the city's architecture, giving local architects the opportunity to express themselves.

Another example is Medeo, the ice skating rink (077) designed by Vladimir

Arman Cinema (052), which Anel Moldakhmetova calls one of Almaty's iconic buildings

Katsev. He cleverly integrated it into the surrounding mountainous landscape. This integration with the landscape can also be found in Hotel Kazakhstan (054), the first high-rise to be built with earthquake resistance in mind.

But earthquake-resistant construction is simply a necessity in Almaty.

Moldakhmetova: Yes, that's true, but it's also about identity. It's about the uniqueness of the local conditions and how local architects deal with them. It's not that they just did functional things. They were inspired by the landscape. And that is a very strong connection for me.

Can you find that identity in contemporary architecture?

Azhiyev: It seems to me that we are losing our identity. As a rule, we now build with reference to Western European or American design, which has been copied and adapted second- or third-hand in Russia and then transferred here. We use building materials from Europe or China. We hardly create anything of our own. All we do is punch the ornament of the Kazakh flag into metal, cut it out with a laser because that's the cheapest and easiest way, and attach it to a façade. We see a lot of glass, which is not the best solution from the point of view of both local identity and local climate – because these glass buildings require air conditioning, you have to cool everything down in the summer, and in the winter it is very energy-intensive to heat.

There are works by earlier architects who worked at a time when materials and technologies were scarce. They found their own technical solutions – for example, creating fountains in courtyards or cooling buildings with air shafts. They made beautiful things out of scarcity. Now that we have all this technology at our disposal, decisions are based more on economic considerations than on identity or beauty. That's why we now have fairly standardised architectural solutions that are used everywhere.

Perhaps there is simply a different, new identity today?

Moldakhmetova: In my opinion, modern architecture reflects the new mentality that has formed since independence. This is a culture of Toy-Khana, of wedding palaces, of presenting oneself to the outside world. People like to go out to eat, to show off, to celebrate even if everything around them is going to hell in a handbasket. This is important in Kazakhstan, and especially in Almaty.

Almaty is the capital of hedonism in general. And when you walk around the city, you can see it very clearly: some people

Adil Azhiyev laments the monotony and lack of identity of modern architecture in Almaty.

Modern glass facades are often unsuitable for Almaty's climate.

Monuments of history and culture of Almaty, 2008

The presidential residence, which was built in Soviet times as the Lenin Museum and was re-dedicated in independent Kazakhstan. Here seen in the year 2000

call it 'Kazakh Baroque'. It's an accumulation of different styles, an abundance of ornamentation, of gold, a kind of grotesque exaggeration. And even if people don't have the money to celebrate an event, they take out loans and celebrate. It's an interesting combination of ambition, and it's also found in the architecture – that opulence on the outside and then these cheap materials. There have been many complaints about the poor quality of the construction, even accidents when elements have fallen off. The exterior splendour is in no way matched by the quality of the interior.

Isn't that what people are told from above, by the state leadership?

Moldakhmetova: No, not at all, the culture of Toy-Khana comes directly from the people, it's something that is deeply ingrained in the Kazakh people.

Are the people involved in the development of the city?

Moldakhmetova: Yes, more and more. People have learned to express themselves by initiating dialogue. This is thanks to the many years of work by various citizens' initiatives. ArchCode has also contributed to this. Especially when it comes to discussing the city's

architectural heritage. Unfortunately, there are also examples of the city's inhabitants being ignored. The presidential residence is one such example. It was badly damaged in January 2022 and was eventually demolished. The discussion about preserving the residence was an important indicator of how engaged people are now. But the building was a political object, ideologically and symbolically incredibly important, including because it was the only building from the time of independence to be included in the register of monuments. After it was set on fire during the events of January 2022, the special interior suffered quite a lot. Unfortunately, the technical report on the damage was not transparent and was withheld from the public.

At the time we initiated a discussion about the fate of the residence. The decision to demolish it and make it impossible to rebuild had already been taken at presidential level. But we wanted this dialogue to take place precisely because the building was so important from a political and ideological point of view. The building was a monument to 30 years of independence, and then it was demolished? This is an incredibly strong ideological point on which the people should express themselves. But you can see the result: in the end the residence was indeed demolished.

After Bloody January 2022 the presidential residence was demolished. A public park will be built in its place.

What is the value of Almaty's historical buildings?

Azhiyev: From a global perspective, you might think that Almaty is provincial, nothing special, a former capital but nothing like Moscow or St Petersburg. So the budgets are much lower, fewer famous architects have come here, the materials are cheaper because there was always cost-cutting here. But that's part of the city's identity, that's what makes us special. And that has to be preserved because it's part of history, and we can't keep rewriting the history of our architecture by tearing it down every year and building anew. Historically, ecologically, and for other reasons, that is completely wrong. We need to preserve collective memory. It is important to preserve these things because we have nothing else.

Moldakhmetova: Buildings are artefacts of history. The one we're in now is the former NKVD building (024), the home of the KGB. And we are talking freely in a place where there were bugs everywhere recording every word, where people were interrogated. The building was used to crack down on political dissidents, including in the 1930s against the Alash Horde, a provisional government of Kazakhs who

A historic building; ArchCode is located at the former NKVD headquarters (024).

Iconic buildings of Soviet Modernism used as decoration on construction site fences

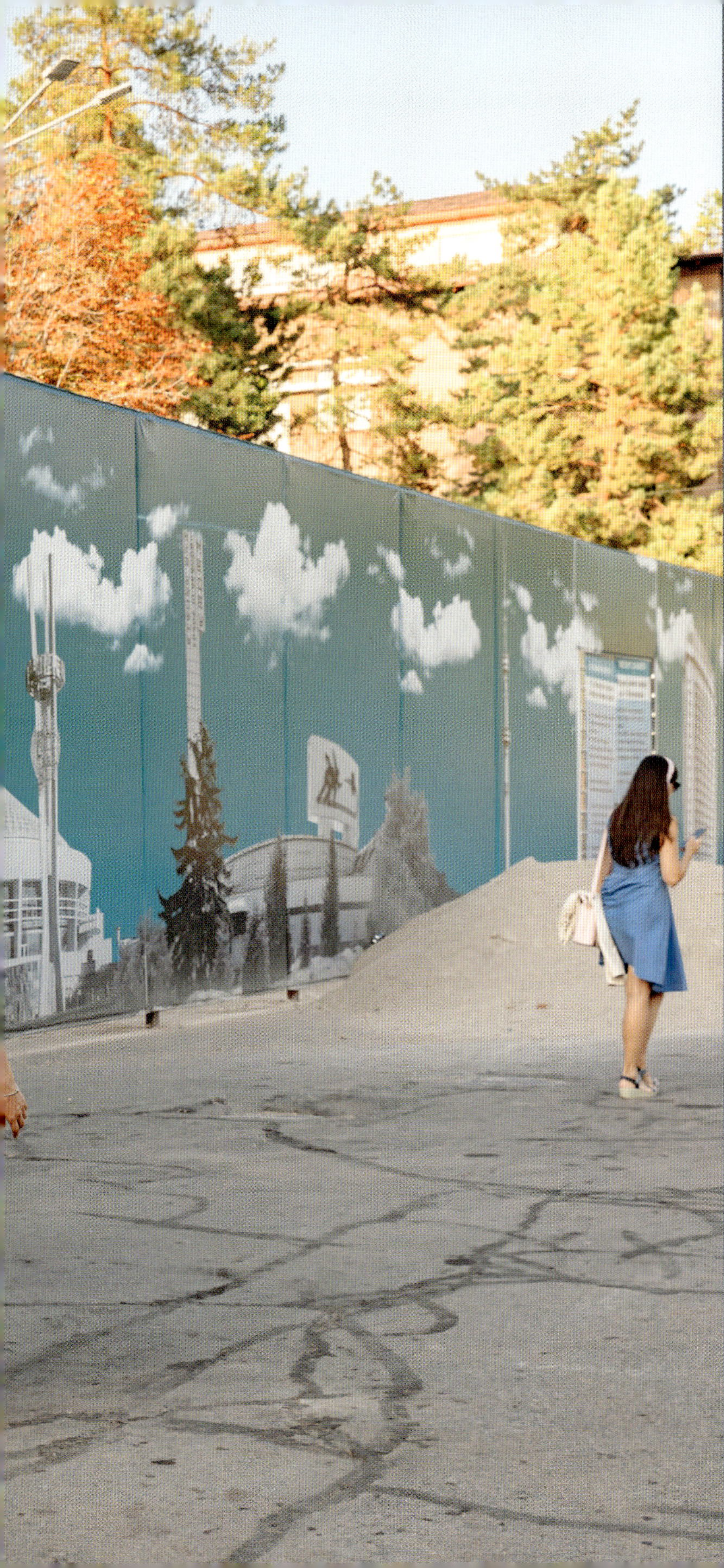

opposed Soviet power. This building is historically extremely important and valuable; it is a monument to the history of this nation – I am not afraid to use that big word. After independence, it became a museum to commemorate the victims of political repression. But in the early 2000s a political decision was made to move the museum to the village of Zhanalyk, north of Almaty, near the mass graves of political victims. And this building was turned into a hotel, can you imagine? That's why it's important for us to be here, so that people are reminded of these events by finding a connection to this architecture. The same could have been done with the demolished presidential residence. There shouldn't be a park on the site, it's a political place. The question of why old Almaty should be preserved is also a political question for me. And there can be different answers. If I answer it as an activist, as an advocate of public engagement, then I say it is important to preserve history and the artefacts of collective memory. But people should also find answers for themselves, and for me that is the main

criterion of social value – whether there is a sufficient number of people care about the fate of a building and look after it. The more people are convinced of the value of a building for our history, the higher its value, the more important it is to preserve it. For me, this is different from the aesthetic value of identifying unique examples of, say, Constructivism or Modernism. This is about typology and aesthetics. Architects can say that Almaty must be preserved because it represents a regional architecture that cannot be found anywhere else. Of course, it is impossible to preserve the whole city. There is constant construction, there are economic aspects, but there is also something like a cultural heritage economy. The value of Abai Opera House, for example, was determined simply on the basis of its material value. They looked at it as an investment project and realised that it was worth practically nothing. But cultural value should also be taken into account from an economic point of view because it can be monetised, for example when tourists come to experience an old building.

The historical city centre is increasingly seen as an attractive residential area.

Are people aware that old houses may be more interesting to live in than new ones?

Moldakhmetova: I think so: something is changing. If you look at krysha.kz, the country's main property website, you can see that a location in the historical centre of Almaty is already considered expensive. Even though the roofs are leaking, cockroaches are running around, and so on. Everyone used to say, 'Yuck, that's *sovok* [slang for 'Soviet'; editor's note]; now it's considered valuable.

Azhiyev: Of course, there were times – in the 1970s, when mass serial housing construction began – when people liked to move out of old houses, shacks, into prefabricated buildings because they were more attractive and offered more comfort. They had their own little kitchen, their own bathroom, their own personal living space. What's coming on to the property market now are usually huge 16- or 18-storey apartment blocks where there are no trees in the courtyard and only one lift per entrance, where it takes ages to get to the top floors, where people fight over parking spaces and kill each other. That actually happened, you know. These are such large gatherings of people that there are bound to be conflicts.
I'm not saying it doesn't happen in Soviet apartment blocks, but people are less crowded there. There are lively courtyards and gardens. People know their neighbours because they have lived together for a long time. In Soviet days the two- or three-storey houses in the city centre were reserved for the elite, politicians, scientists, and artists. The majority of the working class could only afford prefabricated buildings. If you compare the housing estates of that time with those of today, I have the impression that the quality of life was better back then.

As someone who wants to involve the population in urban development issues, do you see any progress?

Moldakhmetova: Absolutely, in terms of people understanding their own rights. This is a very important result. The former ASK-2 television studio complex (061) is a positive example of how the public can accompany reconstruction processes and coordinate with the client, and the result was very good. The opinions of the public were taken into account. We included many experts in the working group, and the result was maximal impact on preserving the authenticity of this monument. The building is still not listed, but that was discussed at the time and we asserted our right to be involved. People have also started to resist infill and gap development. In the past hardly anyone would have dared to do that. More recently, for example, there's been debate about the redevelopment of Sairan Lake, where local people want to get involved and assert their rights. You can't just say to people, 'Here's the project, and here's how we're going to do it.' That used to be possible, but it's not any more.

Will the way in which Soviet and Russian architecture is treated in Almaty and Kazakhstan change? I notice a stronger dissociation from the Russian-dominated past. Does that affect architecture?

Azhiyev: This demarcation was felt immediately after the collapse of the Soviet Union in the early 1990s. Many buildings were rebuilt at that time. But unlike many other cities in the former Soviet republics, most of the Soviet architecture was preserved here because the capital was moved to Astana in 1997. As a result, almost nothing has been touched. If Alma-Ata had remained the capital, it would look very different today; many buildings would have been demolished to make way for piles of glass boxes like in Astana. It was easier to build there because there was plenty of space. The old city was preserved, was redesigned, but mostly new buildings were built. But in Alma-Ata, which is surrounded by mountains, the historical centre would probably have been demolished. In the early 2000s there were plans to demolish the old Stalinist buildings in the centre. But in 2008 the financial crisis hit, the money ran out, and that saved these buildings. In fact, the crisis turned out to be a stroke of luck for the city.

Aksai, one of Almaty's 'sleeping districts', built in the 1970s and 1980s

Prefabricated residential building from the 1970s on Zhibek Zholy and Baribayev streets

Serial Housing in Almaty's Soviet-era Architecture

Gulnara Abdrasilova. Edited by Edda Schlager

With a population of 2.241 million (as of 01.03.2024), Almaty is the largest city in Kazakhstan and the country's financial, scientific, educational, and cultural centre. Due to the city's relatively short history – Vernoye Fortress was founded by the Russian military in 1854; the city was called 'Verny' from 1867 and 'Alma-Ata' from 1921 – one has to live with the disappointment that there is no old architecture to attract tourists. The city also lacks the 'birthmarks' of old cities – dilapidated and disadvantaged neighbourhoods and abandoned buildings. Before the October Revolution of 1917, Verny was a small town of one-storey houses without any comfort or sanitation. In the early years of Soviet rule the state focused on repairing the existing housing stock. The blocks of flats built in Alma-Ata between 1921 and 1928 did not differ much from the pre-revolutionary ones; they were small and single-storey [1, p. 6].

The systematic development of residential architecture in Kazakhstan began in the 1920s. In 1925 a construction office was established in Alma-Ata to deal with housing in the city, and 'in 1926 the construction of the first 19 residential buildings with 54 apartments began' [2, p. 41]. The beginning of active housing construction in the Kazakh SSR dates to the 1930s, after the capital was moved from Kyzyl-Orda to Alma-Ata in 1929. At that time the city began to build residential buildings based on standard designs, including by reusing project templates in the railway station settlement and on vacant lots in the city centre, such as at 6 Kazybek bi Street.

The city began to develop rapidly: housing, cultural, and public facilities were built on a large scale, and water supply, sewerage, and outdoor facilities were improved. 'Two-, three-, and four-storey blocks of flats were built to replace the one-storey rural-style blocks. The concentration of new buildings on several plots in the centre made it possible to create separate

One of the first standard-design residential buildings from the early 1930s in the Turksib railway station settlement at 6 Kazybek bi Street

Rear of a 1930s residential building at 6 Kazybek bi Street

residential, administrative, and public building complexes [1, p. 7].

In the 1930s housing construction in the Soviet Union was gradually industrialised. Under the city's first general plan, drawn up in 1937 by Architecture and Planning Studio No. 1 of the People's Commissariat for Education, extensive industrial, residential, and civil buildings were built in Alma-Ata in the pre-war years. The general plan provided for preservation of the existing rectilinear urban layout; the creation of important

The condition of some of the standardised buildings dating to the 1930s is extremely poor, as they have barely been renovated since they were built.

architectural and urban nodes, such as Central Square, Theatre Square, and Railway Station Square; widening of main roads; enlargement of smaller blocks; and creation of technical infrastructure and open spaces [1, p. 7].

The construction work was carried out on the basis of an urban planning concept that provided for the designation of residential areas with a high quality of life. In the Turksib district, for example, two-storey blocks of wooden houses were built with relatively large living spaces and balconies, but without public facilities.

In the first half of the 1930s 11 apartment blocks with eight flats each were built to the same design on Kazarmennaya (now: Panfilov), Artilleriyskaya (Kurmangazy), Vokzalnaya (now: Abylai-Khan Avenue), and Lagernaya (Shevchenko) streets. Each apartment had three or four rooms, a kitchen, a veranda, and a sanitary unit. These were the first blocks of flats in the city to have a water and sewerage system. The two-storey houses, popularly known as 'slanted houses' because they stood at an angle to the street, were demolished in 2006 and 2007. There is now a park on this site.

During the Second World War many industrial plants were relocated from European parts of the Soviet Union to the southern and eastern regions, and parts of the civilian population were evacuated here. In Alma-Ata many single-storey blocks of flats were hastily built from local building materials near the industrial plants for the workers and employees who arrived with the evacuated factories and businesses. The end of the war brought resumption of construction of three- and four-storey blocks of flats, with improvements in their layout, landscaping, and the architectural designs for their façades. Surviving examples of these residential buildings include the Academy of Sciences block of 18 flats at 15a Shevchenko Street (1950), the Kirov Engineering Works residential complex (049) at 11 Baitursynov Street / 151 Zhibek Zholy Street (1947/49), Zhilkombinat No 9 on the corner of Sovetskaya (now: Kazybek bi) and Tchaikovskaya streets (1950), and the House of Scientists at 60 Zhibek Zholy Street (050).

Residential buildings were designed to new urban planning concepts, but with street-facing façades often in the Neoclassical style. Due to the increased risk of earthquakes in Alma-Ata, these buildings were built no higher than four storeys. The foundations were strip footings; fired bricks were used for the walls, and wooden planks for the floors. The staircases were of monolithic reinforced concrete.

In the post-war period particular attention was paid to the exterior appearance of the houses. This can be explained by the desire to create the most expressive solutions for the development of an independent national architecture, as well as by the location of residential buildings on main streets and squares if they were intended to be particularly respectable. The architecture of the residential buildings of this period in Alma-Ata is characterised by the use of design elements borrowed from Classical and national Kazakh heritage, such as pointed arches, decorative columns, massive cornices, and applied ornamental details.

Among these houses particularly notable are the House of Scientists (050), the residential building for Turksib workers (048) with 68 flats, and the Kazpotrebsoyuz house (038) with 35 flats. Decades after their construction, these buildings in the centre of Almaty still play an important role in the cityscape.

Of course, reliance on one-off, non-standardised architectural design made it impossible for the state to guarantee quantitative growth of construction activity and universal provision of housing for its citizens. In the mid-1950s the volume of housing construction increased: in Alma-Ata construction of standardised buildings, especially two- and three-storey houses, greatly accelerated [1]. During these years the foundations were laid for

Typical Stalin-era residential development at the junction of Akhmet Baitursynov (then: Uighurskaya) and Gogol streets. Facing a main road, this house has balconies and national ornamentation in the form of stucco mouldings. These buildings belong to the residential complex of the Kirov Engineering Works.

Three-storey 1950s residential building

comprehensive industrialisation of the construction industry. Under the Decree of the Central Committee of the CPSU and the Council of Ministers of the USSR 'On the Development of Production of Pre-fabricated Reinforced-Concrete Elements and Structures for Construction', passed in 1954, 400 factories and plants for pre-fabricated reinforced-concrete elements were established in the Soviet Union. In 1956 the Almaty House Building Combine was commissioned to produce prefabri-cated reinforced-concrete elements and products for mass housing construction.

The idea of standardised housing be-came a cornerstone of the Soviet state's social policy.

In Alma-Ata, the capital of the Kazakh SSR, further development using only two-storey residential buildings could have led to serious economic and urban planning problems. For this reason, between 1954 and 1955 the three- and four-storey I-275 and I-275-A series of residential buildings were developed specifically for Alma-Ata on the basis of a single standardised de-sign and, in many cases, built [1, p. 7].

In 1958 the Kazgorstroyproekt design in-stitute (now KAZGOR) developed a pro-posal for the development of new dis-tricts in the west of Alma-Ata, based on the principle of microzoning, which al-lowed for creation of large districts of residential buildings, schools, kinder-gartens, recreational parks, etc.

From 1961 forwards, new residential districts were built on land amounting to more than 500 hectares. These con-sisted of four to six micro-districts, each designed for 6000 to 10,000 in-habitants. Each micro-district was or-ganised as a group of residential build-ings with its own recreational areas and primary service facilities. The housing stock of the first 12 districts, built from 1961 forwards, consisted of 596 residen-tial buildings. Of these, 81 per cent were four-storey; 15 per cent, five-storey; 1 per cent, two-, three- and six-storey;

Laura Aukhadiyeva

Series 1Kz-464DS house, built from large prefabricated panels from the early 1970s on, here in the Koktem micro-district

Dzhansaya Kambarova

Staircase of a series No 1-464A house, one of the the first series of large prefabricated buildings, here in micro-district No 3

Laura Aukhadiyeva

A series 1Kz-464DS house from the 1970s in the micro-district of Koktem. This series is more earthquake-resistant and better adapted to the climate than series from the 1960s.

and 2 per cent, eight- to nine-storey pre-fabricated buildings. By 1965 the construction of large prefabricated buildings accounted for more than two-thirds of all residential construction in Alma-Ata. In 1959 one-third of houses built were single-storey, but construction of such buildings was discontinued in 1962. After the first micro-districts, other residential areas were built in Alma-Ata between 1970 and 1990: Orbita and Taugul in the south west; Zhetysu, Mamyr, and Aksai in the west; Koktem in the centre; Sairan and Tastak in the north east; Samal in the east; Almagul and Kazakhfilm in the south. All these neighbourhoods were essentially built using large prefabricated blocks.

One of the first series of large prefabricated buildings in Alma-Ata was No 1-464A, which was built in micro-districts Nos. 2 to 6. In 1962 this series was improved and adapted to both climatic conditions and the high seismicity in south Kazakhstan, receiving the name '1Kz-464AS/62'. It was

Aiym Iliasova

Aiym Iliasova

The balcony and kitchen of a house from the more advanced Series 1Kz-464DS/84, which was mainly built in the west of the city in Ainabulak and Aksai micro-districts from 1984 onwards

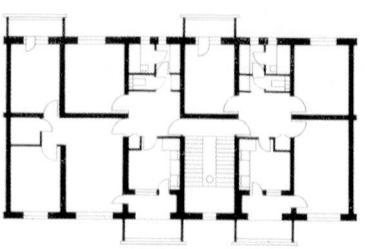

Series 69, a block construction with longitudinal and transverse walls

also used in the construction of micro-districts No. 1 to 12, and partly in areas of dense development in the city centre, for example at the corner of Panfilov and Mametov streets. The more advanced Series 1Kz-464DS was used in mass production from 1971 forwards in the Aksai and Koktem micro-districts, while Series 1Kz-464DS/84 (1984) was built in the city centre, in the west of the city, and in the Ainabulak micro-district.

Four- to five-storey houses from Series 1Kz-464 were built with different staircases and layouts for one- to four-room apartments. They have no garbage chutes

or lifts. The supporting walls are 3.2 or 2.6 metres high; the span is 5.76 metres; and the total width of the building is 11.52 metres. The foundations are monolithic strip foundations of concrete and reinforced concrete. The building's main structure consists of reinforced-concrete cross walls. The floor slabs are 2.6 or 3.2 metres wide and rest on the external wall slabs. When these buildings were built on main roads, their ground floors were used for shops and similar functions.

At the end of the 1960s new housing types were developed with the aim of improving the buildings' structural and aesthetic qualities and comfort of living. The Kazgorstroyproekt state design institute developed series No. 69 and No. 70 for Alma-Ata.

Series No. 70 was designed in 1968 by the architects Aleksey Naumov and

E-147, an experimental series of eight-storey houses from the early 1970s

Façade of an eight-storey building from the E-147 series at the intersection of Kurmangazy Street and Abylai Khan (then: Kommunistichesky) Avenue

Architecture of Soviet Kazakhstan, 1987 (3)

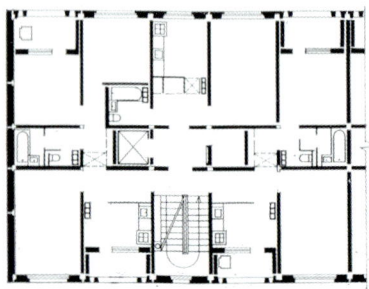

Series 158, a development of Series E-147: five- and nine-storey houses built in the residential areas of Aksai, Almagul, and Tole Bi Avenue in 1978 and 1980

N. Nikonova and the engineers P. Mednikov and Y. Zolotarenko using block construction. Four or five storeys high with ceiling heights of 3.0 or 2.80 metres for different expected earthquake strengths, they consist of a prefabricated monolithic reinforced-concrete skeleton with column spacings of 3.0 to 3.60 metres and spans of 5.40 metres. The walls are brick-faced. The slabs are multi-layered, pre-stressed ribbed concrete slabs.

The large panelled houses of Series 69 were designed in 1970 by the architects Aleksey Naumov, Alikhan Mukhtarov, V. Sokolov, and S. Uspanova with the participation of the engineers P. Mednikov and Y. Zolotarenko. Buildings in this series are four storeys high. The design uses block construction with longitudinal and transverse walls. The distance between the transverse walls is 3.0 or 3.6 metres. The distance between the longitudinal walls is 3.9 or 5.4 metres. The storey height is 3.0 metres. The floors are of reinforced concrete. On the upper floor there are two flats (or three and four rooms). The total floor area of the three-room flat is 62.6 square metres; that of the four-room flat, 77.47 square metres. The living areas (total floor areas minus areas of kitchens, bathrooms, and corridors) are 41.52 and 52.57 square metres

respectively. The sanitary facilities are separate and are illuminated by daylight. The kitchens have a floor area of eight square metres and a loggia – a novelty at the time and a sign of particular comfort. In the three-room flat all the rooms are side by side. In the four-room flat the common room is a walk-through.

As the population of Alma-Ata grew, it became increasingly necessary to increase density of construction and thus the number of storeys in a building. At the Central Research Institute for Housing Construction in Moscow a team of architects and designers led by Boris Rubanenko developed several

Nine-storey house at 36 Dostyk (then: Lenin) Avenue, built in the 1970s

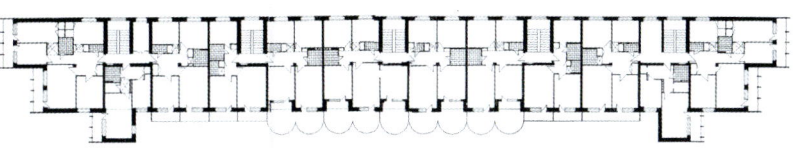

The former Pioneer shop on Kurmangazy Street between Nazarbayev Prospekt and Panfilov Street: skeletal construction with wall infills

experimental projects for eight-storey houses with the designation E-147 [2, p. 146]. The first eight-storey residential building in the E-147 series was built in the city centre, on the southeast corner of the intersection of today's Kurmangazy Street and Abylai Khan Avenue, where it still stands today. Later, this series was also built in the No. 10 and Koktem micro-districts.

Based on the initially experimental Series E-147, a series of five- and nine-storey residential buildings called 'No. 158' was developed and put into production in 1978 and 1980. From 1978 forwards, houses in this series were built in the Aksai, Almagul, and Tole-Bi Avenue residential areas.

More than 90 per cent of residential neighbourhoods were built in this style. To this day, about two-thirds of Almaty's housing stock consists of apartment blocks, most of which were built during the Soviet era.

In the 1970s and 1980s planning solutions for prefabricated housing were continuously improved, taking into account local climatic, geological, and social factors. The Almaty Housing Combine produced special regional series with increased storey heights for greater earthquake resistance.

Rapid urbanisation led to far-reaching changes in planning and housing construction: the construction period was shortened, while the reliability and quality of the buildings were maintained; floor areas and heights of living and ancillary rooms were increased; and each apartment was equipped with a bathroom and household appliances. Technical and social communication facilities were made compulsory for new residential buildings, and more attention was paid to the appearance of residential buildings.

Half-timbered and monolithic construction methods were used in the construction of residential buildings with larger numbers of floors. In 1970 the residential complex on Lenin (now Dostyk) Avenue was built in a timber-framed style. The east part of the avenue from Tole bi Street to Kurmangazy Street was reconstructed: the Three Warriors residential complex (085), three 12-storey, single-section buildings connected by a shared stylobate and transitional galleries, and a group of nine-storey, multi-section residential buildings, including 36, 40, 42, 46, and 48 Dostyk Avenue, were built here. The half-timbered buildings include the nine-storey block at 75 Gogol Street, between Kunayev Street and Nazarbayev Avenue, and the two striking 16-storey, single-section residential towers on the north side of Republic Square at 42 and 49

Baiseitov Street. Today these buildings are among the most important and distinctive residential buildings in the city.

The skeleton construction of these buildings made it possible to use the lower floors for public facilities that complemented the cultural and commercial services offered to the public.

The construction of skeletal residential buildings with different wall infills, such as slabs or bricks, allowed for the development of a variety of volumetric planning solutions – from the 16-storey high-rise on Republic Square (42 and 49 Baiseitov

16-storey residential buildings on Republic Square, at 42 and 49 Baiseitov Street

Street) to large, multi-storey buildings such as the one at 43 Kurmangazy Street with 48 flats and the former Pioneer shop. However, the use of frame and panel construction has disadvantages in the event of earthquakes, including consumption of expensive metal, complexity of joins, and the weight of the façade panels [2, p. 168].

The combination of a frame and strut system with a stiff monolithic core, which has been implemented in a number of residential buildings in Almaty, has opened up new possibilities for improving the earthquake resistance of buildings and extending building designs to a greater number of storeys. Such houses are based on the principle of transferring the seismic load from the frame to the reinforced-concrete core.

'In the 12-storey residential building with 48 apartments at the corner of Krasina and Kalinina streets (now 88 Kabanbai Batyr Street) by architects Kaldybai Montakhayev and Yuliya Skvortsova [...] the 5.24-by-5.24-metre reinforced-concrete core fully absorbs the seismic loads and relieves the lightweight skeleton structure, which is mainly designed to bear static vertical loads. [...] The use of a single design step of 5.1 by 5.1 metres and cellular prefabricated floor slabs supported along their edges made it possible to reduce the number of standard product

sizes and labour intensity during assembly of the structures' [2, p. 171]. The skeleton construction with a stiff core made it possible to create a cross-section with a more complex configuration than in conventional buildings with a rectangular plan in conditions of increased seismicity. The stiffening core contains staircases, lifts, and garbage chutes. The apartments meet all orientation and ventilation requirements. Buildings with a monolithic reinforced-concrete core also include the 12-storey

Elongated nine-storey residential building with a monolithic reinforced-concrete core and 280 apartments at the intersection of Auezov and Dzhandosov streets

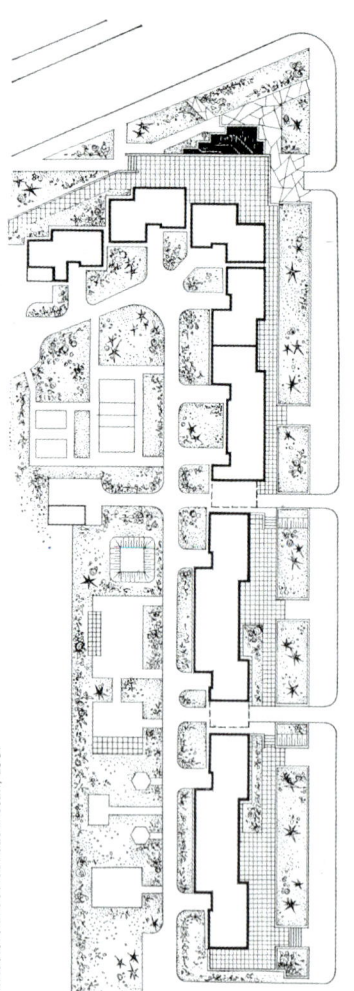

high-rise building with 110 apartments on Timiryazev Street near the Esentai (formerly Vesnovka) River at Mikrorayon Koktem-2, 1 and the elongated nine-storey residential building with 280 flats at the intersection of Auezov and Dzhandosov streets.

It became possible to vary the number of storeys (from five to 16) in houses with rigid cores using a range of prefabricated reinforced-concrete products.

Monolithic construction has proved particularly economical and competitive, thanks to effective complete prefabrication of houses and the technical solutions used during construction. The advantage of monolithic construction is the ability to vary the plasticity of the structure, which increases the architectural expressiveness of the buildings. In Almaty too this method has been used to construct high-rise buildings that serve as urban landmarks. One of the first buildings of this type was a nine-storey residential building with 36 flats of monolithic reinforced-concrete construction on Abai Avenue in Micro-district No. 4 (1971). This project was reused with minor modifications in the centre of Almaty. Almaty's first 12-storey monolithic reinforced-concrete residential building was built in 1978 on the west side of what was then Lenin (today: Dostyk) Avenue between then Kalinin (today: Kabanbai

Aksai-4 micro-district, where serial prefabricated buildings of four, five, and nine storeys were built from the 1970s to the early 1990s

Batyr) and Dzhambyl Streets. 'The basis of the architectural design and layout of this house is a compact layout with four flats per floor, which, unlike the first nine-storey monolithic buildings in Almaty, has a square configuration (21 by 21 metres) with oblique corners based on a structural system with load-bearing walls, which in turn has a favourable effect on increasing its seismic resistance' [2, p. 184]. The presence of loggias in the flats contributes to the improvement of their microclimate in the southern climate. The building was constructed using monolithic prefabricated construction, employing 'room-sized' prefabricated reinforced-concrete slabs for the intermediate ceilings, which made it possible to avoid the presence of cantilevered beams inside the living spaces. The cruciform floor plan with cantilevered volumes and rounded corners, as well as the use of a contrasting combination of monolithic reinforced-concrete façades with a rhythmic system of horizontal transoms on the corner loggias, permitted a degree of architectural expressiveness [2, p. 187].

After the collapse of the Soviet Union in 1991, mass housing construction came to an end. The transition from a planned to a market economy exacerbated the housing problem, and new solutions were needed. In April 2011, 20 years after Kazakhstan's acquisition of independence, the government adopted the 'Programme for Modernisation of Housing and Communal Services of the Republic of Kazakhstan for 2011–2020'. This programme aimed to modernise municipal infrastructure, create an optimal model of housing conditions, improve the quality of housing and municipal services for the population, and establish special financing mechanisms for the repair of common property in condominiums, including thermal upgrading [3]. Due to the rapid influx of people moving to Almaty and the prolonged lack of regulation and control of technical solutions, as well as to the difficult economic situation, the Soviet-era mass housing built between 1950 and 1990 has suffered significantly. There is a huge need for research and development to maintain these buildings and keep them in use. Many have a long service life and are in good structural condition. International experience shows that the comprehensive demolition of Soviet-era housing does not make economic or social sense and that modernisation of housing pays for itself.

In recent years the state has actively promoted the introduction of modern energy-efficiency technologies, including through the drafting of appropriate legislation. This allows for owners to carry out major

On the left: Almaty's first 12-storey monolithic reinforced-concrete apartment building (53 Dostyk Avenue) was built in 1978. Several more of these striking high-rises can be found throughout the city centre.

repairs to their flats at their own expense. In apartment buildings – condominiums – the owners are obliged to bear the costs of general overhauls of common property in proportion to their share in co-ownership [4, p. 73].

In 2022 there were 54,474 apartment buildings in Kazakhstan, almost a third of which were built before 1970; about two-thirds of the housing stock entered use more than 25 years ago. A third of these dwellings are in need of some form of repair. Almost all the housing stock (97.8 per cent) is privately owned, often in condominiums in Soviet-era apartment blocks, while only 2.2 per cent is state-owned. Given the enormous importance of Soviet-era housing to the population, the state is now taking steps to prevent further deterioration and to preserve these buildings. The mass character of standardised construction in Almaty is particularly obvious in the so-called 'dormitories' – housing estates built between 1960 and 1980 using a serial construction method and equipped with social infrastructure such as schools, kindergartens, polyclinics, and commercial facilities.

It is worth noting that the housing stock in Kazakhstan is of a relatively high standard. In cities 100 per cent of residential buildings have a water supply; 96 per cent have a sewerage system; and 90 per cent have central heating. At the same time 97.8 per cent of dwellings are privately owned [3, p. 15]. The common problem of most residential buildings is their low energy efficiency. Research shows that at 270 kW/square metre per year, the heat consumption of blocks of flats is well above the European average of 100–120 kW/square metre per year), with around 30 per cent of heat being lost through the building envelope, i.e. through façade walls, windows, roofs, basements, ground floors, and building entrances [4, p. 43]. In order to maintain and, in the best case, increase buildings' lifespans, there is an urgent need for renovation.

In addition to renovation of residential buildings, landscaping of built-up areas will be upgraded. Accessibility will be improved; passageways and footpaths will be created between blocks; and sports grounds and children's playgrounds will be renovated. After the refurbishment, many of the residential buildings from the early housing series, built in the 1960s and 1970s, will be converted into offices and service facilities, such as clinics, pharmacies, beauty salons, and repair workshops.

At the end of the Soviet era the urban development of the typical socialist city was repeatedly the subject of criticism, sarcasm, and comedy. Just think of the 1976 film *The Irony of Fate, or Enjoy Your Bath!* by the screenwriter Emil Braginsky and the director Eldar Ryazanov, which pokes fun at the uniformity of Soviet

Residential buildings from the 1960s or 1970s, with shops added later, after perestroika

planned cities and the powerlessness of planners and architects in the face of bureaucratic functionaries: the main character confuses his apartment with a similar one in a completely different city, resulting in slapstick-like situations. The uniformity of the buildings and the monotony of residential areas made up of identical houses have been criticised for lack of architectural originality.

Indeed, the obsessive focus on the cost efficiency of standardised designs in the face of economic constraints was reflected in the schematic nature of the compositional solutions, the inadequate landscaping, and the monotonous appearance of the buildings. Geographical and climatic peculiarities were all but ignored in the means and techniques used in urban planning. Almost no methods were explored by which to reveal the identity of the architectural environment through incorporation of street furniture and elements in regional styles. Nevertheless, despite the limited expressive possibilities offered by standardised construction, each successive series of houses had more expressive façades: regional character was manifested through decoration of the facing panels, ornamentation of balconies and loggia roofs, and sun-protection grids.

Over time, our view of the mass of residential buildings in Almaty will acquire a different tinge – warmer, less sharp. These modest, architecturally unpretentious standardised residential buildings allowed the state to solve its most important task – to provide the population with modern housing.

A look back at Almaty's architecture shows that mass housing has not only solved socio-economic problems but also become an integral part of the established cityscape. In the twenty-first century standardised buildings are no longer alien to the ever-growing city. The state is implementing various programmes to redevelop 'dormitory towns'. Over the last ten years, the quality of renovation of mass housing estates erected from the 1960s to the 1990s has improved considerably.

Of course, there is no denying that there are problems today caused by the level of motorisation of the population: the narrow passageways inside the street blocks in Almaty's micro-districts were not designed for such intensive car traffic, and the lack of parking spaces is also a problem for residents.

Overall, however, Almaty's housing estates with their four-to-nine-storey residential buildings and public facilities such as schools, kindergartens, clinics, and shops form a special architectural environment: the block structure with orderly main streets and cosy, densely planted courtyards with playgrounds and recreational areas conveys a sense of scale and the ergonomics of the surrounding space.

In Almaty's modern architecture the 'layers' of different historical periods – pre-Soviet, Soviet, and post-Soviet – are closely interwoven. None of these periods can be ignored; each has contributed to the image of the green, so-called 'garden city' that spreads out at the foot of the majestic Alatau Mountains. And in this mosaic of the city the modest standardised Almatian houses, which, built in different eras, have become a symbol of their hometown to many citizens, occupy a worthy place.

Literature

1. Basenov, T.K., Gershberg, V.S, Greben, V.B., et al., *Urbanism in Kazakhstan* (Alma-Ata: Kazakhstan, 1973).

2. Glaudinov, B.A., Seydalin, M.G., Karpykov, A.S., *Architecture of Soviet Kazakhstan* (Stroyizdat, 1987).

3. 'On the adoption of the concept for the development of housing and communal infrastructure until 2026. Resolution of the Government of the Republic of Kazakhstan of 23 September 2022, No. 736'. URL: https://adilet.zan.kz/rus/docs/P2200000736 (date of publication: 15. October 2022).

4. *National Housing Survey: Republic of Kazakhstan* (Geneva, 2018). URL: https://unece.org/DAM/hlm/documents/Publications/CP_Kazakhstan_web.RUS.pdf (as of 30 July 2022).

'Almaty has the Perfect Landscape for Tiny Houses.'

Entrepreneur Dinara Zhashibekova on the need for tiny houses in Almaty and flexibility in the business world. *Interview by Edda Schlager*

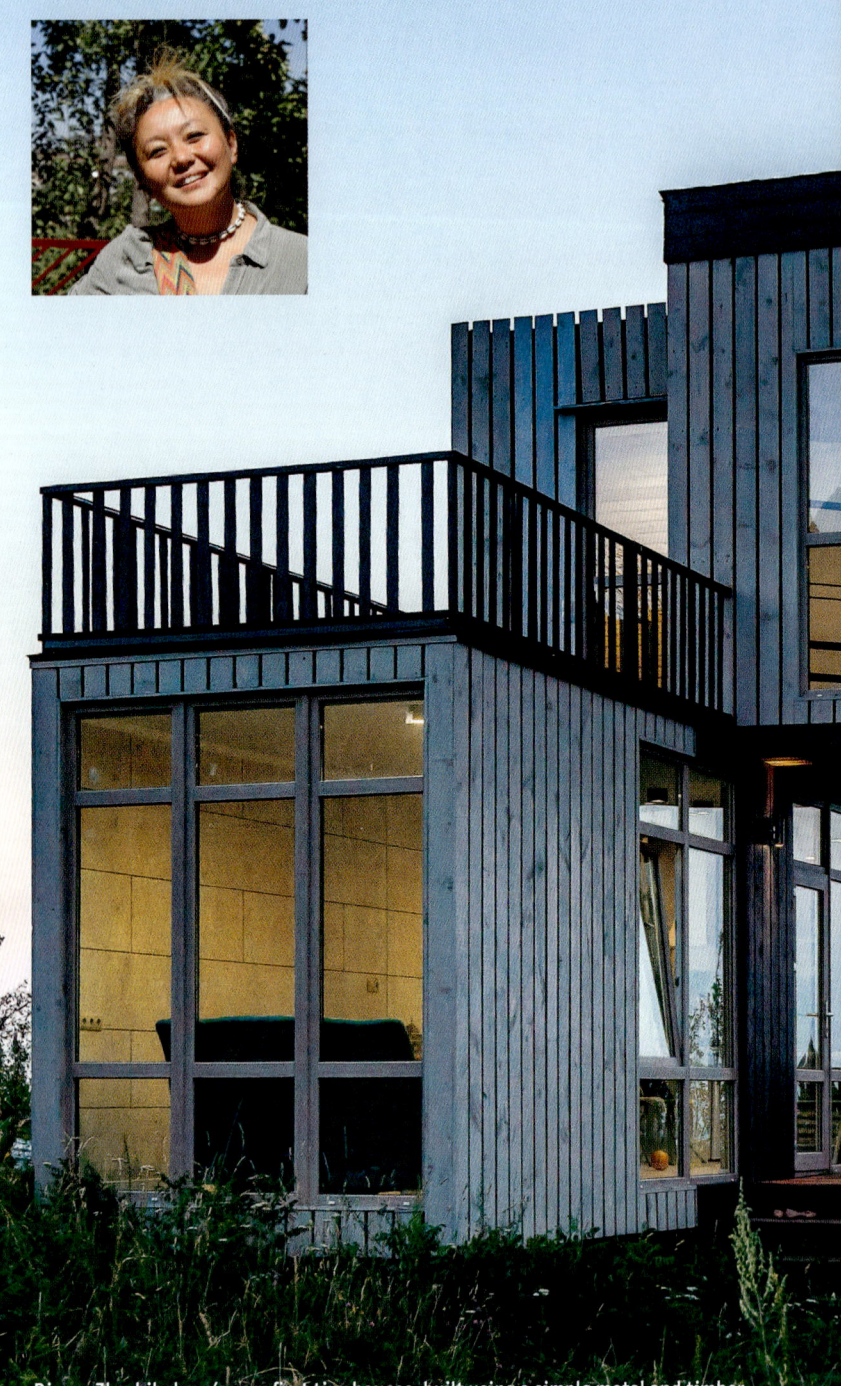

Dinara Zhashibekova's very first tiny houses, built using a simple metal and timber construction. She was one of the first to establish this type of holiday accommodation in Almaty. The one-storey house (background) has a floor area of only 18 square metres; the two-storey house, an area of 40 square metres.

Dinara Zhashibekova is the founder of iHouse Almaty, one of the first companies in Kazakhstan to offer tiny-house holidays since 2018. After building and successfully marketing tiny houses in two locations in the south of Almaty, she took a break for personal reasons. She is now planning to build the next tiny house in a village about 80 kilometres from Almaty, where for the first time she will own the land rather than rent it.

Why does Almaty need tiny houses?

Of all places, Almaty has the perfect landscape for tiny houses. Lots of green hills and fantastic mountains with the best views over the city, rivers, and lakes. All this close to the city, without having to drive for hours to get out into nature. Almaty needs this because the city is full of concrete multi-storey buildings. It also needs tiny houses to preserve nature without burdening the earth with more concrete and bricks. I'd like to leave nature untouched, adding trees to the view and the feeling of living in a tiny house, whether it's for a short time or for life. Tiny houses are quick to build, aesthetic (if you put passion and thought into it), practical, and often more affordable.

Pavel Tenyakov

You do the exterior and interior design of your houses yourselves. Where does the inspiration come from?

Mostly from old Soviet dacha houses, I suppose. Partly because that was my first experience of contentment and happiness, being out on a plot of land in a small village house. I associate such houses with childhood and a time without thoughts, freedom, fresh berries. I have always had this inner feeling that allows me to intuitively know the exact shape of a house for a particular location. I get inspiration from houses I see on my travels, and, of course, social media is also a source of ideas.

What is your entrepreneurial approach? What has been your experience of establishing this novelty in Almaty? Is the city administration open to it? And how do your guests react?

There was absolutely no entrepreneurial approach when I started, to be honest. I had wanted to do this for so long and had had weeks and months of sleepless nights and vivid dreams about tiny houses in Almaty. I am very lucky to have family and colleagues who are there for me and

have supported me and my first houses in many different ways. So, yes, I just had to do it, to tick it off my mental to-do list. I should also say that at that time I felt the urge to get away from the city and the constant competition. I was very surprised that so many people shared this need and very quickly became tiny-house fans. It's been six years since the project captured the hearts of our guests and, amazingly, we continue to receive notes of gratitude and beautiful stories from them. Unfortunately, I don't know much about the local authorities and their views on tiny houses, but I like the idea that some of them have even been my guests.

You had to abandon your first tiny houses, which were running very successfully. Why was that?

Yes, I didn't own the land, and from the beginning I'd had a feeling I would have to leave at some point. Even though my first tiny houses were portable, I didn't move them for a number of reasons. One was the fact that even after several years of looking for a new location, nothing could beat the first place and its magic. So instead of moving the houses for the sake of

Zhashibekova's second project renting small houses to tourists went bigger. This two-storey house has a floor area of 85 square metres and a terrace on each floor.

Gulnur Yesbolat

in Almaty know the problems with water, gas, and electricity supply in some places, and this certainly makes regular work more difficult and more expensive. Road access and infrastructure is another thing that needs to be considered. It would help entrepreneurs immensely if the government could support them by funding tourism projects and see the bigger picture regarding tourism development. Training for entrepreneurs in this area and also proper regulation of quality and service would be an advantage.

continuing the project, I decided to build another in a completely different location in an architectural style that fits perfectly into the landscape. I was also successful but have recently decided to close this site too, for personal reasons.

How difficult is this type of business in Kazakhstan? What problems do you face as an entrepreneur in Almaty?

In the last two or three years, this sector has been growing rapidly in and outside the city. Glamping in remote areas has become a trend. Those who live

What are your future plans for tiny houses? Will you be developing new projects?

Definitely! I now want to move further away from the city and develop rural areas. I already have a certain place in mind, 80 kilometres from Almaty. I'd like to support local women with work and income by having my tiny houses there and bring tourism to the village. iHouse is changing, of course, and I'd like urban people to keep their heads clear by getting out of the city, closer to nature, and really relaxing in Kazakhstan's most natural habitat.

Yenlik-Kebek, a mosaic (1965) by Moldakhmet Kenbayev and Nikolay Tsivchinsky at Hotel Almaty (063)

A mosaic by Moldakhmet Kenbayev and Nikolay Tsivchinsky from the 1960s to 1980s, rediscovered during the reconstruction of a bus stop that is now a tourist information centre on upper Dostyk Avenue, opposite the Royal Tulip Hotel

Murals and Mosaics:
Façade Art in Almaty Over Time

Edda Schlager

'Look at this composition, how sophisticated it is, these lines, the light – the whole work sings. A dream!' Alpamys Kenbayev points to a photograph of a colourful wall mosaic and flips through the pages of a book showing close-ups of sections of the mosaic. The colourful ceramic pieces form a Kazakh folk tale about the girl Yenlik and Zhigit Kebek, who fell in love despite their parents' plans to the contrary, ran away together, and were eventually condemned and killed by their own tribe for violating their traditions. 'This mosaic,' says Kenbayev, 'represents the renaissance of Kazakh art. It is part of the common heritage of the Kazakh people.' What Kenbayev is describing so passionately is the Yenlik and Kebek mosaic, which hangs to the east of the main entrance to Hotel Almaty and is one of the most valuable and best-preserved works of monumental Soviet Modernist art in Almaty. It was created in 1965 by Moldakhmet Kenbayev and Nikolay Tsivchinsky. For Alpamys Kenbayev it is undoubtedly 'the most beautiful of all my father's works'.

In the tradition of Soviet monumental art

Creative chaos reigns in Kenbayev's studio in the southern foothills of Almaty. There are drawings, oil paintings, plaster reliefs, books, canvases, and painting utensils, as well as tiles with glued-on mosaic stones and glass-ceramic blanks in various dull colours, which only reveal their full splendour when Kenbayev smashes them into small pieces. Now in his mid-sixties, Alpamys Kenbayev is the son of Moldakhmet Kenbayev, a distinguished artist of the Soviet Union, People's Artist of the Kazakh SSR, and professor at several universities, who died in 1993. Kenbayev senior's monumental works, often created in collaboration with the Ukrainian artist Nikolay Tsivchinsky, still

dominate Almaty's cityscape today. The eldest of five children, Alpamys Kenbayev followed in his father's footsteps and is a visual artist in his own right. He is passionate about preserving and restoring the works of his father and colleagues. 'People accuse me of only talking about my father's art,' says Kenbayev, 'but of course Nikolay Tsivchinsky and other monumental artists of the period, such as Boris Anisimov, Vladimir Tverdokhlebov, and Sebastian Kirakozov are also important to me. Even if the styles of the generations are very different.'

The thrust of Soviet Modernism

In Almaty many of the monumental works of art typical of Soviet Modernism have been preserved in public spaces: façade mosaics in the Byzantine style, sgraffiti, large-scale murals created by scratching multi-coloured layers of cement or plaster, reliefs, stained-glass windows, and depictions combining several techniques. In the 1950s Nikita Khrushchev

Alpamys Kenbayev shows a sketch of the mosaic in Issyk Restaurant at Hotel Almaty which he was asked to restore.

Sulushash – The Girl with the Souvenir by Moldakhmet Kenbayev and Nikolay Tsivchinsky, 1970, restored by Alpamys Kenbayev. Originally mounted on the façade of a house on Lenina (now: Dostyk) Avenue, it is now exhibited on Kok-Tobe Mountain.

Making smalt from ceramic tiles

arts were praised in theatres, museum, or cinema buildings, the life of the working people in industrial buildings and administrative headquarters, the pursuit of knowledge and progress in university campuses and buildings of scientific institutions, and physical culture in sports facilities. The postulate 'National in content, Soviet in form' was echoed not only in the architecture of Soviet Modernism, but also in monumental art, so that recourse to national characteristics in depiction was seen as a plus. In Uzbekistan and Tajikistan pictorial representation has played an important role in architecture since the Timurids and Samanids, Muslim ruling dynasties in the Middle Ages. This was also reflected in Soviet Modernism – in the elaborate works and techniques of the Jarsky brothers in Uzbekistan, for example. In Kazakhstan, on the other hand, where nomadic life prevailed until Soviet rule and there was virtually no lasting architecture, traditionally inspired monumental art was something new. And Moldakhmet Kenbayev was a pioneer in this field.

ordered cost-cutting rationalisation and mass production in the construction industry – which, along with technical problems caused by climatically unsuitable building materials and technologies, led to aesthetic impoverishment in many Soviet regions; but from the 1960s onwards, decoration of buildings was again explicitly encouraged. As in the Stalin era, monumental art was used for propaganda purposes, and Soviet life was portrayed as positively as possible. Depending on the theme of the particular building, the

Dedicated to his father's art

'What is special about my father's work,' says Alpamys Kenbayev, 'is his depiction of simple Kazakh life. He grew up in the steppe, and the connection to it can be found in all his works. Before

Selection of ceramic tiles and smalt mosaic pieces

Mosaic by Moldakhmet Kenbayev and
Nikolay Tsivchinsky from 1975, restored
by Alpamys. Originally attached to the
façade of a house, it now stands on the
road to Medeo.

Kenbayev senior gave monumental art in Kazakhstan its own style, there were hardly any such high-quality artistic depictions of Kazakh life in public spaces. 'Yes, the Kazakhs had wonderful commercial art,' says Alpamys Kenbayev, 'but hardly any independent fine art that focused on Kazakh traditions.' Alpamys Kenbayev is closely associated with his father's creative period from the 1960s to the late 1980s. He has restored several mosaics by his father and Tsivchinsky and by other monumental artists of the period: *Sulushash – the Girl with the Souvenir,* which can now be seen on the Kok-Tobe; the *Mosaic of Athletes*, which used to hang on the façade of a house and now stands on the road to Medeo; and the mosaic frieze by Sebastian Kirakozov at Narkhoz University, which was obviously made much later than his father's works. He was also supposed to renovate a mosaic in the Issyk restaurant at Hotel Almaty, which is currently being renovated. 'But I have to import the smalt, the mosaic tiles, from Russia, and they are expensive,' says Kenbayev. 'The client seems to have run out of money. Or maybe they just want someone else to do it,' he says, his disappointment evident. Not only at having missed out on the commission, but also at what is happening to Soviet-era monumental art in public spaces in Kazakhstan in general. Some things have improved in recent years. 'There are always wealthy sponsors who have realised that there is

Mosaic by Sebastian Kirakozov at Narkhoz University, restored by Alpamys Kenbayev

cultural value in preserving and restoring the old murals and mosaics,' says Kenbayev. But too much has already been lost and destroyed.

Urbanism takes over

Instead, a new trend in urban art has emerged in Almaty in recent years. More and more large-scale murals, often several storeys high, are being painted on the façades of buildings in the city centre and in new residential areas. Yerzhan Tanayev is one of the artists creating these new contemporary murals. Tanayev and his former fellow student Ali Zakir are behind the tag 'Tigrohaud Crew', which can be found in dozens of places on the walls of houses in Almaty but now also in Astana, Pavlodar, and Öskemen. The four artists started out in the early 2000s with partly illegal graffiti in a typical hip-hop style. Two colleagues have since left the collective. Tanayev also almost gave up for financial reasons. But since taking part in one of Almaty's regular street art festivals in 2007, the team have been able to make a living from their work. They get commissions from private individuals but increasingly also directly from city councils and *akimats*. 'For the authorities, the murals are a welcome advertisement for their work. They have a positive connotation because they beautify the neighbourhood and are popular with the public. And the officials can show their bosses: "Here we're doing something meaningful

Soviet-era sgraffito by Aleksandr Simakov

and visible".' Tanayev himself is particularly fond of Soviet-era sgraffiti, like the one by Aleksandr Simakov at the junction of Gogol and Auezov streets, which sometimes bear a striking resemblance to modern hip-hop street art. The subjects of Tigrohaud's murals often draw on traditional Kazakh symbolism and themes, usually combined with elements of contemporary urban life. 'The *akimat* often commission patriotic themes. We then suggest sketches. In the end, agreement is reached on the concrete implementation.' The Kazakh flag also appears regularly in this way – nation building wrapped in modern street art. The message of the murals commissioned by the authorities is often little different from the politically conscious monumental works of the Soviet past: both position the respective state power in the 'right' light. Tanayev admits that he often doesn't like these works himself – 'but we do it for commercial reasons, and we just execute whatever is desired.'

Commercial pragmatism

Tanayev's approach to the transience of the murals is similarly pragmatic. The paint often lasts only three or four years, then it fades. 'But then we'd rather paint something new than restore an old work,' he says. 'Our style changes quickly anyway, so we prefer to look to the future.' The fact that murals disappear from one day

Caii Kompe

This snow leopard was painted over with a Coca-Cola ad but later recreated.

Yerzhan Tanayev

Street art collective Tigrohaud painting a commissioned mural in Oskemen

to the next doesn't bother him. 'Once the work is done, we no longer have the copyright to it. What happens to it is no longer our business.' The Tigrohaud crew itself painted over the hugely popular mural of a snow leopard in Almaty in 2023 on behalf of Coca-Cola Kazakhstan – with advertising for Coca-Cola, also cleverly packaged as a colourful, cheerful mural with a young Kazakh woman holding a Coke bottle in the foreground. 'The campaign was completely legal, we had all the licences,' Tanayev says today. After an outcry in the media that art was being subordinated to commerce, the company had the advertising removed and the original snow leopard motif painted back on the façade.

Protests from society are effective

The painter Saule Suleymenova herself saw one of her murals in Almaty suddenly disappear without notice. Together with her husband, Kuanysh Bazargaliyev, who is also an artist, she had painted a façade in the centre of Almaty at the request of the Almaty *akimat*. It was based on her 2008 painting *Waiting* – a grandmother with binoculars looking out into the vast steppe with her two grandchildren – which in turn was based on an old Kazakh photograph from the 1970s or 1980s. 'The mural was so popular,' says Suleymenova, 'that it was even listed as a

One of many murals by the street art collective Tigrohaud in Almaty

Saule Suleymenova and Kuanysh Bazargaliyev's mural *Waiting* following restoration

landmark on Google Maps.' In 2022, however, the mural was simply painted over in a single colour as part of a renovation of a large number of historical houses, also ordered by the *akimat*, in order to unify the façades in the city centre. A citizens' initiative then launched a campaign to restore the façade. At first, Suleymenova and Bazargaliyev did not want to do this work themselves, so young graffiti artists were hired. 'But when we went to the site to check what they'd done, we didn't like the result at all, so we corrected the expression of the faces and the whole mural ourselves.' Suleymenova has her own take on the evolution of mural art in public spaces: 'Attitudes to the Soviet-era works have changed recently,' she says. 'People are increasingly recognising their artistic, historical value and restoring the old mosaics and reliefs.' However, she is personally sceptical about the Modernist monumental art of the Soviet era. 'I never liked that mystical exaggeration and whitewashing of reality.' She prefers to use her art to show the beauty of everyday life without glorifying it.

Transience as an essential quality of art

One of Suleymenova's latest works, *Yellow-Blue Bus*, a 50-square-metre mural, depicts such everyday moments on a bus in Almaty. Made of plastic bags on

polycarbonate panels, it was displayed at a festival on the east side of the National Library (065) but subsequently removed. Although Suleymenova would have liked to see the work there for longer, she believes ephemerality is part of art. In her 'cellophane painting', as she calls this technique, for example, it is part of the concept that the plastic bags will fade with the weather, imparting a new texture over time. Suleymenova hopes this painting will find a permanent place in the urban landscape. Almapys Kenbayev, the mosaic artist and restorer, rejects this understanding of façade art in the cityscape. 'Some people like it, others don't. I don't want to judge anyone,' he says, 'but for me, it's not art. These murals come and go; hardly anyone notices. In that sense, they are very much in tune with the fast-paced, non-binding nature of today's world.'

Anton Karmanov

Artist Saule Suleymenova

Anton Karmanov

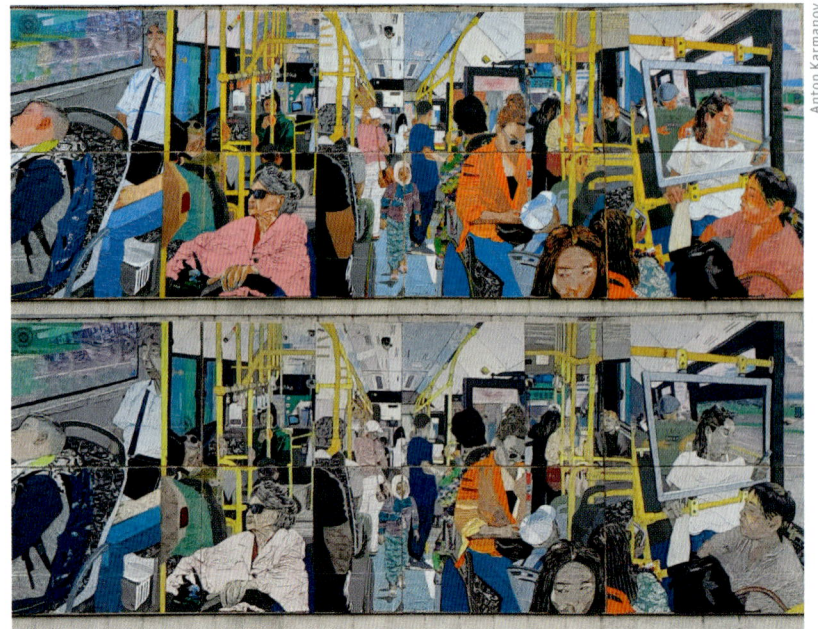

Saule Suleymenova's 'cellophane painting' *Yellow Blue Bus* at the National Library, freshly installed (top) and significantly faded a month after installation (bottom)

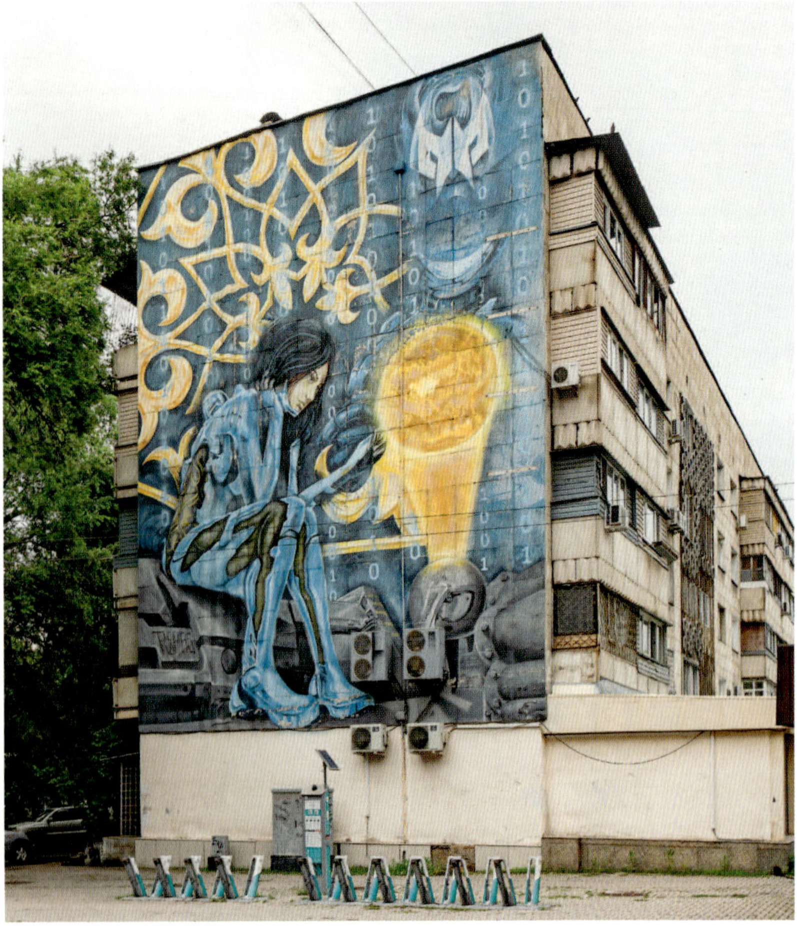

Mural by Almaty's well-known street art collective Repas

Mural depicting the Kazakh poet Abai Qunanbaiuly on Al-Farabi Avenue. The depiction of national heroes is very popular and contributes to the formation of identity.

Mural depicting ranger Erlan Nurgaliev, who died protecting the endangered Saiga antelope

Mural by the artist Alexander Blagy of the Belarusian
street art collective Taktak

Mural by the street art collective Repas

Mosaic by Sebastian Kirakozov on the cornice of the former Soyuzpechat building on the west bank of the Sairan. Soyuzpechat was a Soviet-era state network of organisations for the distribution of periodicals. The colourful mosaic runs around the entire building and depicts stylised newspaper illustrations and headlines.

150

Detail from *Students*, a 1968 mural by Nikolay Tsivchinsky on the rear of one of the buildings of Kazakh State Women's Pedagogical University at the junction of Gogol and Aiteke bi streets

Mosaic by Kanafiya Ospanov from 1994 on the north façade of the older KIMEP building at the intersection of Abai and Dostyk avenues. The mosaic is not actually a Soviet work: it shows elements of Kazakh history from the perspective of independent Kazakhstan. However, Ospanov was trained in the Soviet Union, the technique of mosaic tiles on individual panels that are assembled to form a picture was developed by Soviet Modernism, and the smalt came from the stock of the Union of Artists. This mosaic may therefore be considered the last Soviet mosaic in Almaty.

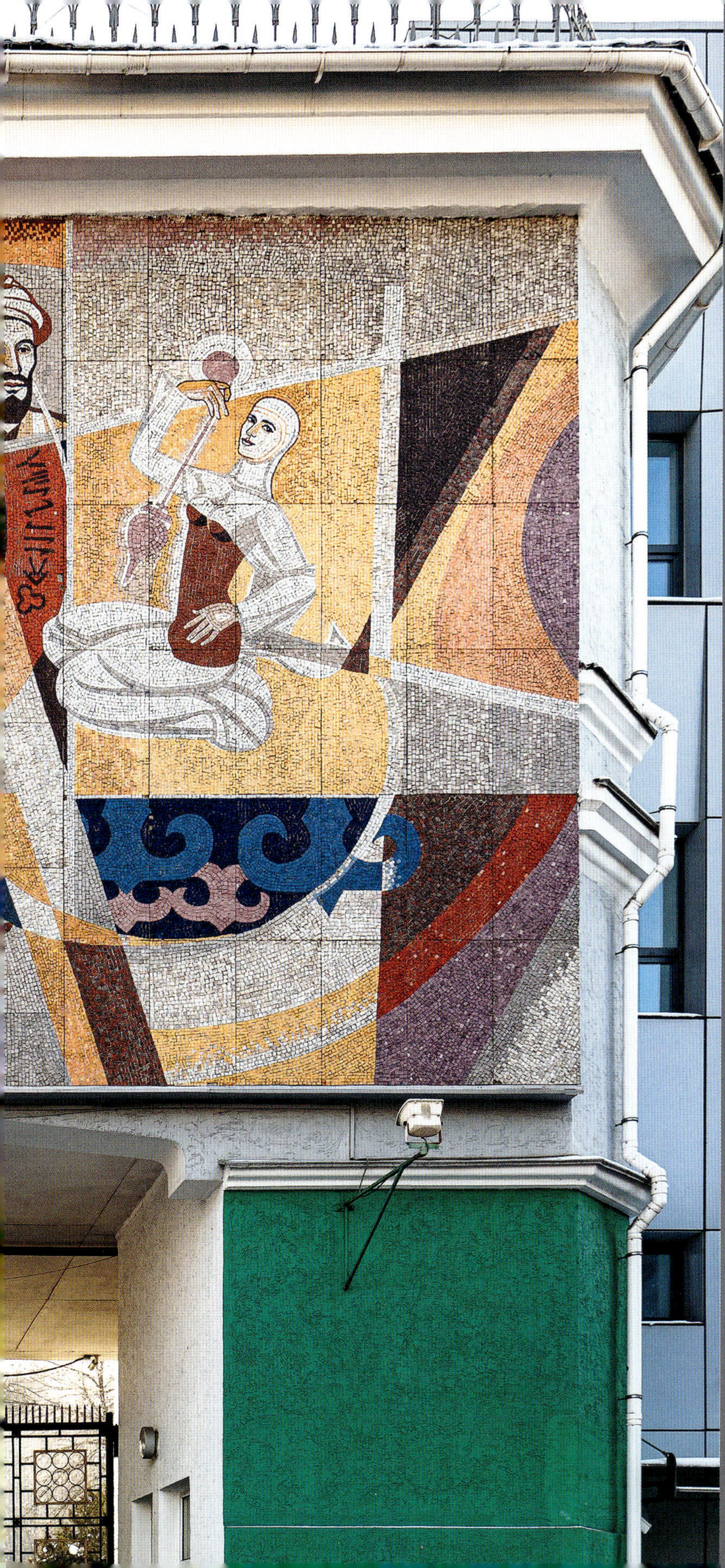

'Eastern Calendar / Sign of the Zodiac, fountain from 1980

'His Time Was the Time of the Soviet Union.'

Interview with Anara Forrester about her father, Vladimir Tverdokhlebov (1937–1922), one of Kazakhstan's leading and most renowned monumental artists.
Interview by Edda Schlager

In recent years many of your father's works have been damaged or even destroyed. What can you tell us about this?

Yes, unfortunately some of his art has been destroyed or lost. For example, the interior decoration he did for the Academy of Sciences (033). His works there include wall mosaics in the Florentine and Byzantine styles, stained-glass windows, murals, and tapestries. The windows are well preserved, and a large Florentine mosaic of Lenin still exists but is not open to the public. However, several of his large tapestries there have been almost completely destroyed. During the restructuring of the Academy of Sciences in the 2000s, the Academy decided to rent out part of its premises and many works of art were damaged. For example, the fresco in the winter garden was painted over and covered with tiles. My father's mosaic *Dragon*, which he created

in 2002 on the façade of a Thai restaurant at the junction of Kurmangazy Street and Dostyk Avenue, was destroyed when the building was demolished. This sad story probably hastened my father's departure from life. It affected him deeply. In 2022, before the exhibition commemorating his death, the administration of a rented part of the Academy of Sciences, the House of Academics in the south wing, showed us many of his tapestries rotting in the attic. The hand-made conference room curtains and tapestries had been removed by the new management and thrown into the space under the roof, where they were eaten by moths and became an unrepairable heap. And just a few days ago, I heard that another of his works, the 1987 mosaic composition *Art and Architecture* for the Palace of Culture in Koldi, about 30 kilometres north west of Almaty, is under threat. With the support of local activists, we were able to save the pieces

Silk Road, mosaic by Vladimir Tverdokhlebov from 2004, to the west of the entrance to Hotel Almaty

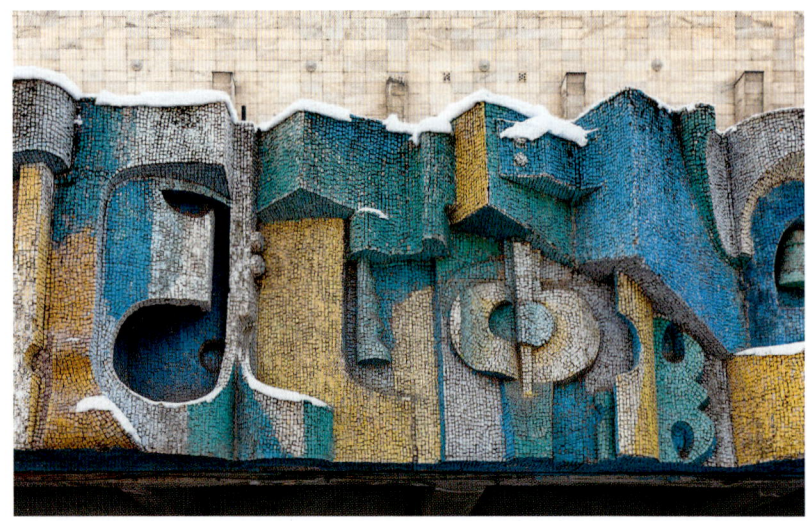

Art and Architecture, relief-mosaic, 1987, at today's Sats Russian Theatre for Children and Youth (formerly: Palace of Culture of the Almaty Cotton and Paper Combine) (088)

and make the city administration aware of their artistic and cultural value.

Why is your father considered one of the most important and renowned monumental artists in Kazakhstan?

When he came to Almaty in 1967, he quickly understood that the development of monumental art was an opportunity. In the 1970s he became a member of the Union of Artists of the USSR and Kazakhstan – which was difficult because you had to be a recognised artist and be

recommended – and he was instrumental in establishing the monumental-art section of the Kazakh SSR Art Combine. This was the Soviet Modernist period; monumental art was beginning to flourish. There was a huge demand for his and his colleagues' work, and they received many commissions. My father became an important part of this movement. For example, he had a decisive influence on the creation of fountains, which were very rare in Alma-Ata at the time but became an important part of the urban landscape in Kazakhstan. His *Eastern Calendar / Sign of*

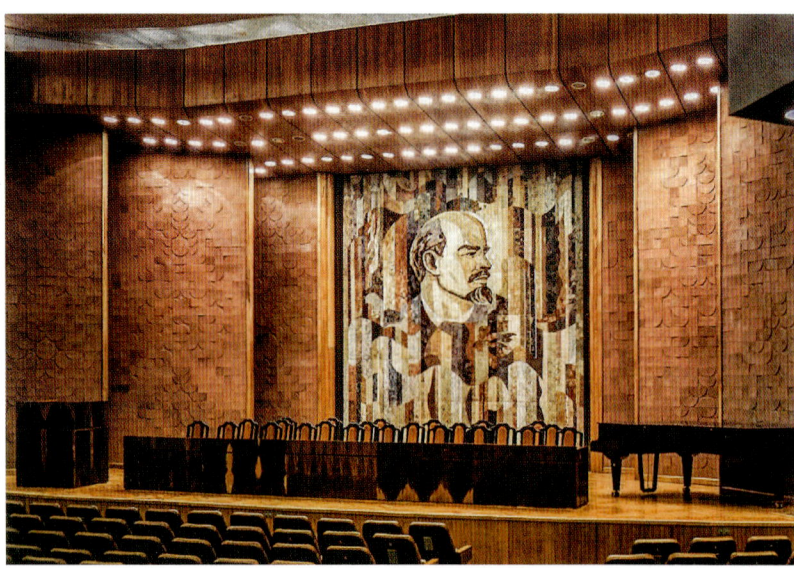

V.I. Lenin, Byzantine mosaic from 1984 in the House of Academics in the south wing of the Academy of Sciences, by Vladimir Tverdokhlebov, Boris Anisimov, Aleksandr Obedin, and Aleksandr Zinenko

The Culture of Kazakhstan. The Link Between the Past and the Present, composition in stained glass; *Sands of Centuries* from 1984 at the National Academy of Sciences (033)

the Zodiac fountain near the Academy of Sciences, which he created in 1980, is still a favourite spot for the city's residents and a well-known Almaty landmark. The fountain was recognised as one of the best works in the field of decorative park sculpture at the sixth congress of the Union of Artists of the USSR in 1978–1982. In 2010 the National Bank of Kazakhstan began issuing gold and silver collector coins based on my father's design of the zodiac animals. In fact, my father's work became the textbook for monumental art in Kazakhstan, and the variety of his art contributed to the formation and development of the distinctive face of Kazakhstan's urban landscapes.

What was your father's relationship with Almaty?

He had lived in St Petersburg, which was Leningrad at the time, before coming to Kazakhstan. He fell in love with what was then Alma-Ata on his first visit – it was a beautiful, green city, welcoming, sunny, with magnificent views of the mountains from every angle. After graduating

Vladimir Tverdokhlebov, right, personally supervising the cleaning of the *Eastern Calendar / Sign of the Zodiac* fountain

from the Vera Mukhina Art Academy, now the Stieglitz State Academy of Art and Design in St Petersburg, he was offered a job in urban planning by the Leningrad city administration. It was a great job to have right after graduation. But in the holidays before starting work he went to Alma-Ata for three months to organise an exhibition at the State Historical Museum. The museum then invited him and other artists to collaborate. He had met my mother during his first visit. And since monumental-decorative art was in its infancy in Kazakhstan at that time, they decided to live here.

What kind of person was your father? Was he different from the artist Vladimir Tverdokhlebov?

I cannot say that the man and the artist were two different people. He was holistic, at one with himself, in life and in work – thorough, responsible, disciplined. He never missed an important meeting, was friendly, honest, and always treated his colleagues decently. He was conscientious in everything he did, completed all his work on time, and never accepted shoddy workmanship. Clients were always satisfied with him and wanted to continue working with him. When approaching his work, he carefully studied the material, spent time in libraries, and consulted specialists and scientists.

What did he do after the end of the Soviet Union?

He worked as a taxi driver. I mean, before that, he had been directing and realising large, monumental artistic projects, government commissions, not only in Alma-Ata but in other regions of the country. And then that government and the Soviet Union ceased to exist. He simply became unemployed. It was during this period that my father found time to paint. He travelled all over Kazakhstan, Kyrgyzstan, Uzbekistan, France, Britain, Russia, Turkey, and found inspiration for painting there. He was quite prolific, producing more than 250 paintings, most of which are kept in the family and have yet to be exhibited or acquired by collectors.

In the 2000s there was renewed interest in his monumental work. That's when he created the mosaic in Hotel Almaty, commissioned by the hotel owner. But his greatest success and recognition came during the Soviet period.

How do you think the city of Almaty deals with your father's work today?

After some years of lack of appreciation, I think the city now looks at his work with great respect and pride. Almaty residents and visitors alike appreciate the originality of his works and the ennobling effect they have on the cityscape. And this applies not only to his work, but to public art in general! Residents have begun to notice urban art and architecture much more. They are writing about it, analysing it, discussing it on social media. Several active groups have been formed to help notice any changes, such as action aimed at destruction, demolition attempts, etc., and to take steps to prevent this by asking the city authorities to pay attention to them. There has been an idea to install information boards on monumental works of art in public places, with information about the works of art. But this hasn't happened yet, partly because the officials in charge are constantly changing. The lack of continuity in the duties of public

Remains of the *Dragon* mosaic of 2004, which was completely destroyed in 2021

authorities is a big problem in Almaty and in Kazakhstan in general.

Why are you doing all this? Why are you so committed to Almaty?

First of all, because I love my city, it's where I was born and raised. Having travelled and lived in many places abroad, I know that Almaty deserves to be listed among the most beautiful, authentic, and comfortable cities in the world. And, of course, because my father had a hand in creating the city's unique, distinctive face. I will continue to work to preserve my father's legacy. And I also believe I can contribute to a greater interest in art and architecture, in the artistic and cultural heritage that has shaped the face of Almaty today. I am working on educational programmes in Kazakhstan to develop an understanding of architecture and art, for example for children, which will help to raise a more enlightened and culturally aware generation. I am currently working on a book, a biography of my father. I am the director of the Vladimir Sergeyevich Tverdokhlebov Foundation of Monumental Art. And I am working on exhibitions of my father's paintings, mosaics, tapestries, and posters that are worthy of representing Kazakhstan on the world's most important art platforms.

A lot is changing in Kazakhstan at the moment. Reforms have been announced, and the *akim* of Almaty says he wants to involve the city's inhabitants more. How do you see this?

I think there is hope. Of course, much more could be done if the city administration had more open-minded, experienced, and proactive professionals who cared about the city. I myself am an urban sociologist, and urban management is my speciality. So if I am invited, I would gladly consider helping.

Archive of Anara Forrester

Anara Forrester, Tverdokhlebov's daughter, before the demolition of his mosaic *Dragon*

Wall mosaic in Auezov Theatre metro station, by Gaziz Yeshkenov, Aidar Zhamkhan, et al .

One Line After Three Decades: the Slow but Steady Construction of the Almaty Metro

Edda Schlager

Construction of Central Asia's second metro – after Tashkent – began in 1988 but soon proved extremely complicated. This was not only due to the stringent technical requirements in earthquake-prone Almaty but also for political and economic reasons: with the collapse of the Soviet Union, funding from Moscow dried up, and the Kazakh economy went through an existential crisis that lasted several years, bringing construction of the metro to a virtual standstill by the end of the 1990s. It was not until 2003 that the project was revived. In December 2011 the first 8.5-kilometre section of the line, with seven stations, finally opened. This did little to relieve Almaty's road traffic, as commuters from the densely populated suburbs were not connected at all. Since then, however, the metro has been extended westwards, with two more stations added in 2015 and two more in 2022. Today the only metro line, Line 1, which is now at least 13.5 kilometres long, at least connects the dormitory districts to the west of the city centre with the north part of the centre, mostly along Abai Avenue. It carries about 90,000 passengers a day. The stations are at different depths, with the

Metro lines for Almaty as planned in 2007

deepest station, Abaia, at 78 metres below ground level. As in the Soviet Union, each station is dedicated to a theme, which determines the design using colourful tiles, mosaics, murals, and reliefs. The stations differ accordingly (also in terms of quality): Baikonur Station, for example, is rather plain and modern – one might even say unimaginative – while Auezov Theatre Station is inspired by Neoclassicism, and its imagery and fascination with jewellery are based more on models from the Stalin era and Socialist Realism. The newer stations are simpler and in what Kazakh architectural parlance calls the 'high-tech style' – possibly just to save money. Of these new stations only Saryarka has a more Classical design, with pylons and vaults. It echoes the steppe theme with wall panels

Architecture and urban development, 1998

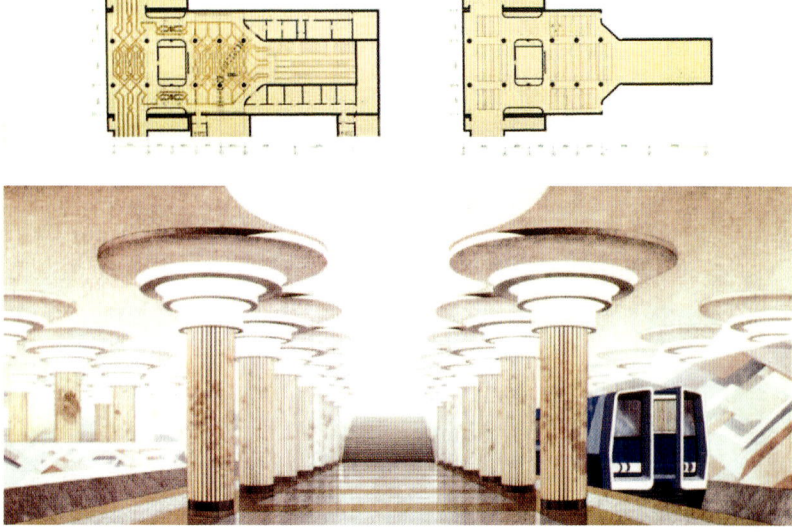

Design studies for Baikonur, Alatau, and Raiymbek metro stations by Almatygiprogor

Depiction of Saiga antelopes at Saryarka Station

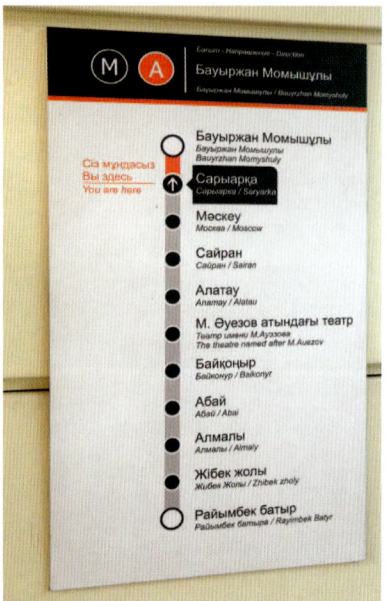

16.4-kilometre, line from Sairan Station northwards and then east to the line connecting the two stations. 300,000 people will be able to use the metro every day. There are also plans for around 80 kilometres of light rail transit (LRT), modern trams with their own track bed by 2040, and an extension of the existing bus rapid transit to almost 300 kilometres by 2030. Some of the plans published by the *akimat* and the planned routes for all modes of transport are contradictory. The transport concept as a whole has been criticised for not taking sufficient account of seismic conditions, financial viability, and, above all, the needs of an expanding city with a rapidly growing population and high mobility requirements. The plans are ambitious. But if the rail-based public transport system in particular is developed at the current rate, the metropolis, which is already regularly on the verge of gridlock, is likely to be stuck in traffic jams for many years to come.

and depictions of Kazakh flora and fauna. Originally, plans dating to the 1990s called for the construction of three underground metro lines that would have almost completely connected Almaty with a network that would have been 45 kilometres long. However, after the first section of the metro went into operation and the technical and financial challenges became apparent, the plans changed several times. A new transport development plan was also presented as part of Almaty's new general plan of 2023, which envisages a total of almost 40 kilometres of additional metro lines being built by 2030. One line will run from Almaty-2 Station to Almaty-1, another from Zhibek Zholy Station to the airport, and another,

Metro lines and one of the main BRT lines as planned in 2024

Auezov Theatre metro station

Philipp Meuser

Baikonur metro station

Philipp Meuser

Zhibek Zholy metro station

Philipp Meuser

Bauyrzhan Momyshuly Station, the current terminus of the metro in the west, opened in 2022.

A

Ascension Cathedral

001 A

40v Gogol St
K.A. Borisoglebsky, N.I. Stepanov,
S.K. Troparevsky, A.P. Zenkov
1904–1907

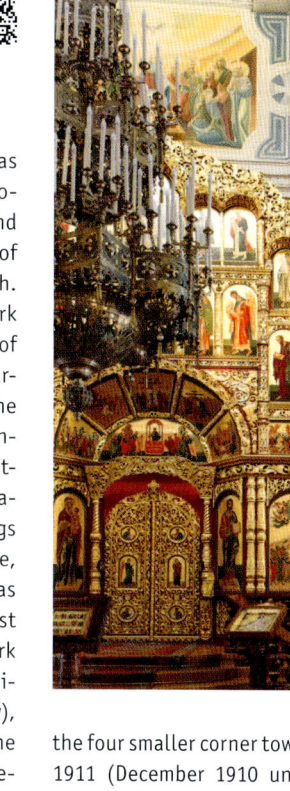

Ascension Cathedral was built as St Sophia Cathedral of the Turkestan diocese after its bishops decided at the end of the nineteenth century that the city of Verny needed a Russian Orthodox church. Today the cathedral located in the Park of the 28 Panfilov Guardsmen is one of Almaty's oldest and most striking architectural monuments. It is also the first example of earthquake-proof construction. One year after the devastating earthquake of 1887, a set of regulations for the construction of buildings more resistant to earthquake damage, based on science and experience, was adopted – and applied here for the first time. This was also the first time that work was divided between the designing architects (Borisoglebsky and Troparevsky), whose plans were ready in 1898, and the implementing engineers (Stepanov, Zenkov). The church was built from local coniferous wood and metal pins on a reinforced-concrete slab. At the time of its construction, this was the tallest building in the city at 53.34 metres. The bell tower on the west side surmounts the dome and the four smaller corner towers. In January 1911 (December 1910 under the Julian calendar) Ascension Cathedral survived a severe earthquake in which more than 700 people died, with only minor damage. The cathedral has been reconstructed three times since 1973, most recently from 2017 to 2020.

Consulat Général de France

99 Nazarbayev Ave
attributed to A.P. Zenkov
1890

A number of residential and commercial buildings from the tsarist era have survived in the historical centre of Almaty. The former house of the Shakhvorostov merchant family, built shortly after the devastating earthquake of 1887, is one of the most beautiful and oldest to be preserved from this time. Entirely in the Russian Historicist style, the house has a high basement and richly moulded cornices and stucco decoration, making it a typical example of Russian colonial architecture from the turn of the last century. In 1920 the Shakhvorostov family was dispossessed and their property nationalised, after which the building was used by various state institutions. After Kazakhstan's acquisition of independence, it briefly housed the US Embassy before passing into the hands of the French Consulate General. Over recent decades it has been completely renovated, including technical equipment. In 2009 the palace was restored to its original state by Berlin-based Meuser Architekten, in keeping with its status as a listed building. At the same time it was structurally reinforced against earthquake damage.

Philipp Meuser

During renovation in 2009

St Nicholas Cathedral ⌃
56 Baitursynov St
N.I. Lavanov, S.K. Troparevsky,
1906–1908

Kazan Cathedral ⌄
45a Khaliullina St
P.M. Zenkov
1871/1898

In 1904 the inhabitants of the south-western part of Verny began to collect money for the construction of a church on Zubovsky Square. Consecrated in 1908, the church has an axial shape with seven domes, high vaults, and a bell tower. During the Second World War it served as a stables and a military prison and was severely damaged. Afterwards, the domes and the destroyed bell tower were rebuilt and the church was reconsecrated in December 1946.

In 1871 St Sophia's was moved from Bolshaya Stanitsa to Malaya Stanitsa and renamed 'Kazan Cathedral'. The new church was partly built with materials from the old wooden building. Badly damaged in the earthquake of 1887, it was extended in 1889–1898, when it was given its distinctive eight domes. A lengthy renovation from 1991 forwards has left it dominated by the oversized, orientalised roofs of the front and south porches, supported by disproportionately thin columns.

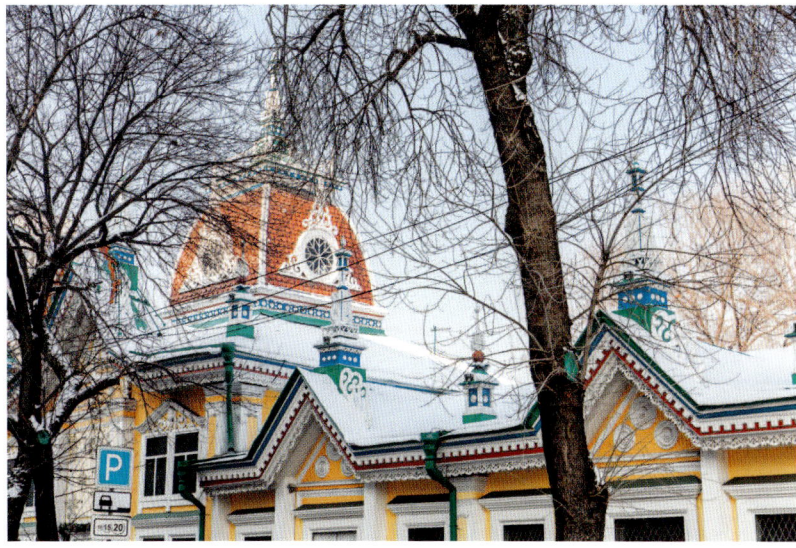

Kyzyl-Tan
63 Zhibek Zholy
P. Gourdet
1896

005 A

The textile and haberdashery shop near the Green Bazaar is one of the most splendid and famous merchant houses in the city. It belonged to Iskhak Gabdulvaliev, a merchant from Tashkent. The building has a rectangular floor plan and is symmetrical: in the centre is a hip-roofed dome with a tower, to the east and west of which are two wings, each with its own entrance. The roof, façades, and gables are richly decorated with additional towers, columns, carved cornices, and plinths. Although the interior has been extended and rebuilt several times over more than 100 years of use, some stucco carvings and carved wooden panelling from the building's early days have survived. The house was long attributed to the architect Pavel Zenkov, the first mayor of Verny, and supposedly built in 1911. However, Nelya Buketova, a local historian from Almaty, discovered in the town archives that Gabdulvaliev had applied for the building as early as 1895 with the following words: 'I hereby submit a two-sheet project for the construction of a shop on the land I own, no. 441, and I have the honour to humbly ask the town council of Verny to approve it and allow me to build it.' The request was granted, and the shop was built a year later by the French architect Paul Gourdet, who had lived in Verny since 1875. Gabdulvaliev and Gourdet fought over the building – to the point of battling it out in court. What remains is a piece of Russian Eclecticism, inspired by Gourdet's time in Russia.

Monuments of history and culture of Almaty, 2008

Some of the old plastered carvings inside Kyzyl Tan have been preserved.

Kazakh Museum of Folk Musical Instruments ⌃

24a Zenkov St
A.P. Zenkov
1908

006 A

Built as an officers' club, this magnificent wooden house in the Park of the 28 Panfilov Guardsmen served as a post and telegraph office after 1918, as a cinema, then as the officers' house for the Central Asian Military District and, until 1982, as a puppet theatre. The building's most distinctive feature is its central tower with its raised tent-roofed spire rising from a hipped roof with a viewing platform. The façade with its mullioned windows is complemented by carved wooden cornices, decorative canopies, and gables.

Almaty Museum ⌄

132 Kabanbai Batyr St
P. Gourdet
1892

007 A

The construction of the former orphanage in Verny was financed by donations from benefactors. The architect designed the project free of charge as his own contribution. The building is symmetrically divided into a central section, with a staircase leading up to it, and two side wings, which are given a three-dimensional appearance by the use of distinctive risalites, richly carved wooden window casings, and wooden window brackets and cornices, also skilfully carved. Inside the building, stucco carvings have been preserved on the ceilings and walls.

House of the orphanage director ≈

008 A

551 Seyfullin Ave
unknown
before 1892

Probably built as an apartment building, this house was later acquired by the city as the home for the director of the orphanage (007), only a few streets away. It is one and a half storeys high, like almost all private houses built at this time. Seen from the front, these houses appear single-storey, but from the rear courtyard – facing south in this case – you can see a balcony on the first floor. The reason for this was that extra tax had to be paid on a second storey of a house. As the rooms on these floors had no windows facing the street, they were not considered to be full floors.

House of merchant Radchenkov ≈

009 A

25 Tulebayeva St
unknown
1890s

The house built by the family of the merchant Ivan Radchenkov is relatively unremarkable compared to other houses of this period. The Radchenkovs, who came from the former governorate of Yekaterinoslav, now Dnipro in Ukraine, settled in Verny in the 1870s. They owned several businesses here, including a mill and a brewery. The house was used as an apartment building and is accordingly quite plain, with simple wooden window casings and some carving on the cornices. It was bought by the city in 1910 to house a telegraph office and was used as such until a new post office (021) was built in 1931.

House of physician Fiedler ⌃ 010 A

18 Kazybek bi St
unknown
early 1900s

House of merchant Filippov ⌄ 011 A

20 Makatazev St
S.K. Troparevsky
1901

This simpler house from the same period is square in plan, single-storey, with a brick base and a plastered timber frame. Protruding structures organise the façade: vertical wall projections between the windows and at the corners; horizontal belt courses above the plinth and under the roof cornices. Facing away from the street, a staircase leads inside the house via a covered terrace. The former owner of the house was Leiba Neivohovich (Lev Nikolaevich) Fiedler, a doctor who was considered a luminary in Verny. The writer Mukhtar Auezov dedicated several chapters to Fiedler in *Abai Zholy* ('The Path of Abai'), his famous book about the life of the Kazakh poet Abai Qūnanbaiūly, which vividly describes life in Verny at the time.

Standing on a high brick plinth, this two-storey building has wooden pilasters on the upper floor, carved window frames, and intricate cornices. There is an open veranda on the courtyard side. The interior, which has been redesigned several times, is characterised by long corridors and a number of rooms without windows. The house was originally built for the town's girls' gymnasium. However, when the school moved to a larger building one street to the west, the house was bought by the merchant Filippov – a rather unusual move as at that time the municipality tended to buy houses from private individuals. Today it accommodates the Kazrestavratsiya State Restoration Research Centre.

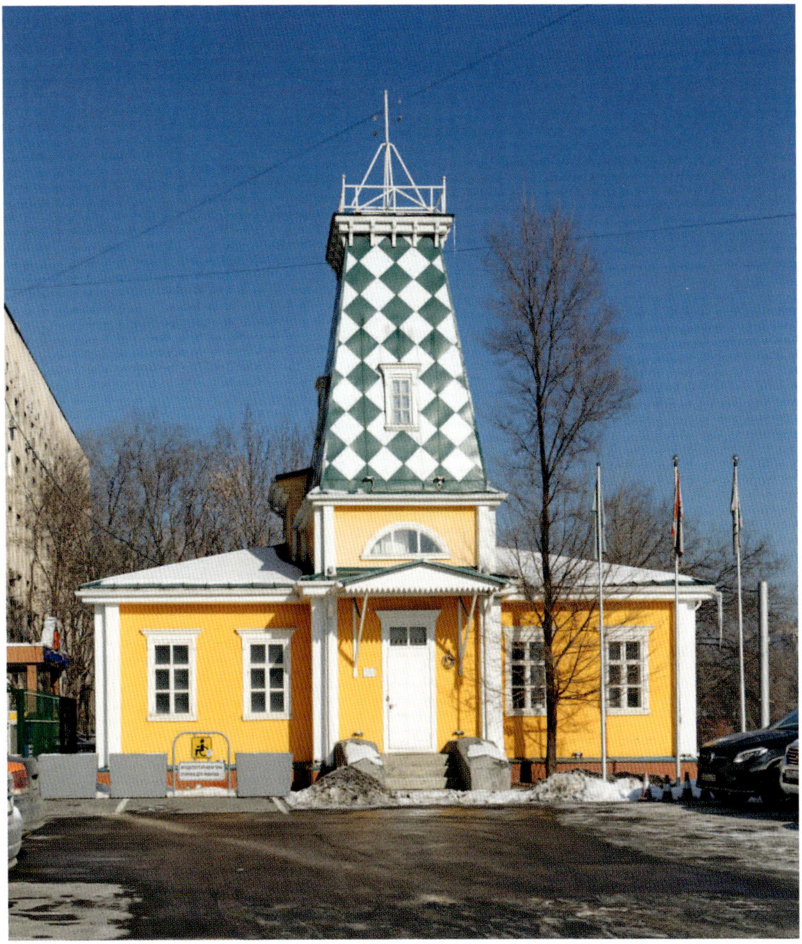

Verny Observatory ⌃

599b Seyfullin Ave
I. Ponomarev
1915

012 **A**

In 1913 St Petersburg's Main Geophysical Observatory decided that, as the administrative centre of Semirechyenskaya Oblast, Verny, needed its own meteorological observatory. Previously, weather observations had been carried out at various stations; however, the frequent changes of location and constant reinstallation of the instruments had affected their technical condition and reduced the effectiveness of the observations. Two years later, this dedicated observatory was constructed, based on the design of Pulkovo Observatory in St Petersburg and located on the southern outskirts of the city. With its striking tower, this building is one of the few surviving examples of Art Nouveau in Kazakhstan. The main façade of the rectangular, single-storey building faces south. The façade has double casement windows with wooden surrounds on all sides. The four-sided hipped roof is covered with metal shingles. Both the main building and the tower are made of spruce from nearby Tien Shan and are plastered inside and out. The Bredikhin Tower, named after the Russian astronomer Fyodor Bredikhin, contained a telescope. From 1918 to 1921, during the Russian Civil War, this was the headquarters of the troops of Semirechyenskaya Oblast. For many decades Verny Observatory was the most important geophysical and meteorological measuring centre in the region. When the property was about to be privatised in the 2000s, the Almaty prosecutor's office placed a ban on the transaction, in order to protect the building. Until a few years ago, the observatory remained in poor condition. It was reconstructed in 2019, when it was given its current colourful coat of paint.

House of the Cossack Ataman 013 A

40 Ashimbayeva St
unknown
before 1918

This house with its bright blue, richly decorated window casings and carved roof cornices was the home of the Cossack ataman of Bolshaya Stanitsa. In the architectural register of the *akimat* of Almaty the year of construction is given as 1918. But this is probably not correct. In 1918 the Soviet regime was also fighting opponents in distant Central Asia, with uncertain prospects for an end to the civil war. The Soviets took repressive action against the Cossacks in particular, and Lenin and Stalin began a process of de-Cossackisation. The Cossacks had helped the Russian Empire expand; now they were deprived of their privileges, rights, and property. During these years there was less building activity in Verny. However, many houses in the architectural register are dated 1918 although they must have been built earlier; 1918 is merely the year in which these buildings were inventoried when they were confiscated by the Soviet authorities. After the expulsion of the ataman, the house continued to be used as a residential building. In the late 1930s the famous dancer and teacher Alexander Seleznev, after whom Almaty Ballet School is named, lived here. The house has been in private hands ever since.

House of Mayor Lutmanov ≫

115/1 Kazybek bi St
unknown
before 1887

Ivan Lutmanov came to Verny as a merchant from Yelabuga in Siberia, where he was born in 1846. He quickly established himself as a respected member of the merchant community of the Semirechen Cossack Army. On 17 November 1877 he was elected a member of Verny's town council and deputy to the first mayor, Pavel Zenkov. Lutmanov was a successful businessman. He ran tobacco and fruit plantations, three tobacco and cigarette factories, a brewery, wool laundries, a mill, warehouses, and grocery shops. After the earthquake of 1887, he left his undamaged house to his colleague Zenkov. Lutmanov himself was elected third mayor of Verny on 24 June 1890, a post he held for eight years.

Vladimir Proskurin

Pavel Zenkov, Verny's chief architect at the time, in front of Lutmanov's house

House of mechant Gavrilov ≪

167 Zhelttoksan St
unknown
early 1900s

Originally built at the intersection of Shtabnaya (now Gogol) Street and Lepsinskaya Street (now Nazarbayev Avenue), this house was first owned by the Gavrilov merchant family, who specialised in growing and trading in tobacco. After the death of M.A. Gavrilov in 1928, the house was nationalised. For a long time it was the seat of the Regional Council of People's Deputies of Semirechenskaya Oblast. In 1973 the structure was completely taken apart and rebuilt at its present address. In the 1990s a second reconstruction was constrained by the lack of building materials and expertise in the early years of Kazakhstan's independence, as can be seen from the façade, which is clad in cheap plastic panels. The layout was also changed to incorporate a restaurant with two banqueting halls. The house originally had 12 rooms and was equipped with one Russian and eight Dutch tiled stoves; these were lost during the move. Only the ornate wood carvings on the windows, the massive veranda roof, and the carved cornices give us an idea today of how splendid the house must have been when it was built. The house is currently owned by the city of Almaty and is used for receptions.

House of mechant Golovizin

162 Nazarbayev Ave
unknown
1905–1908

016 A

A

The house of Tit Golovizin is one of the most famous merchant houses in Verny built in the early 1900s – not surprisingly given its prominent location on Almaty's Golden Square on one of the city's busiest main streets. Built in the Russian Eclectic style, it combines elements of Historicism and Art Nouveau. The main, north-facing, façade is characterised by a purely decorative composition of four Ionic half-columns, the capitals of which even have lateral volutes and floral ornaments. The visual centre of the façade is emphasised by a decorative rectangular pediment. Pilasters are found on the east side of the main façade and on the west façade. A notable feature is the round corner facing the crossroads, which, due to the dome attached to it, resembles a tower. The entire façade is richly decorated with floral stucco, enhancing its three-dimensionality. The entrance to the house is situated not on the splendid outer sides, but on the courtyard side, diagonally opposite the 'tower room'. Here too it is clear that the house is not single-storey, as the street side would suggest, but has an additional storey, hidden for tax reasons, as in other buildings of this period. The balcony, supported by Ionic columns, spans a small veranda. After Soviet rule was established in 1918, the house was nationalised and used as a kindergarten and a polyclinic. It was later taken over by the Kazakh Council of Ministers and hosted prominent guests including Zhumabay Shayakhmetov, First Secretary of the Central Committee of the Communist Party of the Kazakh SSR, and Leonid Brezhnev, the future leader of the USSR.

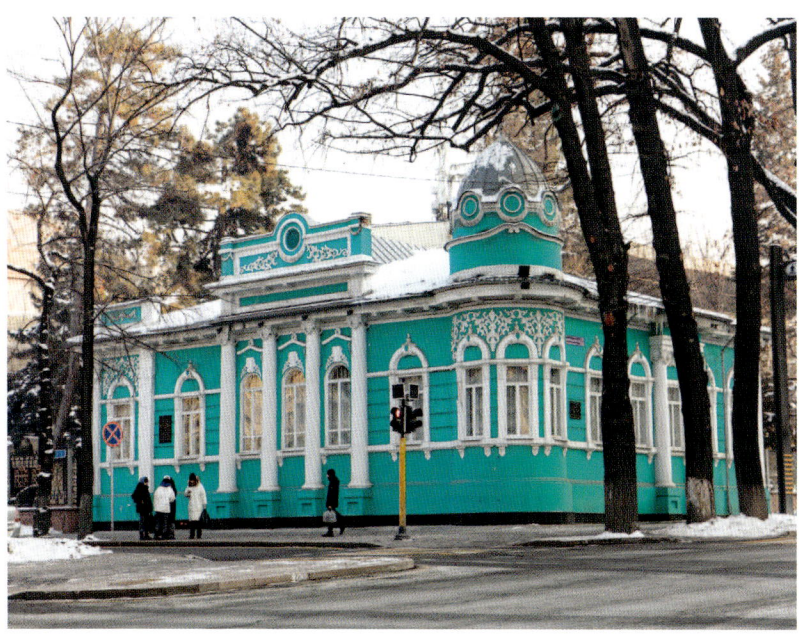

Gabdulvaliev mansion

017 A

38a Tulebayev St
A.P. Zenkov
1909

Behind the dense trees on Tulebayev Street, this two-storey Art Nouveau building is barely visible. The impressive size of the rectangular building is accentuated by the two domes with mansards. The façades are clearly structured both horizontally and vertically. The unusually large windows are surrounded by moulded plaster bands and consoles. The profiled cornice and the columns of the parapet, crowned with spheres, are decorated with floral ornaments carved in wood. However, the roof structures have suffered considerable damage in recent decades. The curved parapet walls no longer exist, and the playful turrets on the domes have also disappeared. Now a pub, the building has lost much of its former splendour. The mansion was commissioned by the wealthy family of merchant Iskhak Gabdulvaliev, who ran the Kyzyl-Tan department store (005) just 300 metres away as the crow flies. The Art Nouveau building belonged to Kutdus, the second of Iskhak's four sons, who was as successful a merchant as his father. This Tatar family, originally from near Kazan, was also involved in philanthropy, directed in particular at Turkic-speaking young people, and supported pan-Islamic and pan-Turkic ideas, which aroused the suspicion of the authorities. Iskhak Gabdulvaliev died in 1911, shortly after construction began on the house in what is now Tulebayev Street, and his son Kutdus left Verny that same year. Other members of the family saw to the mansion's completion. The building's purpose is not entirely clear. It might have been intended as a residence for the Gabdulvaliev family, an apartment house, a bank, or a department store. In 1918 all the Gabdulvalievs' property was nationalised. This house was also used by the Soviet authorities.

The Gabdulvaliev mansion with its original Art Nouveau appearance, 1910s

Ivan Nikolaevich Panov

A

House of merchant Pugasov ≫
70 Bogenbai Batyr St
unknown
end of 19th century

Pink house ≫
33 Tole bi St
unknown
probably before 1918

Nikita Pugasov was one of the richest merchants in Verny, possessor of a vast trading empire. He owned distilleries, vodka factories, and a tannery in the Semirechye region. The house does not even remotely reflect this wealth because for Pugasov, who did most of his business in Tashkent, Verny was only his second home. He came to Verny when he had business to do or to visit his sons Yakov and Pavel, who lived here. The house is poorly preserved and is an example of the gradual destruction of historical buildings through modern reconstruction.

This pink house with the stunning carved window casings on the corner of Tole bi and Valikhanov streets is exceptionally well preserved. It is probably one of the houses built at the end of the nineteenth century that were inventoried by the Soviet authorities in 1918 and are therefore listed as having been built in that year. The occupants in Soviet times were teachers and academics. Inside, the stucco ceilings have been preserved, as have the original doors and a large cast-iron cylinder stove, which the owner says is still in full working order.

B

House of Government

020 B

127 Panfilov St
M.Y. Ginzburg, I.F. Milinis
1931

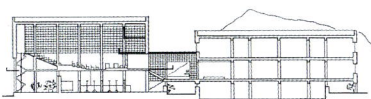

The former House of Government (originally: the House of the Council of People's Commissars) is one of the few surviving examples of Constructivism on the Soviet periphery but may also be considered one of the masterpieces of Avantgarde architecture of the early Soviet era. Completed in 1931, the building was designed by Moisey Ginzburg and Ignaty Milinis, who had already worked on the Narkomfin House in Moscow. The current home of the Kazakh Academy of Arts has undergone many disfiguring changes over the years. The east façade, for example, originally featured large expanses of glass, intended to demonstrate the openness of the Bolshevik government, in keeping with the revolutionary aspirations of the architects and their times. However, this glazed front was soon reduced to a narrow strip, which means that the original impression can no longer be experienced.

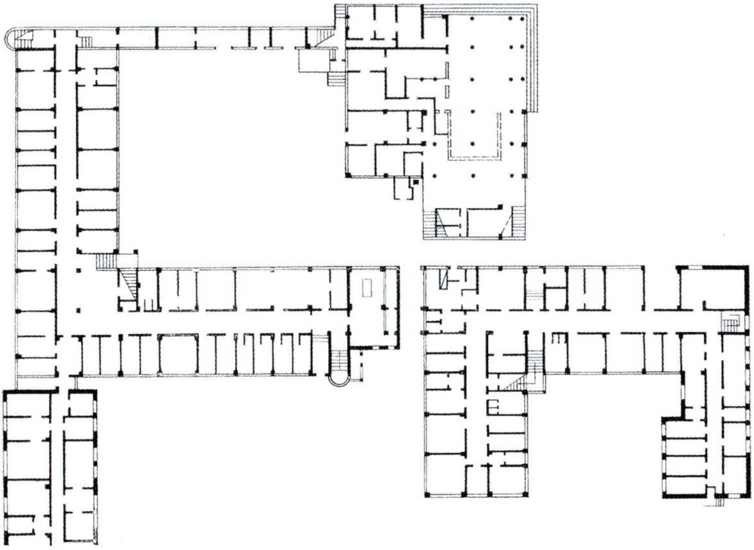

Architecture of Soviet Kazakhston, 1987

Philipp Meuser

General Post Office

134 Bogenbai Batyr St
*M.Y. Ginzburg, I.F. Milinis,
G.G. Gerasimov, Y.K. Dyatlov*
1931–1934

021 B

This building, which still serves as Almaty's main post office, was built as the House of Communication. Designed to meet the needs of modern communication in the growing young capital of Alma-Ata, it became one of the central buildings in the newly built government district on the former Cossack Square, not far from the House of Government (020). Moisey Ginzburg and Ignaty Milinis, who designed the House of Government, are also credited with designing the General Post Office. However, Georgy Gerasimov is often cited as its architect too, so the three may have worked together on this project. The House of Communication was the home of the post office, the telegraph office, and the telephone exchange for city and international connections. The round shape on the east side of the two-storey building is repeated in the original glass-tiled staircase that initially bookended the building on the west side. However, in the 1960s a bell tower with a carillon was added to the Constructivist structure by the architects Yevgeny Dyatlov and Kim Do Sen and the engineer Y. Skrinsky. Fully restored in 2003, the building is today a distinctive landmark in Almaty's city centre.

The General Post Office in late 1960, early 1970, after the bell tower was added

Archive of ArchCode

Management of Turksib ⌃
100 Panfilov St
M.Y. Ginzburg, I.F Milinis
1928–1934

022 B

House of Narkomats ⌄
108 Nauryzbai Batyr St
G. Korostin, S. Shevyrev
1934

023 B

The headquarters of the Turkestan-Siberian Railway was designed as part of a state contract that also included the Narkomfin building in Moscow. The similarity between the two buildings is obvious. The Alma-Ata headquarters, however, was smaller and designed to resist earthquakes. Like its Moscow counterpart, it was assigned to the engineer Sergey Prokhorov. In the 1930s it was given curtain walls as a decorative element.

Originally the seat of several people's commissariats (*narkomats*), the ministries of the Soviet government, this building stretched from today's Panfilov Street to Nazarbaev Avenue. It housed the people's commissariats of finance (Narkomfin), agriculture (Narkomzem), and construction (Narkomstroy). The east wing burnt down in the late 1980s or early 1990s. A residential building was erected in its place.

NKVD ⌃

108 Nauryzbai Batyr St
V. Burovzev
1932

024 B

Uyghur Theatre ⌐

83 Nauryzbai Batyr St
V. Burovzev
1932–1935

025 B

On today's Nauryzbai Batyr Street there is an almost completely preserved ensemble of Constructivist buildings built in the early 1930s. Designed for the People's Commissariat for Internal Affairs (NKVD) and its staff, this complex was located west of the city centre, away from the government district with the other *narkomats* (023). The so-called 'Chekgorodok' ('Chekist city') – named after the Cheka, the Soviet secret service – included the building of the Kazakh headquarters of the NKVD, four houses for employees (one of which has been demolished), the NKVD Club (025), and two other buildings for the Joint State Political Directorate (OGPU), the state security service and secret police of the Soviet Union and the successor organisation of the Cheka. After Kazakhstan's acquisition of independence, the building housed the Museum of Victims of Political Repression. In the early 2000s, however, the museum was moved to a village north of Almaty and the NKVD building was turned into a hotel. Today it is home to Archcode Almaty, an initiative dedicated to preserving Almaty's historical architecture. It has long been earmarked for reconstruction. So far, public protests have prevented this.

Originally built as a club for the NKVD, the building diagonally opposite the former NKVD headquarters (024) now barely betrays its Constructivist origins: its reconstruction between 1994 and 2002 was carried out in such a way that the 1987 decision to protect it as a historical monument had to be revised in 2010. Originally, the NKVD club had a multi-level central semicircular façade framed by two corner buildings with vertical strips of glazing. A large balcony was attached to the central façade. The redevelopment involved enlargement of the upper floors, resulting in the loss of the multi-storey façade and a radically changed overall appearance. The two end buildings became a single unit together with the entrance area and were covered with a glass façade. In 1969 the building was handed over to the Uyghur Theatre, whose home it still is today.

The NKVD club building in the 1950s

Residential buildings for NKVD employees ⌄

 026 B

81, 104, 106 Nauryzbai Batyr St
V. Burovzev, Skvortsov
1935–1936

Four residential buildings completed the complex of NKVD buildings. Here lived the organisation's employees, just a few steps away from their workplaces at the NKVD headquarters (024). One of the residential houses, situated further down the street, burnt down. Three buildings are still standing: 81 Nauryzbai Batyr Street, north of the NKVD club (025) on the west side of the street, and numbers 104 and 106 on the east side, north of the NKVD headquarters. The houses are four storeys high and set back from the street. Their façades are geometrically structured with accentuated staircases. Despite their monumental, almost intimidating appearance, they are made of wood and their façades are plastered. These houses mark the end of Constructivism in Almaty. At this point the age of Stalin entered architecture – much later in distant Kazakhstan than in Russia – and demanded an imperial aesthetic.

One of the residential buildings in Chekgorodok, on the east side of Nauryzbai Batyr Street

Bread factory »

33 Valikhanov St
unknown
1933

This former bread factory was one of the first industrial buildings to be built in the Constructivist style in the early 1930s. The building was remodelled in the mid-1930s, with the addition of Classical elements. Today it houses a supermarket, the façade is clad, and there is little to be seen of the original design. The building's original pilasters, extending over the two lower floors, are, however, still visible on the courtyard side.

Archive of ArchCode

Philharmonic »

21 Tole bi St
D.G. Fomichev, E. Tseytlin
1933–1936

The House of Culture, now the Zhambyl Kazakh State Philharmonic, was designed by the Leningrad architects Demyan Fomichev and E. Tseytlin. It was built on the orders of Anatoly Lunacharsky, the Soviet People's Commissar for Culture and Education, who had decided that the young capital of the Kazakh SSR finally needed a fully fledged concert hall – as there had been none in Alma-Ata to that date. From 1941 to 1944 the building housed the Central United Feature Film Studio (TsOKS). The Second World War had forced the two film studios Mosfilm and Lenfilm to evacuate from Moscow and Leningrad to Alma-Ata, where they merged with the local film studio to form TsOKS. The equipment, sets, and costumes were housed in this vast building. In the 1960s the structure was extensively renovated and extended, retaining its Constructivist style. However, further alterations in 1985 stripped the building of its simple, unadorned appearance. Brutalist porticos were added to both the main and west wings, probably to create a more stately appearance, according to officials at the time. On the east side of the Large Auditorium, however, the structure of the façade is still recognisably Constructivist.

Sports School ⌃

029 B

61 Dosmukhamedov St
unknown
1929–1935

Zhilkombinat No 4 ⌄

030 B

118 Nazarbayev Ave
Y.-I.I. Stankevich, T.K. Basenov
1937

Schools for working youth existed throughout the Soviet Union from the 1920s forwards. Here older teenagers and young adults who had not received an adequate primary education could catch up on their secondary education while continuing to work. The building of this school in Alma-Ata playfully breaks with the chessboard-like street grid of the old city centre and its strict east-west and north-south lines by orienting itself at a 45-degree angle to the street. The classroom windows therefore face south east. The building is made of wood and has a plastered façade. The blocks of glazing on the staircase, which interrupts the main façade with its circular body, have been replaced. Otherwise, the building now housing the Sports School for Gifted Children is well preserved.

The so-called *zhilkombinats* (residential combines) nos. 2, 3, and 4 on the east side of Nazarbayev Avenue, between Kabanbai Batyr Street and Bogenbai Batyr Street, were built as residential buildings for employees of the nearby *narkomats*. They are of brick; some of the non-load-bearing interior walls are half-timbered. No. 4 on the corner has two three-storey wings and a central four-storey section. Its façade is characterised by square windows and vertical rows of loggias above the entrances and balconies. A wide two-part band from the lintel of the ground floor window opening to the floor level of the first floor is complemented by a somewhat thinner but also two-part parapet band on the first floor. A narrow frieze band merges into a serrated cornice.

Architecture of Soviet Kazakhstan, 1987

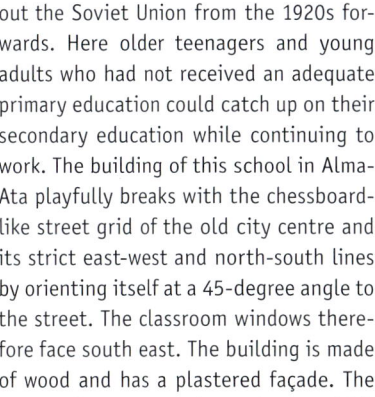

Plan of the 2nd floor of Zhilkombinat No 4

C

Abai Opera House

110 Kabanbai Batyr St
N.A. Kruglov, T.K. Basenov,
N.A. Prostakov, N.V. Tsivchinsky
et al.
1936–1941

031 C

This opera house heralded the arrival of the Stalinist Empire style, which combined pompous Classicism with national elements. The opera house was modelled on the Alexandrinsky Theatre in St Petersburg, which had been built about 100 years earlier. The main building has a projecting four-columned portico with square columns on the main façade, complemented by semi-columns of the same shape framing the opening of the loggia and its inner wall. On the ground floor, below the columns, are massive pillars on an extended base. Between the columns are the large doorways of the main entrance. Compositionally, the ground floor serves as a kind of stereobate for the entire building. The portico has massive pylons that merge into blind side walls. Originally, quotes by Lenin on art issues were inscribed in the decorative stucco frames of the pylons, which form pointed arches. The main façade is crowned by a frieze that recalls Kazakh culture but also points the way to the birth of Soviet man. The opera house was rebuilt between 1995 and 2000. The ornamental pattern of the figurative grid of the roof was partially altered and only remains on the central risalite.

C

Railway Station Almaty-2

1 Abylai Khan Ave
A.P. Galkin, M.I. Kudryavtsev
1937–1939

032 C

The main entrance to this station is highlighted by a monumental portal with four pairs of columns and a semicircular window above the doors. In the frieze of the portal niche above the round window is a bas-relief depicting scenes from everyday socialist life. When the station opened before the Second World War, only the east wing was complete. Here there is a waiting room with an attic that leads to a single-storey, semicircular volume. The west wing, planned in the same way but without the attic,

was not completed until 1976. The extension brought further changes to the station's interior. The station building was renovated in 2012, when the façades were covered with marble panels. A fundamental reconstruction, which has been planned for several years, has not yet taken place.

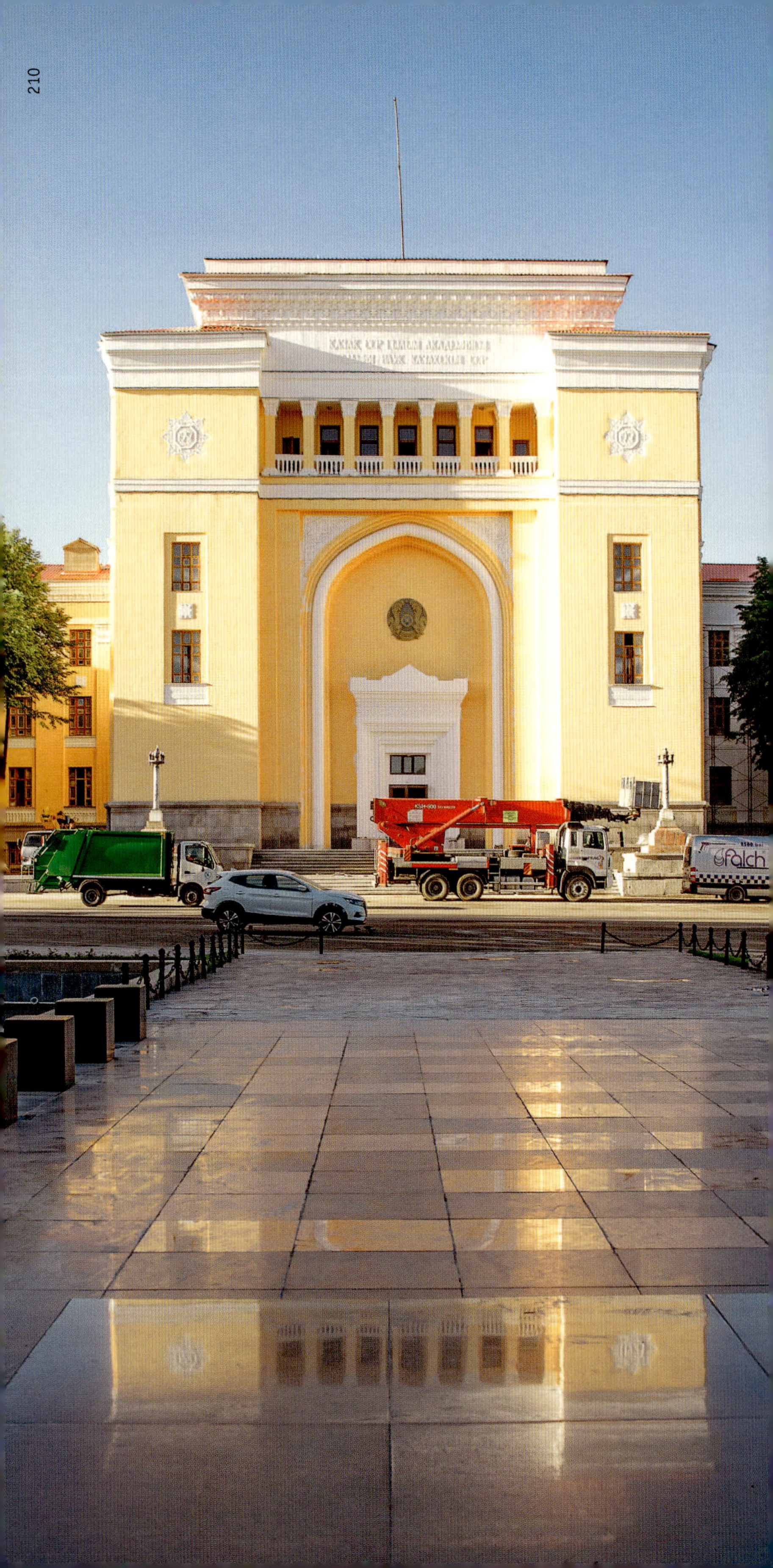
falch

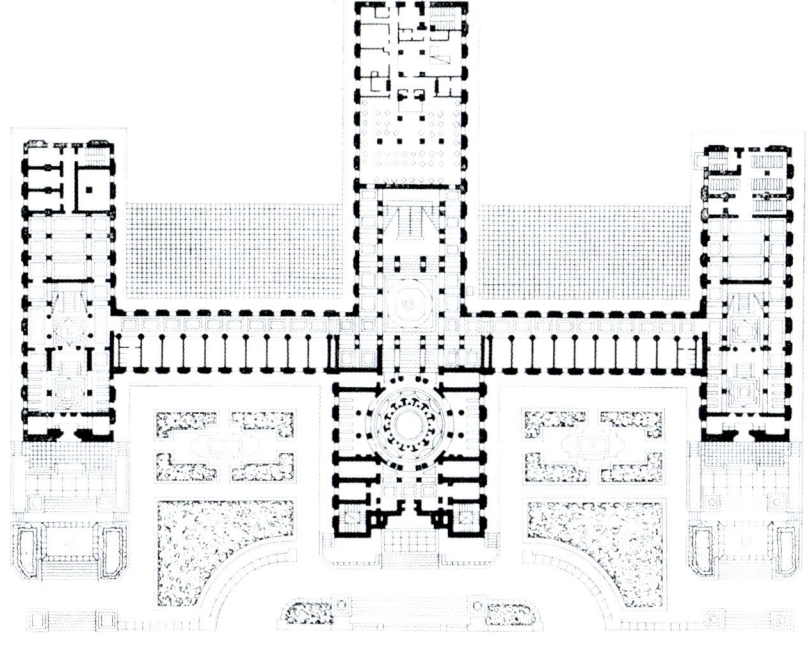

C

Kazakh National Academy of Sciences

033 C

28 Shevchenko St
A.V. Shchusev, N.A. Prostakov
1953

The main building of the National Academy of Sciences is a typical example of late Stalinist architecture, comparable with the very similar Palace of Culture of Railwaymen in Tashkent (A. Pavlov, 1939). However, Aleksey Shchusev, this building's architect, was unable to match the quality of his masterpiece, the Navoi Theatre in Tashkent, which was completed in 1947. It is true that Shchusev and his colleague, Nikolay Prostakov (whose work includes the Abai Opera House, 031), were experienced in the appropriation of oriental architectural language. However, the traditional interplay of monumental form and filigree ornamentation that is one of the features of Central Asian architecture does not come into play here: the yellow plastered entrance portal of the multi-winged complex appears too massive. Nevertheless, the magnificent vestibule with its grand staircase is worthy of note.

Kazakh National Medical University ⌃

 034 C

94 Tole bi St
A.I. Gegello, B.N. Stesin,
D.L. Krichevsky
1932–1952

The first Kazakh medical university was built over a period of about 20 years. The ensemble consists of the main building, the laboratory, and the rectorate. The façades are a synthesis of Constructivist and Classical tendencies, successfully combining large-scale ribbon glazing with elements of Classical architecture. The buildings are of plastered and whitewashed brick. Decorative elements are of cement.

Kazakh National Agricultural University ⌄

  035 C

8 Abai Ave
N. Petrov, V. Biryukov
1934/1954

The main building of Kazakh National Agricultural University – not to be confused with the Veterinary Institute's surgical clinic building at 26 Abai Avenue, which is also part of the university – was built in two stages. First, the east wing was erected in 1934 to plans by N. Petrov. Then, 20 years later, in 1954 the central part and the west wing, designed by Vasily Biryukov, were completed. This building is an example of Classicism combined with Kazakh national decoration.

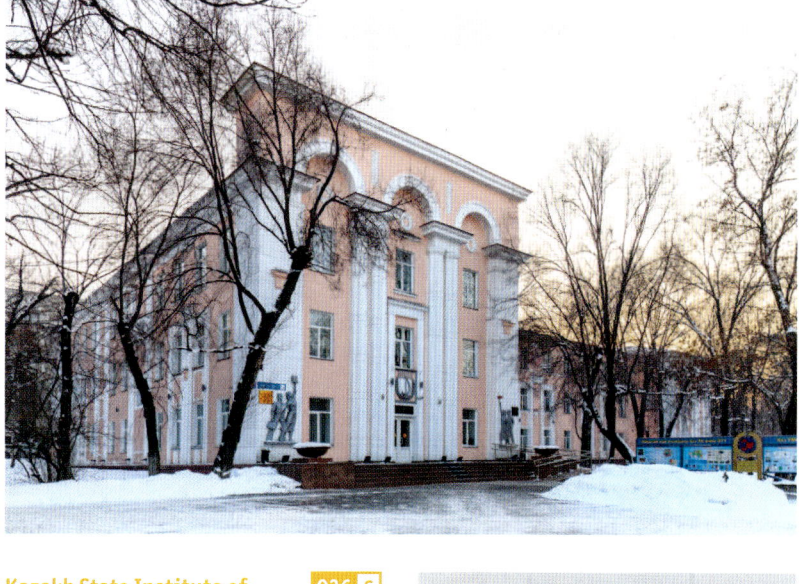

C

Kazakh State Institute of Foreign Languages

036 C

84 Tole bi St
G. Voznyuk, Y.M. Kudryavtsev
1940

The Institute of Foreign Languages is part of the Abylai Khan University of International Relations and World Languages, whose new main building is located at 200 Muratbayev Street. The historical building, with which the university was founded, is now Building 2 and houses the Faculty of Translation and Philology. The three-storey building is asymmetrical, extending from east to west, and is flanked by a risalite at each end. The central entrance is located in the larger corner risalite on the east side and is accentuated by elements of Classical architectural decoration – two pairs of narrower pilasters and two wider corner pilasters, ending in three round arches on multi-part consoles at the level of the attic. The building is crowned by a cornice with a complex profile. Below the cornice, a band of stucco medallions with a hammer and sickle on a book, framed by a wreath of honour, runs around the entire building. The hammer and sickle was the main state emblem of the Soviet Union. The reliefs to the left and right of the entrance, depicting young people seeking knowledge with a book and torch in their hands, also echo the Soviet symbolism of Socialist Realism.

Figures and a corn wreath from the Soviet era are accompanied by the new Kazakh national coat of arms on the main building of Kazakh Agricultural University.

Kazakh-British Technical University

037 C

59 Tole bi St
*B.R. Rubanenko, T. Simonov,
G. Kalinin, P.A. Mamontov*
1934–1957

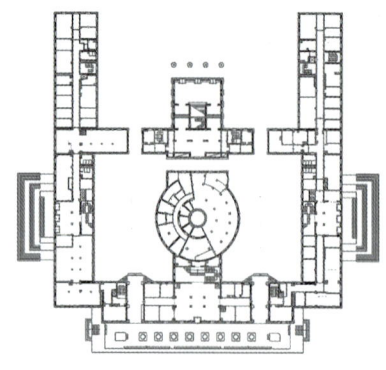

Architecture of Soviet Kazakhstan 1987

For more than 30 years from the late 1950s, the building that is now the Kazakh-British Technical University was the seat of the Central Committee of the Communist Party of the Kazakh SSR. It later housed the Supreme Soviet and, after independence, the Kazakh parliament until the capital was moved to Astana in 1997. Preparations for the construction of an imposing building on the central parade ground in Alma-Ata began in 1934, but only slight progress had been made by 1941, when war broke out. Construction resumed in 1951 and was completed in 1957. The building consists of four-storey pavilions surrounding a conference hall in the centre of the courtyard. On the south side, where the central part of the building is five storeys high, entrance is by a wide staircase and two ramps. The monumental architecture of the Government Building is underlined by a symmetrical composition built around a main axis. The centrepiece is the majestic portico with eight octagonal columns and a high attic on the south façade. The columns are clad in marble and crowned with Ionic capitals in the Kazakh national style with a five-pointed Soviet star in the centre. The massive pylons on the sides of the portico are connected to the rest of the building by two bridges. A narrow cornice runs above the columns, while an arcade frieze runs even higher up, surmounting a massive, richly decorated figural cornice. The main entrance to the building, behind the portico, is emphasised by a massive marble slab and a stained-glass window in an ogival arch. The two side passages to the courtyard are also pointed archways. The rest of the façade is characterised by the rhythm of its pilasters with herbaceous capitals separating the rows of rectangular windows. The building is crowned by a high parapet with a moulded cornice. At the back, on the north side, is another portico with four columns. Two symmetrical extensions at the edges of the north façade were built in 1972 to a design by the architects G. Kalinin and P. Mamontov of Kazgorstroyproyekt. The new buildings are far removed from the original building and close off the side view of the north portico. The architecture of the main building is recreated in the appearance of the annexes.

The main façade of the decades-long seat of the government of the Kazakh SSR

C

Kazpotrebsoyuz «

038 C

55 Tole bi St
B.N. Stesin, G.A. Bobovich,
M. Bekker, V. Lukhtanov
1953–1955

Writers' Association «

039 C

105 Abylai Khan Ave
A.A. Leppik, A.F. Ivanov,
I.V. Shcheveleva
1955

C

What used to be the building of Kazpotrebsoyuz, Kazakhstan's consumer association, originally had 35 apartments and a residential and administrative section. The two parts are separated by an arch and passageway leading through to the courtyard in the centre of the south façade. The prominent five-storey octagonal tower with a spire in the south-west corner of the building is set back from the two façades and tapers towards the top with cornices whose edges are decorated with moulded cornices and balusters. The tower's lower level, above the fourth floor, is crowned by a cornice of stalactites borrowed from the Central Asian architectural tradition. Oriental ornamentation is found throughout the façade. The windows on the ground and upper floors of the tower have pointed arches with ornamental inlays. The pilasters are decorated in the same style, and the cornice of the main façade consists of a narrow band of stalactites and a Classical moulded band. The abundance of ornamentation is characteristic of this period, when even residential buildings, especially on boulevards, were designed to make a statement.

Diagonally opposite the House of Communication (021), this building was the headquarters of the Ministry of Foreign Affairs of the Kazakh SSR before being assigned to the Kazakh Writers' Union, which is still based here. Built in the Neoclassical style, this was an important landmark of Alma-Ata at the time and is a good illustration of Soviet civil and public architecture. The architectural and urban composition of the three-storey building is central-axial with a rectangular ground plan. The main entrance is at the front of the central risalite. There are side entrances on both sides of the building, decorated in a similar manner to the main entrance. The composition of the façade is based on a contrast between the horizontal band of window openings and the vertical rhythm of pilasters between the windows and at the corners of the building. The supporting structure is a reinforced-concrete frame with brick infill. In 1972, in the run-up to an international writers' conference, a conference hall and a café were added to the building, based on a design by the architect I.V. Shcheveleva.

The 1930s saw the construction of the government district along the main axis leading south from Almaty-2 Railway Station (032). Vokzalnaya Street was renamed 'Stalin Avenue'. The buildings of the former people's commissariats of the food industry, health, and agriculture, between Gogol and Aiteke bi streets, form a courtyard. All three buildings are in the Neoclassical style and incorporate national architectural elements and ornaments. The entire complex was designed by Kazgosproyekt and constructed by Almatastroy.

People's Commissariat of the Food Industry ↗

040 C

75 Abylai Khan Ave
G.P. Kushnarenko, K.F. Simkachev
1936–1938

The northernmost building in the ensemble on the corner of Abylai Khan Avenue and Gogol Street, this used to house the People's Commissariat of the Food Industry. The four square columns with mouldings in the portico on the east side of the corner volume are clad with 1980s panelling almost up to the Ionic capitals. A smooth, thin architrave transitions to a frieze and simple cornice finished with flat, stepped dentils. The portico is crowned by a parapet with bollards above the columns, with simple three-quarter shafts and a dentilled balustrade. The rest of the building has the same horizontal articulations as the portico. Above the pilasters are stucco rosettes carrying a replica of a *shangyrak*, the roof section of a Kazakh yurt, often used as a national pattern. The capitals of the columns of the portico are of a simple square shape; instead of an abacus proper, they have decorative details in the form of a paper scroll attached to their sides. This shape may have been the result of a 'creative' reworking of the Ionic order of Classical architecture. The capitals of the pilasters are likewise primitive, differing from the column capitals in the 'wooden' character of their workmanship.

C

People's Commissariat of Health &

77 Abylai Khan Ave
M.D. Shugal, A. Stremenov
1937–1938

People's Commissariat of Agriculture ≈≈

79 Abylai Khan Ave
G.P. Kushnarenko
1937–1938

The former People's Commissariat of Health stands in the middle of the other two former *narkomats*. Its central risalite contains an arch supported by two Tuscan columns, extending over two floors, with a pronounced entasis. The columns are doubled by pilasters of the same shape. The edges of the risalites have Corinthian half-columns extending over all three storeys. Between them are balconies with balustrades, intricately moulded panels, and consoles. This building is certainly the most expressive in the ensemble.

The southernmost of the three buildings mirrors the L-shaped layout of the north building. Here too the corner risalite containing the main entrance has a portico – here with pylons standing on plinths and decorated with rich Corinthian capitals. There is a wide granite staircase. The portico is surmounted by a tall parapet. The pattern established by the portico is continued on the façade in pilasters with the same Corinthian capitals. A massive cornice with dentils runs round the entire building.

People's Commissariat of Finance

043 C

97 Abylai Khan Ave
M.D. Shugal, V. Biryukov, V. Kroshin
1938

Like the Square of the Three Narkomats, the former People's Commissariat of Finance (Narkomfin), is located on what used to be Stalin (now: Abylai Khana) Avenue. It was originally the seat of the Presidium of the Supreme Soviet of the Kazakh SSR. Later, Narkomfin, which had previously been housed in the House of Narkomats (023), moved here.

The building remained the seat of the Ministry of Finance until the Kazakh capital was transferred to Astana in 1997, after which the city's financial administration moved in, followed by offices. The three-storey building has an L-shaped floor plan and consists of three volumes connected by earthquake-proof joins. The entrance is accentuated by a corner risalite with a four-part portico. The columns and semi-columns have a circular abacus and a tri-partite architrave. The the east, main, façade has a tall frieze designed by V. Kroshin with a relief depicting themes of military might, patriotism, education, and work.

C

Qazgeology ⌃
110 Nazarbayev Ave
G.P. Kushnarenko
1938

 044 C

This L-shaped building consists of two three-storey volumes. The main entrance at the corner rests on a semicircular stylobate and is emphasised by Doric columns culminating in a tall, semicircular parapet. Above the entrance are balconies between the columns; the space below the tripartite windows on the third floor is decorated with coffers. Until Kazakhstan's acquisition of independence, this building was the headquarters of the Geological Service. In the 1990s the National Oil Company of China and the Commercial and Industrial Bank of China were based here. Today this is a hotel, also owned by a Chinese company.

Book Museum ⌄
120 Kunayev St
V.A. Tverdokhlebov, I.B. Vakhek
1936

045 C

Despite its eye-catching asymmetrical portico at the corner, the Book Museum building still seems to recall the minimalism of Constructivism. This was the seat of the People's Commissariat for Social Security, the Ministry of Bread and the Fodder Industry, and the Kazpivo Trust. A striking feature of the building is the band of relief panels depicting scenes from socialist life, created by the Czech sculptor Ivan Vakhek, who lived in exile in Alma-Ata.

School No. 55 ⪢

046 C

36 Auezov St
unknown
1939

Stakhanovites' House ⪡ ⪢

047 C

8 Abai Ave
Y.-I.I. Stankevich, M.I. Kudryavtsev
1938

There are more splendid school buildings from the 1930s than School No. 55, but this was one of the last large buildings built in the west of Almaty before the Second World War. Today's Auezov Street was built in 1936 under the city's general plan as Fifth Line and at the same time as the city's western border. School No. 55 not only demonstrates the understanding of pragmatic simplicity in utilitarian buildings of this time but also marks the boundary between early Stalinist architecture and that of the 1940s–1950s.

In the 1930s Alma-Ata's housing stock mainly consisted of apartment blocks; barracks for factory workers, railwaymen, and other labourers; and merchants' houses from the tsarist era. Unlike in Moscow or Leningrad, *kommunalki* (communal flats shared by several tenants) never became a widespread phenomenon in Alma-Ata. But the privileged classes of the new Soviet state needed new forms of housing. The possession of one's own apartment was a sign of status. That is why the so-called *stalinki* (Stalinist houses) were built at this

C

time. These are three-, four-, and some-times even five-room apartments with high ceilings and spacious corridors and rooms, some with shared bathrooms, others with separate bathrooms, in prestigious build-ings in the city centre. Civil servants, mil-itary personnel, artists, and academics in particular were entitled to these flats. However, at a plenary meeting of the USSR Architects' Association in 1937, it was de-cided that standardised housing should be built instead to save money. This led to the design organisations for the first time de-veloping a series of standardised flats with reduced floor areas, designed for single-family use. Building layouts with four two-room apartments on each floor of a stair-well became common. In addition, this

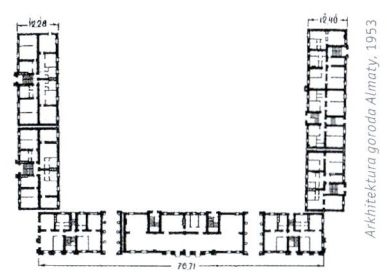

Arkhitektura goroda Almaty, 1953

approach made it possible to build using industrial methods and standardised ele-ments. The Stakhanovites' House is an ex-ample of this new type of construction; its apartments have a floor area of only 26.2 square metres. The house was designed for young communists who had joined the Stakhanov Movement, a socialist campaign to increase labour productivity.

Residential building for Turksib workers

048 C

104 Kabanbai Batyr St
M. Ilyenko
1953

Built for the employees of the Turksib railway, the symbol of this building's original inhabitants is visible from afar: the emblem of the People's Commissariat for Railway Transport, a hammer and a wrench crossed on a laurel wreath, is emblazoned on the balustrade of the tower above the hexagonal corner volume. The building's two wings are only three storeys high, whereas the corner volume is four storeys.

The gates and many of the windows have pointed arches. The façades are structured by risalites, balconies, ornate consoles, cornices, and bands of stucco. A café in the building has a carefully preserved historical interior, with which its design has been tastefully blended – so you can still feel this building's flair today. Critics of the time noted that the ensemble of the square in front of the Opera House, not far to the west, would be disturbed by the exuberant decoration of the façade of the Turksib house. However, the now tall trees in the small park next to the opera house prevent a visual connection between the two buildings.

![Photograph of the white tower and upper façade of the Turksib workers' residential building, with a bird flying in the sky and bare tree branches in the foreground]

Residential building of Kirov Works

049 C

151 Zhibek Zholy St
G.A. Bobovich
1937/1947

This Neoclassical residential building is part of a large, only partially completed project from 1937, which envisaged a cour d'honneur surrounded by a symmetrical ensemble of buildings, the central axes of which are today's Dosmukhamedov Street and Zhibek Zholy Avenue. Construction was delayed by the Second World War and completed in 1947, but not to the extent originally planned. The entire block to the south of Makatayev (then: Yunykh Kommunarov; later: Pasteur) Street and to the west of Akhmet Baitursynov (then: Uighurskaya) Street was used as a residential district for the Kirov Engineering Works. The territory of this once important armament factory lies to the north of Makatayev Street, directly opposite. The architecture of the ensemble of residential buildings is characteristic of the pre-war period. Its centrepiece is the house on the north side of the complex, pierced by a three-storey arch with half-columns and cassette vaulting. Above the archway is a massive parapet with cornices and stucco decoration. Both the central part of the building and the adjoining east and west wings have second and third floor balconies on all sides of their façades, framed by balustrades. The entrances are in the form of rectangular portals with the keystones protruding from the top. The planned west side of the ensemble, intended to mirror the east side, was never built, and other buildings were erected in its place. Nevertheless, the original plan was modified, and the southwest side of the complex was built much later. The entire courtyard exudes a historical atmosphere in which time seems to have stood still.

C

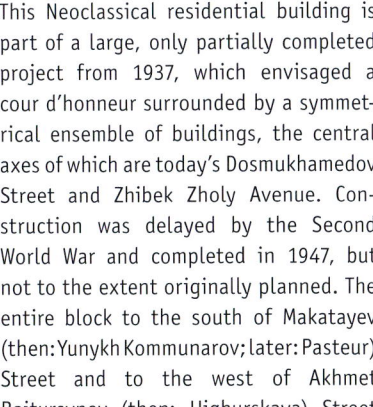

Arkhitektura goroda Almaty, 1953

Original plan (not realised in its entirety) of the complex between Makatayev, Gogol, Akhmet Baitursynov, and Sharipov streets

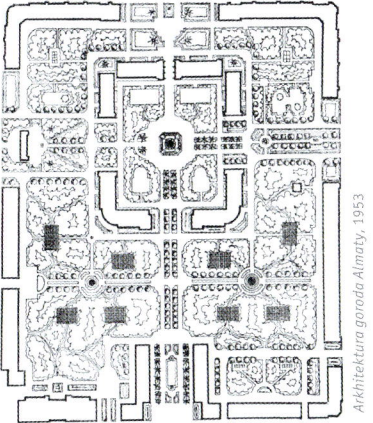

Arkhitektura goroda Almaty, 1953

South façade of the complex's north building, late 1940s or early 1950s

House of Academics ⌃ `050` `C`
60 Zhibek Zholy St
G.A. Bobovich
1949

In the post-war period much emphasis was placed on the exteriors of residential buildings. The House of Academics – so called because it was intended for the academic elite – is an example of this. The façades of the U-shaped, three-storey building are characterised by references to the Orient – pointed arches, floral stucco ornamentation, and arcade-like balconies on the central risalite. The main windows face north, which prevents the building from being overheated. The building is crowned by a massive cornice with a complex profile. The walls are of brick, plastered and whitewashed. The plaster on the ground floor imitates natural stone masonry, giving it a rustic look. The original layout consisted of three and four-room apartments with a room for servants and an internal rubbish chute.

City Executive Committee »   `051` `C`
74a Abylai Khan St
V. Katsev
1963

The Gorispolkom (City Executive Committee) building is a throwback to Stalinist Neoclassicism by the architect Vladimir Katsev, who played a key role in shaping Soviet Modernism in Almaty. Already atypical for the early 1960s, it marks the transition between two architectural eras. The main entrance, with a balcony above, is located in the rounded south-west corner of the building, which is crowned by a dome. A colonnade of stylised octagonal columns forming loggias runs along the entire south and west façades, supporting a high frieze with a moulded cornice. The building was the seat of the City Council until 1994, when the council was moved to Republic Square (058). When the *akimat* building was destroyed in January 2022 during the so-called 'Bloody January' unrest, the administration moved back to its former headquarters until reconstruction of the *akimat* was completed in October 2023.

C

Soviet Modernism

Arman Cinema

052 D

104 Dostyk Ave
I. Slonov, V. Panin, A.I. Korzhempo
1968

Opened in 1968, Arman Cinema is an important example of Soviet-Kazakh architecture of the late 1960s, a moment of transition from the still strictly internationalist architecture of the Khrushchev era to the more independent architectural language of the 1970s. This is particularly evident in the wall relief on the east façade, which is entirely devoted to the cosmonaut aesthetic of the space age and its belief in the future. At the same time it features the traditional Kazakh ornamentation that was to characterise Kazakh architecture in the late-Soviet era. Plans for a major renovation of the cinema have been on the drawing board for several years but have yet to be implemented. Instead, the cinema has had to make do with less sensitive additions and alterations, including such barbarities as a new door in the middle of the wall relief.

Philipp Meuser

D

Palace of the Republic ⤵

56 Dostyk Ave
N.I. Ripinsky, V.N. Kim,
Y.G. Ratushny, L.L. Ukhobotov
1970

053 D

In the early 1960s construction began on Abai Square at the east end of Abai Avenue. First came a nearly 14-metre-high monument to the Kazakh national poet Abai Kunanbayev. Planned as a cultural club for the Kazpotrebsoyuz Consumers' Association, what is now the Palace of the Republic opened as 'the Lenin Palace'. Seen as part of the ensemble surrounding the square, the building volume still looks as originally planned: although much lower than the flanking buildings, it dominates the square; the cable car to Kok Tobe Mountain and Arman

Cinema (052) hang back in the background, providing a view of the mountain panorama. The visible promontory in the east and the ice-covered peaks of Alatau in the south emphasise the palace's monumental presence. However, this building's appearance has changed dramatically following a rigorous reconstruction in 2010, during which the load-bearing and partition walls were reinforced to make them earthquake-proof. The palace's original materials and design were in the style of Regional Functionalism. The main façade was vertically structured by white marble sunshading panels, an element found throughout Central Asia. The rest of the façade was clad in shell limestone from Mangyshlak on the Caspian Sea. The compositional structure of the façades was formed by the wide balconies and panels

Architecture of Soviet Kazakhstan, 1987

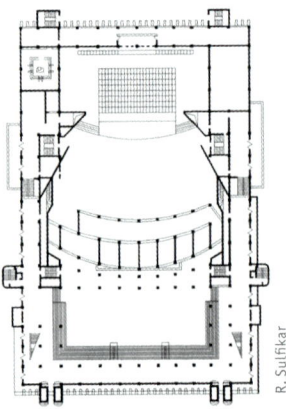

R. Sulfikar

D

of the stepped foyer, while the glazing of the upper level was complemented by thin horizontal lines. Despite its size and monumentality, the main façade remained light and airy thanks to the continuous glazing of the ground floor. The 100-metre-wide staircase of Balkhash granite supports the compositional line of the massive, unusually constructed roof. This is borne by eight reinforced-concrete columns. The walls, which do not extend to the bottom of the roof, give the impression that the roof is suspended in mid-air. The upwardly curved canopies merge seamlessly with the ceiling inside the building, linking the exterior with the interior. A unique feature of the original design was the decorative, illuminated roof covering with a golden honeycomb surface diagonally clad with aluminium pyramid elements in chrome. This was used again in Hotel Kazakhstan (054), built a few years later on the north edge of Abai Square. The reconstruction project, however, replaced the original materials with new ones with no regard for authenticity. The front façade, whose vertical lines gave it a rich plasticity, was replaced with a continuous glass façade, and the paired columns were given capitals. The result was a complete change in the building's architectural appearance.

Architecture of Soviet Kazakhstan, 1987

Collection of Philipp Meuser

D

Bedside lamp as an interior-design object

Hotel Kazakhstan

054 D

52/2 Dostyk Ave
Y.G. Ratushny, L.L. Ukhobotov,
A.Y. Anchugov, V. Kashtanov
1973–1978

In 1978 what was then the most magnificent and modern hotel in the Kazakh SSR opened its doors. The first skyscraper in the city, Hotel Kazakhstan was a major engineering achievement by Soviet engineers as Almaty is located in an area of high seismic risk. Due to the quality of its load-bearing structure and design, this striking building quickly became a symbol of Soviet Alma-Ata and a point of identification for the capital's inhabitants, appearing on the cover of numerous

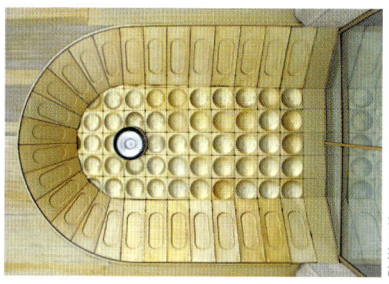

Philipp Meuser

Ceiling ornament in the foyer

official travel guides and on postcards. This was partly due to its prominent position on Abai Square, next to the Lenin Palace (now the Palace of the Republic, 053). With its shimmering golden crown of anodised aluminium enclosing an attic storey for the building services, the hotel long dominated the panorama of the entire city against the backdrop of the Alatau Mountains. More recently, the 25-storey building has faced increasing competition from new glass towers. Its interior is characterised by fine woods, natural stone cladding, and – like the cladding of the base building and the 'crown' – gleaming golden elements, which originally corresponded to the golden roof of the Lenin Palace (since disfigured by renovation).

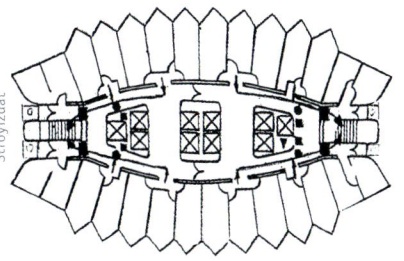

Floor plan, standard floor

KIMEP, Corpus 2 ⌃
4 Abai Ave
D.S. Kim, D. Melnikov, B. Voronin,
N.A. Nikonova, G. Belousova
1978

055 D

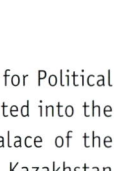

Caspian University ⌄
85a Dostyk Ave
Y.G. Ratushny, O.N. Balykbayev,
T.Y. Yeraliyev
1982

056 D

The western of the two KIMEP University buildings was built 24 years after the main building with its distinctive tower. Both belonged to the Higher Party School, founded in 1946. The most important means of expression are the bays, which are flat on the three-storey north wing but noticeably protrude from the plane of the façade on the five-storey west wing. The continuous ribbon glazing of the bays contrasts with the building's simple rectangular fenestration.

What used to be the Centre for Political Education had to be integrated into the ensemble formed by the Palace of the Republic (053) and Hotel Kazakhstan (054), as well as into the complex of buildings of the Higher Party School (056) south of Abai Avenue. The solution: a horseshoe-shaped main building between two long administrative buildings, the east of which is offset to the south and the west to the north. The latter was replaced by a new office building in 2016.

Circus

50 Abai Ave
V.Z. Katsev, I.V. Slonov
1972

057 D

D

The 80 million who visited circuses in the Soviet Union in 1979 alone illustrate the enormous popularity of this Soviet institution. The circus buildings in the capitals of the republics of the USSR were correspondingly prominent. Almaty Circus, which opened in 1972, is a case in point: designed by Vladimir Katsev, the building is an icon of Soviet Alma-Ata. At the same time it demonstrates the importance of the Kazakh SSR and the architecture of its capital. If the circus buildings in Dushanbe, Frunze (now: Bishkek), and Ashgabat are identical versions of a single standard project, the circus in Almaty, with its expressive domed roof, is subtly modelled on the shape of a traditional Kazakh yurt without copying it. The three fountain figures in front of the circus were created by Pavel Shorokhov, while the colourful tiled cladding of the ticket office pavilion was designed by Jan Nimets and Gennady Zaviziyonny.

The tiled cladding of the circus ticket office pavilion

Architecture of Soviet Kazakhstan, 1987

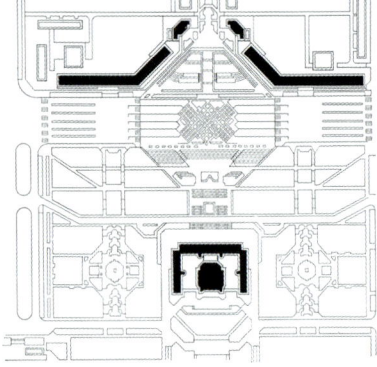

Republic Square
Republic Square
K.Z. Montakhayev, M.P. Pavlov
1977–1980

In the 1970s it was decided to create a new and imposing urban centre for the then capital of the Kazakh SSR. Today's Republic Square (formerly: Brezhnev Square and New Square) was built between 1977 and 1980 under the direction of Mark Pavlov and Kaldybai Montakhayev. The main element is the former building of the Central Committee of the Communist Party of Kazakhstan, now the seat of the *akimat*. Up the slope, 14 metres higher than the buildings on the north side of Satpayev Street, this massive rectilinear volume, clad in the shell limestone typical of Almaty, towers over the ensemble. The north side of the square is dominated by two symmetrical 16-storey residential towers. They flank the Independence Monument, built between 1996 and 1998, which consists of a central 28-metre-high stele and four surrounding sculptures. The *akimat* building was badly damaged during the political unrest in January 2022, forcing the administration to move to its former seat on Abylai Khan Street (051). The building was renovated by October 2023, since when it has been back in use.

D

The *akimat* building, which was partially destroyed in 2022, during reconstruction

Auezov Kazakh State Academic Drama Theatre ⌃ 059 D

103 Abai Ave
M.F. Zhaksylykov, A.S. Kainarbayev, O.Z. Baimurzayev
1980

Arasan Sauna Complex ⌄ » 060 D

78 Tulebayev St
V.T. Khvan, M.K. Ospanov, K.R. Tulebayev, V. Chechelev
1983

This building is an expressive example of late Soviet Kazakh architecture. Only the stage tower protrudes from the otherwise strictly rectangular building. The theatre is notable for its massive, brutalist dimensions and the sloping, closed surfaces of its façade. Despite this, it has a certain lightness: the white marble-clad upper floors seem to float above the dark, deeply recessed glass surfaces of the entrance floor, supported only by the vertical structure of the slightly protruding columns. The façade surfaces feature an abstract relief structure based on Kazakh ornamentation. The architects were awarded the Valikhanov State Prize of the Kazakh SSR in 1982.

The Arasan (Kazakh for 'warm spring') Sauna Complex includes a Finnish and a Russian sauna (*banya*), as well as an oriental *hammam*. This western-eastern use is reflected in the architecture, which eschews flat orientalism and extensive ornamentation. Instead, the architects have created a remarkable modern adaptation of Central Asian building traditions with a massive, elegant façade of marble, shell limestone, and granite. To ensure seismic stability, the complex is composed of seven pavilions. The west building, which dominates the spatial composition, has a semicircular floor plan and is crowned by a ribbed dome. Smaller domes surmount the bathing halls. The foundations are of monolithic reinforced concrete.

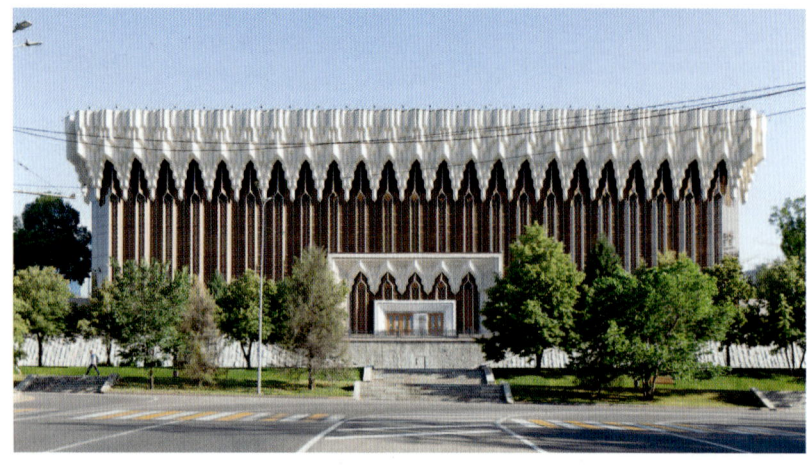

ASK-2 Television Studio Centre ⌃

061 D

185 Zheltoksan St
A.I. Korzhempo, N. Ezau, V. Panin
1983

In the early 1970s it was decided to build a functional but imposing studio building for Kazakh television at the junction of Zheltoksan (then: Mir) and Timiryazev streets. Two high-rise buildings were originally planned, but in the end only a five-storey main building and a two-storey technical pavilion were approved. The main building was the first in Alma-Ata to have an almost entirely glazed façade; this consists of folded volumes of windows of darkened tinted glass. Above, a complex cornice of stalactite-like elements rises from the flat roof, while also reaching down to the height of the fourth floor. The cornice is clad in limestone on a metal frame, while the high stylobate is clad in light-green granite. On the south side, adjacent to the technical pavilion, the façades have ribbon glazing on each floor, without any decoration. The building blends organically into the surrounding landscape, as is emphasised by the terraced design of the site with retaining walls and staircases clad in light-coloured granite. The water basin on the north side, formerly part of the building's air-conditioning system, was reconstructed in 2007 and transformed into a fountain.

Obkom (Regional Committee of the Communist Party) ⌄

062 D

67 Aiteke bi St
K.Z. Montakhayev, N. Ezau
1986

The Regional Committee of the Communist Party was the last government institution to move into a new building in Alma-Ata

before the collapse of the USSR. This brutalist U-shaped building, framing an open square on its south side, completes the axis running from Republic Square (058) along Baiseitova Street, past the first House of the Government (020) and through the Central Committee of the Communist Party of the Kazakh SSR building (037) in the centre to the north. Today it is the seat of financial institutions.

Hotel Almaty

85 Kabanbai Batyr St
N.I. Ripinsky, Y.A. Kartasi
V.G. Chirkin, A.Y. Kossov,
1967

063 D

Hotel Alma-Ata (now Almaty) was the central and most imposing hotel of the early Soviet Modernist period. This was a time when there was an accelerating move away from the strict standardisation prescribed by Khrushchev and it became clear that architects in the Soviet Union were not isolated from international trends. Hotel Alma-Ata was designed by a team of architects from the Kazakh State Planning Bureau (Kazgorstroiproyekt) and built under the supervision of the Ministry of Heavy Plant Construction (Mintyazhstroy). In 1972 the architects received the USSR Council of Ministers Award for this project. Situated opposite the Opera House (031), this eight-storey building with its elegantly curving south-facing façade is notable for its deep bands of balconies, whose simple horizontality meets internationalist requirements while providing adequate shade for the hotel rooms behind them. The main entrance is highlighted by a projecting canopy and a wall mosaic by the monumental artists Moldakhmet Kenbayev and Nikolay Tsivchinsky. The latter depicts scenes from the national epic 'Yenlik and Kebek', which tells the story of Zhigit Kebek and his lover Yenlik. On the north side of the hotel is a restaurant on a high plinth. The restaurant's kitschy, yurt-like roof structure is of recent origin and destroys the clear lines of the original. In 2003 the light-blue glass that originally covered the balconies was replaced with the then popular light-blue Alucobond. Following privatisation in 2007, Hotel Alma-Ata was due to be demolished and replaced by a new, modern building but was ultimately preserved. In 2016 and 2017 the hotel underwent extensive reconstruction, during which the historical appearance of its façade was restored. This is now a listed building.

D

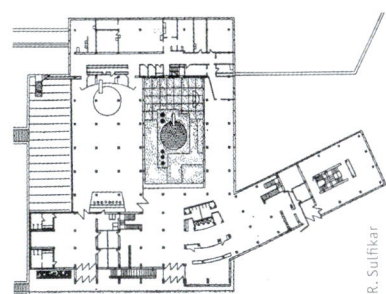

R. Sulfikar

Lermontov State Academic Russian Drama Theatre

064 D

43 Abai Ave

G.P. Gorlyshkov, V.P. Davidenko, N.A. Shebalina

1969

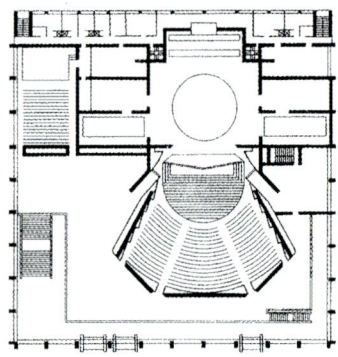

From 1934 to 1969 the Lermontov Russian State Academic Drama Theatre and the Auezov Kazakh State Academic Drama Theatre shared a venue in the building of the Club of the People's Commissariat for Internal Affairs (NKVD) (025). In 1964, as part of the development of Abai Avenue and the south of the city, the capital's building department decided to provide a site for a new theatre building. The National Library building (065) was planned to stand diagonally opposite, and the State Archives complex was already located to the east. Together with them, the Lermontov Theatre building forms a cultural centre around the city's main north-south axis between Baiseitova Street and Abylai Khan Avenue and its intersection with Abai Avenue, which at the time was developing into one of the city's most important west-east axes. The compact theatre building with its square floor plan is separated from the alignment of the adjacent main streets by a green space, now densely planted with conifers. Several steps and terraces follow the relief of the site. On the east side of the building,

for example, there is a terrace that forms an open space below. This has been partially enclosed by a wall since the 2000s, but the large entrance gate has been preserved. The theatre's façades are characterised by a contrast between the large expanses of wall on the upper tier and the continuous glazing of the lower level. The ribbed reinforced-concrete panels on the upper floor create a strict geometric pattern and an interplay of light and shadow on the façade. They can also be opened to create more shade and regulate the building's climate. The 844-seat auditorium, designed as an amphitheatre, is connected to a two-wing foyer with asymmetrical staircases. There is also a small 200-seat hall on the first floor. The latter was reduced in size during a reconstruction in the second half of the 2000s. The glazing and interior decoration were also renewed at this time. The flat roof of the auditorium was covered with a pitched roof.

National Library

14 Abai Ave
V.N. Kim, V.P. Ishchenko
E.K. Kuznetsov, K.N. Kalnoi
1970

The rectilinear building of the National Library, towards which Abylai Khan Avenue runs to the south, is a shining example of early Soviet Modernism in Almaty. A ramp serving as an extension of the street that ends here leads up to the entrance of the three-storey building, which consists of two elongated sections running east-west, connected by three transverse wings. The narrow, north, part was intended for administrative and technical spaces; the wider, south, section with views of the mountains, for readers. The main entrance is in the central connecting wing, from which a large staircase leads to the upper floors. Two inner courtyards serve as light wells for the library rooms. The building's supporting structure is a prefabricated, monolithic reinforced-concrete skeleton; the slabs are of ribbed reinforced concrete; the walls are of lightweight steel cement with mineral wool insulation. Natural and artificial marble, wood, metal, and glass were used in the interior. A distinctive feature is the continuous glazing of the north and south façades – a masterpiece of engineering for the late 1960s which emphasises the building's transparency. All rooms are centrally air-conditioned. Special acoustic and interior design makes the reading rooms especially quiet.

D

Palace of Pioneers

124 Dostyk Ave
V.N. Kim, T.S. Abilda, A.P. Zuyev
1983

066 D

The ensemble of the Palace of Pioneers (now: the Student Palace) consists of 12 pavilions arranged in a spiral around a central volume with a massive dome. The 19-metre-high dome rests on a metal structure and covers a circular ballroom. The chandelier in the ballroom has 288 lights, is seven metres in diameter, and weighs 3.5 tonnes. Glazed ribbon openings in the upper part of the dome provide natural light for the hall. The corrugated surface of the dome is clad with ribbed scales of golden aluminium. There is an observatory in the 40-metre-high tower, but it has not been in use for years. Due to the rounded floor plans, most of the building is made of monolithic reinforced concrete, an advanced construction technique for the time. The pavilions can be used independently – for exhibitions, sports, and major events – but are all accessible from the central volume. The building's façades are clad in marble and shell limestone, while the base is of granite. Reconstruction carried out in 2015–2016 kept the building's appearance essentially unchanged. The cupola and glazing units have been renewed, as have parts of the interior.

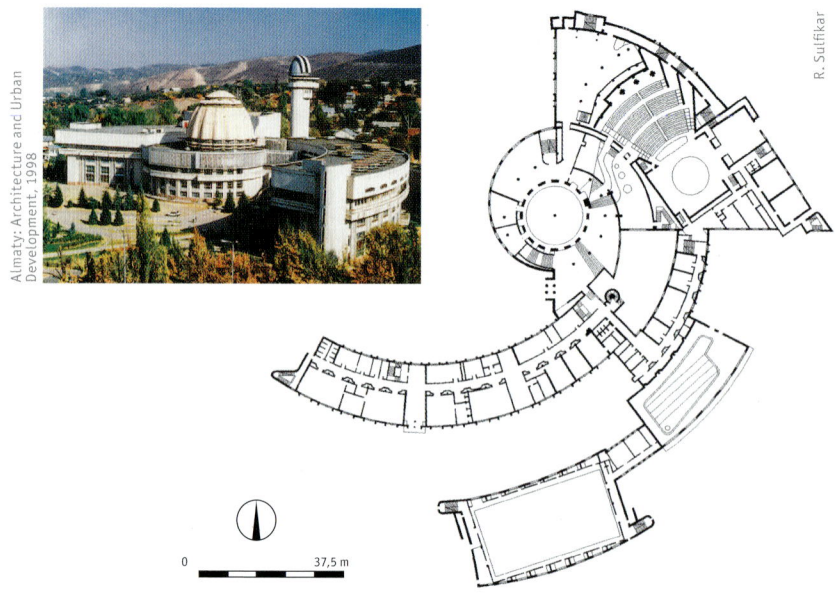

Almaty: Architecture and Urban Development, 1998

R. Sulfikar

0   37,5 m

Palace of Weddings ⌃⌄

101a Abai Ave
M.M. Mendikulov, A.A. Leppik,
N. Orazymbetov
1971

067 D

This three-storey building with a diameter of 34 metres is supported by a hollow frame of reinforced concrete. The façade is clad in white marble and has all-round glazing, which is shaded by a metal façade curtain. The mosaics on the north and south sides were created by Moldakhmet Kenbayev and Nikolay Tsivchinsky. The original decoration of the lobby and halls in marble, gabbro, and polished oak, as well as the murals on the first floor, fell victim to several renovations. Now the front and back entrances have an anteroom, and the interiors are lavishly decorated in the Neoclassical style of the Toy-Khana culture.

Theatre for Children and Youth ⌄

38 Abylai Kjan Ave
A.A. Leppik, V.Z. Katsev,
N.I. Ripinsky
1962

068 D

D

The originally Neoclassical exterior and interior were gradually simplified by removing ornamentation, following the spirit of Modernism. The main entrance on the west side is highlighted by a stylobate staircase and two broad rectangular columns supporting a pediment decorated with a mosaic by Oleg Bogomolov and Yevgeny Sidorkin. Before reconstruction in 2006, the side façades had rows of rectangular windows divided vertically by flat slats, the façade cladding was of grey concrete slabs, and the west side of the building was glazed. Only the two simplified Neoclassical belfries that adorned the top and the red granite of the plinth on the side façades have been preserved.

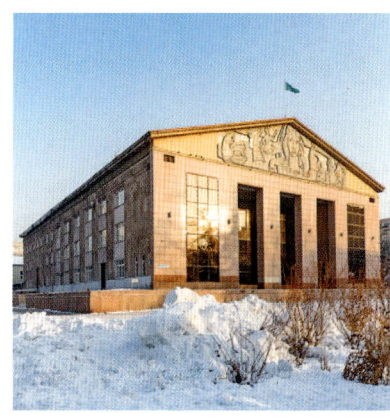

Hotel Otrar

73 Gogol St
M.R. Kabylbayev
1981

069 **D**

In 1970 Almatygiprogor, the Kazakh urban planning institute, was commissioned by Glavintourist, the Soviet state tourism agency in Moscow, to design a hotel for this site. The planned 12-storey Hotel Intourist would have been comparable in size with Hotel Kazakhstan (054) and capable of accommodating 1000 guests. Permits took several years to obtain, and in the meantime preparations for the 1980 Olympic Games in Moscow were underway. The enormous costs meant that many projects on the periphery of the Soviet Union had their budgets cut. The hotel in Alma-Ata was reduced to a budget of three million roubles, five storeys, and 300 beds, resulting in a completely new design project. For its construction prefabricated, standardised reinforced-concrete frames were used for only the second time. What was new was that the huge H-profile sections were delivered from the concrete factory to the construction site, where they only had to be welded together, which speeded up construction enormously. Madeniyet Kabylbayev, the building's architect, was inspired by the medieval Timurid buildings of Khiva, Bukhara, and Samarkand in Uzbekistan, giving this Modernist hotel an oriental flair. Distinctive arched forms can be seen on the façade and in the portal, which is covered with colourful ceramic tiles on the inside. A renovation carried out in the 1990s replaced most of the original interior design, which interpreted national motifs in a Modernist way, with pseudo-Classical motifs.

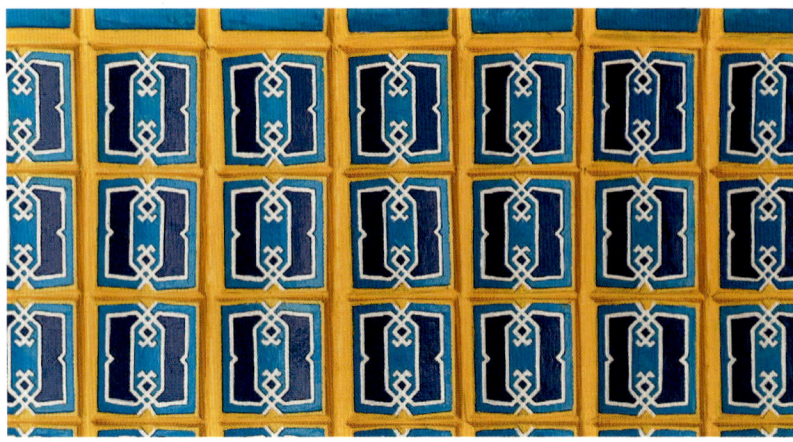

Green Bazaar ⌃
53 Zhibek Zholy Ave
M.P. Pavlov, S.I. Rustambekov
1975

070 D

As early as the second half of the nineteenth century, a market with accommodation for merchants and travellers was established on the square between Zhibek Zholy Avenue and Pasteur (now: Makatayev), Proletarian (now: Zenkov), and Pushkin streets. In the 1940s the bazaar consisted of rows of wooden stalls and warehouses, which were demolished and replaced by permanent structures in the 1970s. Now the rectangular, three-storey building houses the main market hall, as well as storage and administration rooms. The building's façades have wide, continuous bands of windows that are set back into the façade plane, forming an open loggia on the first floor. The two upper floors of the building are cantilevered.

Nine hipped roofs sit on top of the flat roof, with ribbon glazing in the lower section providing natural light to the market hall; the upper pyramidal sections are clad externally with aluminium scales. The windows in the hipped roofs provide natural ventilation. The insides of the roof pyramids are clad with decorative white aluminium panels, while the ceiling of the main hall is clad with gold-coloured anodised aluminium panels. The walls of the market hall are partly tiled and partly clad with aluminium panels. The balcony and stair railings are of wood. The roof rests on four symmetrical massive pylons that structure the main hall. It houses lifts for the delivery of goods from the lower part of the building, as well as cafes and shops. Since the 1990s, many other buildings have been constructed on this site. The catacombs, corridors, staircases, and passages form a labyrinth that showcases the typical life of a busy market.

ГҮЛДЕР

ЦВЕТЫ

ШӨПТЕР

Main hall of the Green Bazaar

D

House of Officers

24 Zenkov St
Y.G. Ratushny, O.N. Balykbayev,
T.Y. Yeraliyev
1978

071 D

This Brutalist building stands on the east edge of the Park of the 28 Panfilov Guardsmen, stretching north-south opposite the Monument to the Fallen in the Second World War and the Eternal Flame. Standing on a high stylobate, the five-storey building consists of two pavilions: the original Officers' House to the south and the north part, added in 1985, which replicates the main building. The foundations are of reinforced concrete, and the supporting structure is a prefabricated, monolithic reinforced-concrete frame with brick infill walls. The façade, clad in gabbro-diabase and shell limestone, is structured by pylons serving as vertical elements between the windows, sloping stone columns as sun screens, and a massive top floor. The upper floor is accentuated by a strip of light-coloured stone that frames the entire façade. The same material is used for the top floor, which is flanked by a row of narrow, set-back windows. Originally, a ceremonial square (Lenin Square) was planned next to the building, which was to have been even taller and more majestic. The intention was to enclose the entire east side of the park from Gogol Street to today's Dostyk Avenue, ending with a rotunda for

D

an operetta theatre. The current Museum of Musical Instruments (006) was also to have been demolished. In the end, however, the building turned out more modest than planned, and the small wooden building at its foot was retained because it emphasised the monumentality of the new building.

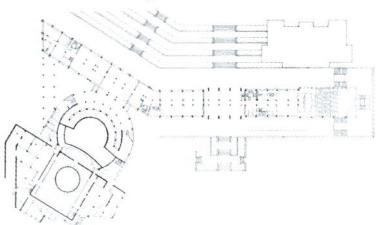

Original design with unrealised operetta theatre

TsUM ⌃
072 D

62 Abylai Khan Ave
*M.A. Gura, P.G. Mikhaldyk,
Mironenko*
1961/1970

The Central Universal Department Store
(Tsentralny Universalny Magazin or TsUM)
consists of two buildings built less than
ten years apart due to a rapid shortage of
space. The first is in a spartan Neoclassical
style. A reconstruction project in 2014
created new entrances and replaced the
windows but preserved the marble interior staircases. The second building to the
east originally had a façade with bands of
glazing overhanging the ground floor. After the renovation, however, little remains
of its stunning Modernist character.

Aerovokzal ⌄
073 D

111 Zhibek Zholy Ave
A.A. Leppik, I.V. Shcheveleva
1976

Until the early 2000s the Aerovokzal
('Aero-station') was the airport's outpost
in the city centre. Passengers could check
in directly. The two-storey building is a typical example of 1970s Functionalism. The
ground floor housed ticket and check-in
counters, waiting areas, and shops, while
the upper floor contained a restaurant
and service facilities. The staircase in the
east part of the building no longer exists.
A parapet runs around the entire building, concealing the flat roof. The composition of the main façade is based on a vertical, rhythmic row of twin pylons, which

D

contrast with the wide horizontal bands of the window openings. The pylons rise above the cornice. The bands of glazing on the first and second floors are set back to reveal the pylons. The façade lattice, in the style of a traditional carpet pattern, is both sun protection and decoration. Up until a few years ago, one could buy train and plane tickets in the building. Today, the Aerovokzal houses small shops for electronic devices and their repairs, with separate booths built directly into the hall.

Sairan Bus Station

294 Tole bi St
V.V. Nerovnya, V.D. Tyaglovsky,
O.Y. Burgimbayev
1983

074 D

As part of the 1978 master plan for Alma-Ata, a site for a second bus station was chosen near Tole bi Street, which was built at this time as an arterial road leading to the west. The three-storey building has a total area of more than 12,000 square metres and is dominated by a massive, nine-metre-high cantilevered canopy. The central section of the main, north-facing, façade is highlighted by large expanses of glazing. Marble, shell limestone, and granite have been used in the building's cladding. The large waiting room occupies the central part of the building; administrative and service rooms, drivers' toilets, and check-in desks are in the side sections. The ceiling of the waiting room has geometric elements in anodised aluminium and luminaires with louvres to diffuse the light. Some elements of the interior panelling and façades have been lost.

Almaty-1 Railway Station ⌃

1 Stantsionnaya St
S.O. Mkhitoryan, Z.M. Soldatova
1976

Kok-Tobe TV Tower

35 Omarova St
N.G. Terziyev-Tsarukov,
A. Savchenko, N. Akimov
1983

Construction of the Turksib (Turkestan-Siberian Railway) began in 1927. The railway was built towards Alma-Ata from two directions – from Semei (then: Semipalatinsk) in the north and from Lugovaya, a village near Taraz (then: Auliye-Ata), in the west. The southern branch of the line reached Alma-Ata in 1929, with the first train arriving on 19 July 1929. The first single-storey station building, built in the Constructivist style, was demolished in the early 1970s to make way for a modern station. The new building was modelled on Almaty Airport, which opened in 1973, and characterised by laconic, straightforward modern architecture. The façade featured large expanses of glazing with aluminium frames, and the cantilevered canopy was supported by a series of rectangular pylons. A reconstruction in 2007 stripped the previously listed building of its sober exterior. The façades and pylons were covered in cheap-looking cladding, and the building was partially extended, destroying the original balanced composition.

The television tower on Kok-Tobe (in Kazakh: 'Green') Hill, south east of the city centre, is one of the most recognisable buildings in the city. The hill, to which a cable car ascends from Abai Square, is 1130 metres high, and the tower itself has a height of 257 metres; it is topped by a 114-metre antenna. The tower's 16-sided monolithic shaft is clad in aluminium panels and has a diameter of 18.5 metres at its base. It tapers upwards to nine metres below the antenna. The foundation extends three storeys into the ground to ensure sufficient stability in this seismically active area. The tower was the first in the Soviet Union to be built in such a geographically and climatically challenging environment. It has a one-storey viewing platform at a height of 146 metres and a second, two-storey, platform at a height of 252 metres. A panoramic restaurant with glass windows and a marble interior was to be located on the lower, enclosed platform. However, no provision was made for the high-capacity lifts or evacuation systems that would have been required. From the two-storey service building at the foot of the tower technicians can reach the top by two high-speed lifts. This is because the television tower is used as such and is equipped with numerous transmission systems. However, it has never been open to tourists and probably never will be.

Wikimedia Commons, Torekhan Sarmanov

Medeo Speed Skating Rink

077 D

465 Kerei-Zhanibek kandar St
V.Z. Katsev, A. Kainarbayev, et al.
1972

The highest ice stadium in the world in terms of altitude, Medeo had a legendary reputation throughout the former Eastern Bloc. In the 1970s and 1980s more than 120 world records were set on the speed skating rink here, located just a few kilometres south of the centre of Alma-Ata. This made this Soviet prestige project, which opened in 1972, unique in the world. Surrounded by the snow-capped peaks of the Tien Shan mountain range, which rises to 5000 metres, the stadium lies in the valley of the Little Almatinka River at an altitude of around 1700 metres in a picturesque setting. A nearby 150-metre-high dam protects the city and the stadium from mud slides. In addition to the 400-metre-long ice rink, the facility has an ice surface of 10,500 square metres. Since Kazakhstan's acquisition of independence, this former Soviet 'record factory' has been used mainly by day-trippers from Almaty. To return it to its glory days for the 2011 Asian Winter Games, the stadium was extensively renovated and now has capacity for 8500 spectators (previously: 12,000). Rather unusually for post-Soviet Kazakhstan, the original design by the architect Vladimir Katsev, which won the State Prize of the Soviet Union in 1976, was left largely unchanged, perhaps due to Medeo's high profile. The gigantic relief of speed skaters by the monumental artists January Nimets and Viktor Konstantinov still adorns the back of the 250-square-metre scoreboard.

Speed skater, a relief by the artists
Jan Nimets and Viktor Konstantinov
(1972)

Medeo Speed Skating Rink in front of the threatening backdrop of the dam in 1978

RIA Novosti

D

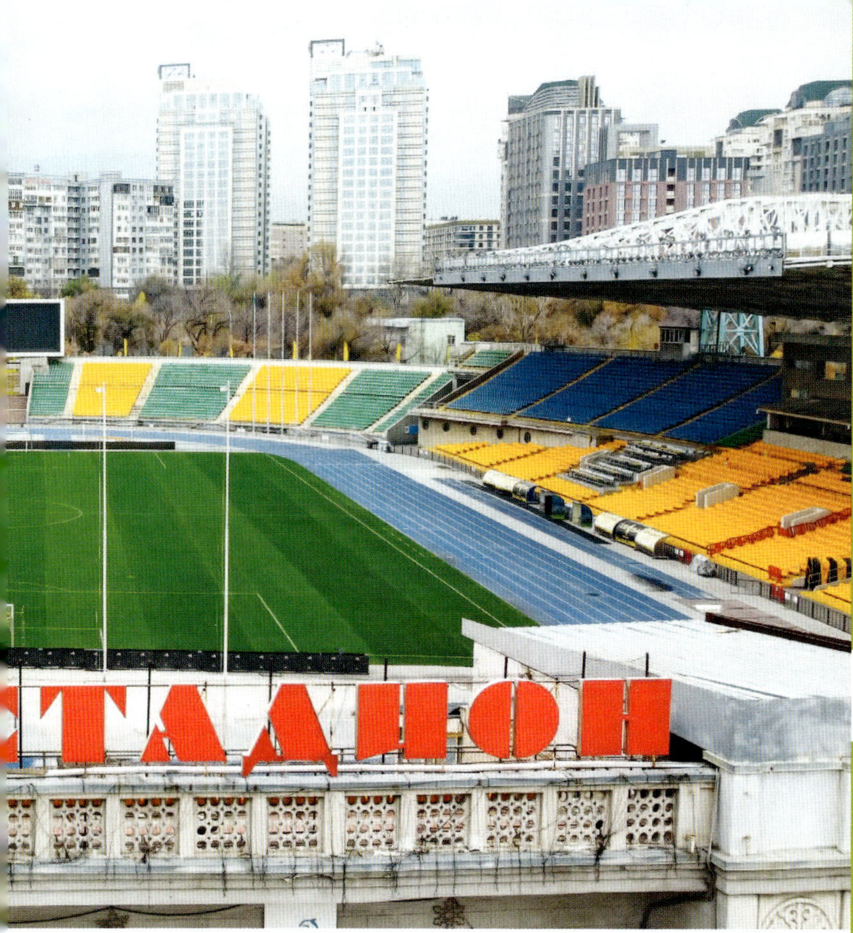
ТАДИОН

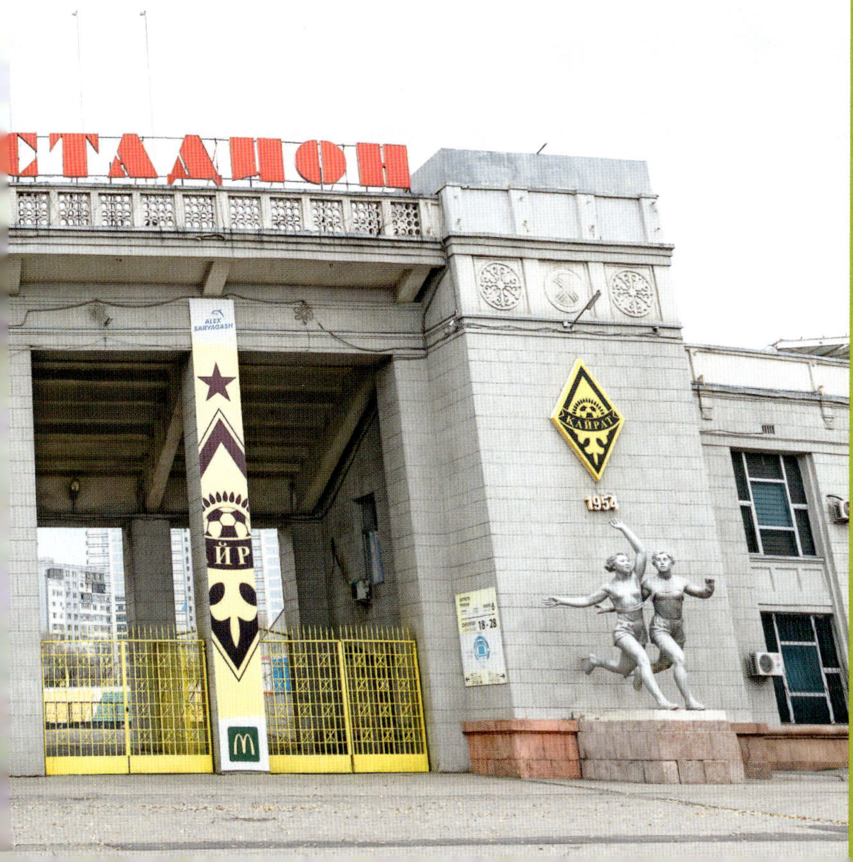
ТАДИОН
ALEX SARYAGASH
КАЙРАТ
1954

Central Stadium

29/3 Satpayev St
A.A. Leppik, A.Y. Koosov,
A.K. Kapanov
1958

078 D

Opened in 1958, the Central Stadium was the first of several sports arenas in Alma-Ata. It is still the home of the legendary football club Kairat, founded in 1954. The stadium comprises a football pitch, Tartan tracks, and stands for 23,800 spectators. The Central Lenin Stadium in Moscow (now: Luzhniki Stadium), built two years earlier, was the model for this project. The structure rests on a rigid monolithic framework of prefabricated beams and L-shaped slabs supporting the rows of stands. The stadium is designed in a simplified Neoclassical style. The flat pylons are separated by recessed rectangular windows, and the façades are clad in a rustic grey plaster that imitates brickwork. The main entrance on the north side of the stadium is a wide portal set into the plane of the façade. At its centre are two rows of four columns, one behind the other, flanked by sculptures of athletes. Above the four side gates of the stadium, which interrupt the façade plane, are decorative friezes with bas-relief depictions of 16 different sports, with four athletes on each frieze. The west stand was covered with a metal roof in 2004, and the pitch was reconstructed in 2009–2010.

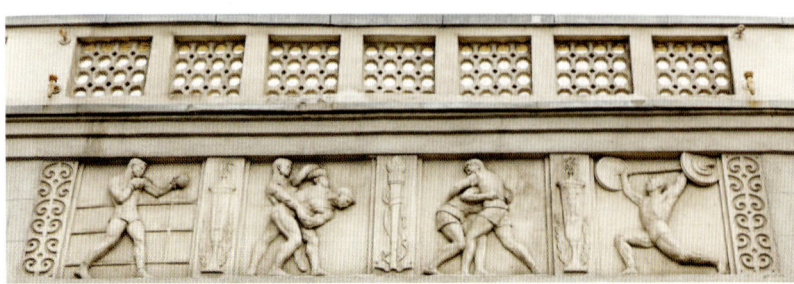

Republican College of Sport

41 Timiryazev St
N. Shalabanov,
S.N. Martemyanov,
A.I. Korzhempo
1979

079 D

D

The athletics hall and the swimming pool of what is now the Republican College of Sport were built as an extension to the former Olympic Reserve School. The architects were faced with the difficult task of integrating the new buildings into the existing complex, which included school and boarding buildings. The result is a surprisingly dynamic composition, with the façades of the two new buildings facing east towards Mursepov Boulevard.

The two buildings are elegantly interlocked with one another and with the adjacent block of student dormitories to the south. A steeply sloping monopitch roof rises above the swimming pool, which houses a diving tower and two pools. It is flanked by a three-storey elliptical cylinder that conceals the staircase. The façade is distinguished by cantilevered balconies and by portholes in the basement, which provide natural lighting for the swimming pool. On the upper floor of the low-rise building is a sports hall with spectator stands. The ceiling of the swimming pool consists of sloping metal trusses. On the walls are mosaics with scenes from the world of water sports.

Contemporary murals in the style of Soviet Modernism at the Republican College of Sports

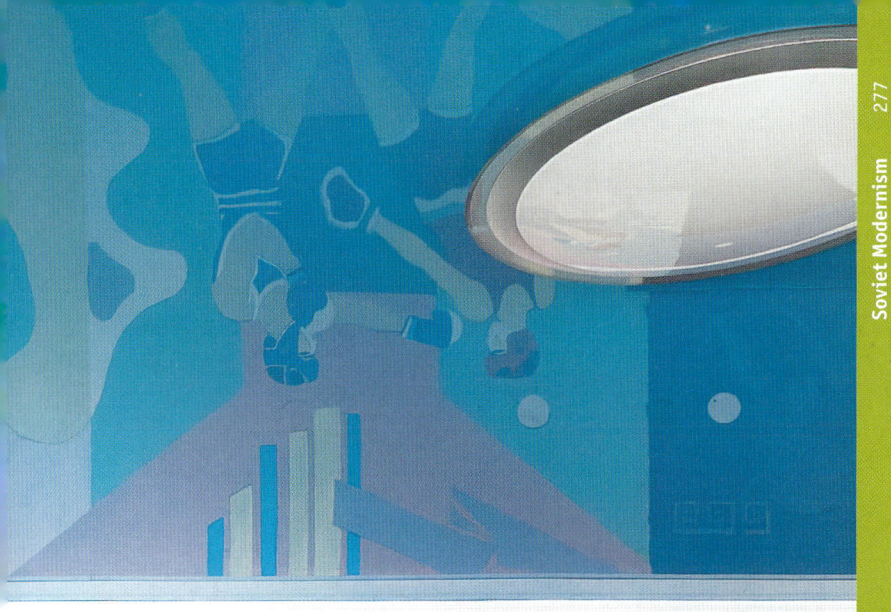

Мұражай

Central Committee of the Komsomol

080 D

67 Tole bi St
S.G. Kosmeridi, V.K. Alle
1970

Kazakhtelecom

081 D

129 Panfilov St
V.A. Babenko, A.A. Petrova,
A. Petrov
1983

The former building of the Kazakh Central Committee of the Komsomol is no longer a prestigious landmark. It joins a long list of neglected administrative buildings scattered across the former Soviet Union that bear only a passing resemblance to the progressive design of their time. There are clear references to the lightness and simplicity of Hotel Yunost in Moscow (1961) and the asymmetry of Le Corbusier's Carpenter Centre in Cambridge (1963), with the ramp as an individual element running counter to the natural relief. In the six-storey main building rooms and staircases are arranged along the main west-east axis. The façades were designed with expanded concrete panels, with vertical aluminium sunshades on the north and south sides; the latter have been removed. On the flat roof is a semi-open pavilion above the lift shaft. Its canopy originally was decorated with a Komsomol insignia that glowed at night. As this building blocks Tchaikovsky Street, there was a passageway at the level of the lowest floor. This also provided access to the auditorium in the one-storey volume on the north side. Today the passage is closed.

The city's central telephone exchange was originally built to manage 25,000 telephone numbers. It still fulfils similar functions today, housing the state communications provider Kazakhtelecom as well as other companies in the communications sector. The building's most striking feature is the diamond-shaped latticework with spherical girders protruding from the façade. This is a similar technical solution to that used for Bush Lane House (1976) in London by Arup Associates. It allowed the internal construction to be freed of some of the load-bearing structures and optimised to accommodate the heavy technical equipment. The windows for the technical rooms are narrow vertical slits. Only on the upper three floors, housing the administration, are the windows wide and rectangular. The building rests on a single-storey podium that protrudes beyond the limits of the main volume. The main entrance is on the east façade, the south part of which has continuous glazing extending to the full height of the building. The volume containing the staircase and lifts is separated from the main volume in an extension on the west side of

D

the building. Consideration was given to the possibility of replacing this system as it wears out. The original blue enamelled steel panels that clad the façade were also an innovation, used in this form for the first time in Alma-Ata. They provided maximum insulation that was not only lightweight but also fire- and moisture-resistant. In 2005, however, the façade was completely re-clad in gold, the windows were replaced, and a small balcony was added to the fourth floor on the east side. The podium was significantly altered by extensions and the original shell limestone cladding was replaced with Alucobond.

Kasteyev State Museum of Arts

082 D

22/1 Mikrorayon Koktem-3
*E.K. Kuznetsova, B.M. Novikov,
O.N. Naumova*
1976

This building communicates its function to the outside world with a simple design that is at once visibly Modernist and Central Asian. From the very beginning of the design process, the lighting and air conditioning were focused on the task of exhibiting art. The three-storey building has a rectangular floor plan and an atrium. The architectural design and layout are based on a clear functional division of the space into a lobby and ancillary rooms on the ground floor, various administrative rooms on all floors

with their own access, and the exhibition rooms on the second and third floors. The square, central entrance hall is crowned by a striking glass pyramid that provides natural light. This is supported by four diagonal metal trusses resting on a reinforced-concrete base. The exhibition spaces are lit by skylights designed as translucent suspended ceilings of reinforced glass in aluminium structures. The north façade, facing Satpayev Street, is distinctive for the rhythm of its wall panels, arranged at an angle of 45 degrees. They form a series of one-sided illuminated bays that limit direct sunlight into the exhibition halls. The bays are repeated at larger intervals on the west façade containing the entrance. The latter is accentuated by a low colonnade with a projecting canopy and a water basin with a fountain that runs almost the entire length of the building on each side. The small park surrounding the building contains a monument to the Kazakh painter Abilkhan Kasteyev, after whom the museum is named, and other sculptures.

Almaty: Architecture and urban development, 1998

View from the south east, mid-2000s

Alatau Sanatorium

50a Mikrorayon Tausamaly
Y.G. Ratushny, O.N. Balykbayev,
T.Y. Yeraliyev
1986

083 D

Built in the late Soviet era, Alatau Sanatorium was originally intended for use by members of the Communist Party. After Kazakhstan became independent, it was an events venue, for long retaining its Soviet charm. Following closure in 2017, it underwent reconstruction over the course of several years. Since 2021 Swissotel has been operating Alatau Almaty wellness resort here. The sanatorium is located in the west of the city, in the middle of a 5000-square-metre park. Integrating the building into the surrounding landscape was a key concern from the outset. As a result, the main building, with its double-curved floor plan, appears to 'wind' between hills, ponds, and small canals, while retaining a certain compactness. On the north side are three smaller buildings, a circular swimming pool reminiscent of a yurt, a cinema, and a restaurant. The two lower levels – containing a conservatory, the foyer, and a dance hall– merge into one another, creating a sense of monumentality. The large spaces are made possible by a reinforced-concrete frame that provides bracing to increase the building's resistance to earthquakes. During the reconstruction, the design of the façade, which reflects the building's volumetric and spatial structure, was largely retained.

Almaty: Architecture and urban development, 1998

D

Kunayev Home Museum
119 Tulebayev St
B.V. Dmitriyevsky, M. Trofimov
1975

084 D

The former home of Dinmukhamed Kunaev, the long-serving leader of the Communist Party of the Kazakh SSR, is now a museum in his honour. Before Kunaev moved into the 230-square-metre apartment in late 1969, he and his wife had lived in a Stalinist building a quarter the size at 107 Kommunisticheskaya St (now: Abylai Khan Ave) and a little further south on Tulebayev St, at the corner of Dzhambyl St. Kunaev's apartment was one of nine in this two-storey building. It is notable for its panoramic windows and rounded frames around the loggias, reminiscent of Bauhaus architecture and Constructivism. These give the building a modern look despite its poor state of repair.

Close-up of the built-over façades of the Three Warriors residential complex

D

Three Warriors residential complex ⌃

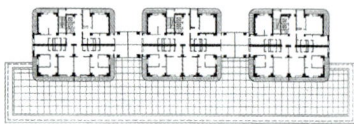

44 Dostyk Ave
A. Petrov, A.A. Petrova,
G.S. Dzhakipova, B.A. Churlyayev,
V.S. Gershberg
1970

The three-tower, twelve-storey residential building on the eastern side of Dostyk (formerly: Lenin) Avenue was designed as a vertical accent in an ensemble built in the 1960s and 1970s. The complex is set back from the street, leaving space for a lively forecourt. The three towers stand on a shared stylobate that houses a cinema and shops. They are connected by metal frames with open exits at the junctions to increase resistance to earthquakes. Each tower has an entrance on its east side with its own staircase and lift. A distinctive feature is the bands of balconies that visually unite the sections of the building. Today the building's façades have been robbed of their original appearance by a chaotic profusion of built-on additions: balconies and exits have been built over by the residents.

Almatygiprogor ⌄

60 Abylai Khan Ave
A.I. Korzhempo
1971

The State Institute of Urban Planning was founded in Almaty in 1966 and moved to its new premises in 1971. The most

striking feature of this building is the grid of solar shades consisting of metal profiles arranged in circles that covers the entire west façade from the second to the seventh floors. This contrasts sharply with the rest of the light façade, whose simple modernity is accentuated on the north and south side ends by balconies and round windows on the third floor. Aleksandr Korzhempo, the designer, originally envisaged a flowing curtain of water extending from the top of the cantilevered roof into the basins of the ground floor terrace to enhance the cooling effect. Only the pools with fountains were included in the final design. The firm of architects, whose other works include Medeo Ice Rink (077) and Republic Square (058), is still active and has also been involved in developing the city's current master plan.

Auyl Residential Complex ⌃

278 – 284 Tole bi St
B. Voronin, L. Andreyeva, V. Vi,
M. Dzhakipbayev, Y. Rykov
1983

087 D

D

The redevelopment of Tastak District, south of Tole bi Street and east of Lake Sairan, was intended to include a group of 33 monolithic towers of different heights. Only four towers, however, were actually built – at the west end of the planned district. They were constructed using monolithic reinforced concrete and slip forming. The design offered three different configurations, allowing the towers to be oriented differently. The rounded balconies, bays, and projections give this complex its distinctive appearance. The collapse of the Soviet Union was another factor that put an end to this project.

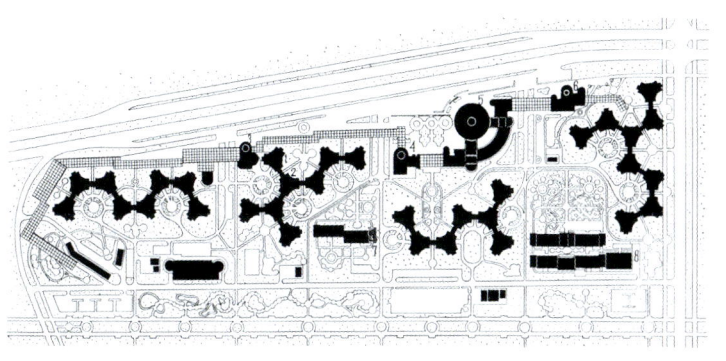

Architecture of Soviet Kazakhstan, 1987

Planned neighbourhood of Auyil. Only the four towers at the far left (west) were realised.

Sats Russian Theatre for Children and Youth ⌃

088 D

22 Shalyapin St
G.S. Dzhakipova, A.A. Petrova, Z.M. Mustafina
1981

The building that now houses the Russian Children's and Youth Theatre, named after the Russian musical theatre director

Natalya Sats, was originally built as the Palace of Culture of the Almaty Cotton and Paper Combine (AKhBK). In the 1980s this factory employed around 9000 people, providing them with housing in the Zhetysu and Aksai microdistricts as well as medical and cultural facilities. Situated in the west of the city, the theatre building immediately catches the eye with its voluminous brutalism, its imposing appearance making a sharp contrast with the surrounding park, which is now rather neglected. On the east side of the theatre a covered gallery leads from the forecourt to the main entrance. As you walk through, you see the wide, monolithic grid of reinforced-concrete girders forming the ceiling of the gallery, adding to the feeling of oppressiveness exuded by the building. However, the façade of the gallery is decorated with a three-dimensional relief mosaic by the monumental artists Yury Funkorineo and Vladimir Tverdokhlebov; this playful depiction of art gives the building a sense of lightness. The façades of the main volume acquire plasticity from the rhythm of variously profiled pylons in the vertical

plane and mezzanines and crowning cornices in the horizontal plane. The upper floor, designed as a parapet, is connected to the balcony on the fifth floor by a wide diagonal frieze with a windowless end and ribs. The façades and interior of the building are clad in shell limestone, marble, granite, and exotic woods. The interior of the main building houses the foyer, a 900-seat auditorium on the second and third floors, and club and administration rooms on the fourth and fifth floors. At the centre of the main foyer is a symbolic column – the Tree of Life – whose ribs form a decorative grid on the ceiling. The column not only gives the room an original figurative character but also supports the auditorium slab. The walls of the lower level of the foyer and the staircase are decorated with concrete reliefs with mosaics in the same style as on the east pediment. The fountain in the square next to the theatre was originally designed in the same style but was 'modernised' in the mid-2000s.

Central State Museum of Kazakhstan

44 Mikrorayon Samal-1
Y.G. Ratushny, Z.M. Mustafina
1984

089 D

D

The Central State Museum building is a clear expression of Kazakh national character – with a large dome occupying almost the entire depth of the central section and multi-sided pylons fixing the corners of the building and likewise crowned by small domes. The main façade derives its rhythm from triangular pylons. Yet the traditional forms of oriental architecture, such as domes, pylons, and pointed arches, do not have a historicising effect but, on the contrary, emphasise this building's elegant modernity. The originally light-blue roof, which matched the shell limestone of the façade, also contributed to this. Today the roof is coloured the blue of the national flag, which gives the building a rather ponderous appearance and detracts from the skilful composition.

KAZGOR (former Kazgosproyekt)

The museum with the original roof in the 1980s, a few years after its construction

Concrete solar shading elements on the rectorate building at Al-Farabi University

090 D

Students' Palace at Al-Farabi Kazakh National University

D

Al-Farabi Kazakh National University

71 Al-Farabi Ave
V.P. Bondarenko, Y.S. Zimin,
V.M. Yegorov, L.P. Samartsev
1971–1991

090 D

Situated between the Vesnovka (today: Esentai) River in the east, the Botanical Garden in the west, Timiryazev Street in the north, and Al-Farabi Avenue in the south, Kazgugrad, the campus of Al-Farabi Kazakh National University, covers an area of approximately 90 hectares. Construction of the new campus of what was then Kirov University, founded in 1934, began in 1971. The plan was to complete it in two stages: the main administrative, teaching, and dormitory buildings by 1986; and the extension by 1995. Perestroika threw a spanner in the works. The campus was designed by the architectural collective of the Kazakh branch of Giprovuz, the State Institute for the Design of Higher Education Institutions, which designed educational facilities throughout the Soviet Union. The principal buildings on campus are the rectorate, built in the late 1970s, and the Students' Palace, completed in 1989, located opposite each other to the west and east of the main alley and campus axis. Between them is a square designed as a forum. Both buildings perfectly combine the principles of Modernism with characteristics of Kazakh national architecture. At the time of its construction the 18-storey, 75-metre-high Rectorate Tower was one of the tallest buildings in Alma-Ata. Its structural system consists of a metal frame with vertical girders and horizontal bars to which the external reinforced-concrete walls are attached. This solution allowed for a fast construction process and for large spans for free-standing areas inside the building. The skyscraper has a simple, unpretentious form but makes a striking impression thanks to the complex system of solar louvres and the decorative framing of the balconies. Together with the ribbon and panoramic glazing, the louvres give the façade a dynamic, three-dimensional expression. The Students' Palace was designed as a central event hall with seating capacity for 1537. It is built on a hill, which emphasises its monumentality. A wide staircase leads to the main entrance on the west side, with symmetrical fountains on either side. The building is octahedral in plan,

Development of the campus west of the Vesnovka River in the early 1970s

D

with four wide sides forming the main façades and four narrow sides to which the risalites containing the staircases are attached. The risalites rise above the roof level and visually draw the building upwards. They have no decoration, but their axes are marked by rectangular windows. The building's recessed ground floor is accentuated by a clear rhythm of pylons. The fifth, technical, floor is also set back; this visually separates the roof from the building, giving it the appearance of floating in the air. The main façades are divided into five sections by vertical columns. Stretching to the full height of the three middle storeys are reinforced-concrete grilles with ornamentation based on traditional Kazakh forms in front of the large windows, offering protection against the sun. The entire building is clad in shell limestone, a link with the rectorate building. After the collapse of the Soviet Union, construction of the second phase of the campus was postponed for almost 20 years; it resumed in 2005, when more dormitories, buildings for three faculties, a new catering centre, and a swimming pool were added. The old student residences have undergone maintenance work. For a number of years there has been talk of a major redevelopment of the campus. A preliminary project by Envicon has been presented to the public. This includes construction of a new rectorate building on the south side of the campus as well as a number of new student residences and faculty buildings.

Visualisation of further development envisaged for the university campus

D

Enicon

Kazakh Modernism

E

Central Mosque

16 Pushkin St
S.K. Baimagambetov
1999

091 E

As you drive from the airport to the city centre, the golden dome of the Central Mosque, built between 1996 and 1999 to designs by Sultan Baimagambetov, can be seen from afar. Clad throughout with white marble slabs, this building, which has space for around 3000 worshippers, was the first major new mosque to be built after the end of the Soviet Union and its atheistic state doctrine. Modelled on 'classical' Central Asian mosques with their high tambours, it is surprisingly simple in its details. This is particularly striking when you compare it with the richly decorated new mosques in Astana. Unlike many medieval mosques in Central Asia, the rectangular building, measuring 70 by 50 metres, is not arranged around a central courtyard – the only sensible solution given the city's continental climate. In addition to four small minarets at its corners, the mosque also has a freestanding 47-metre-high minaret.

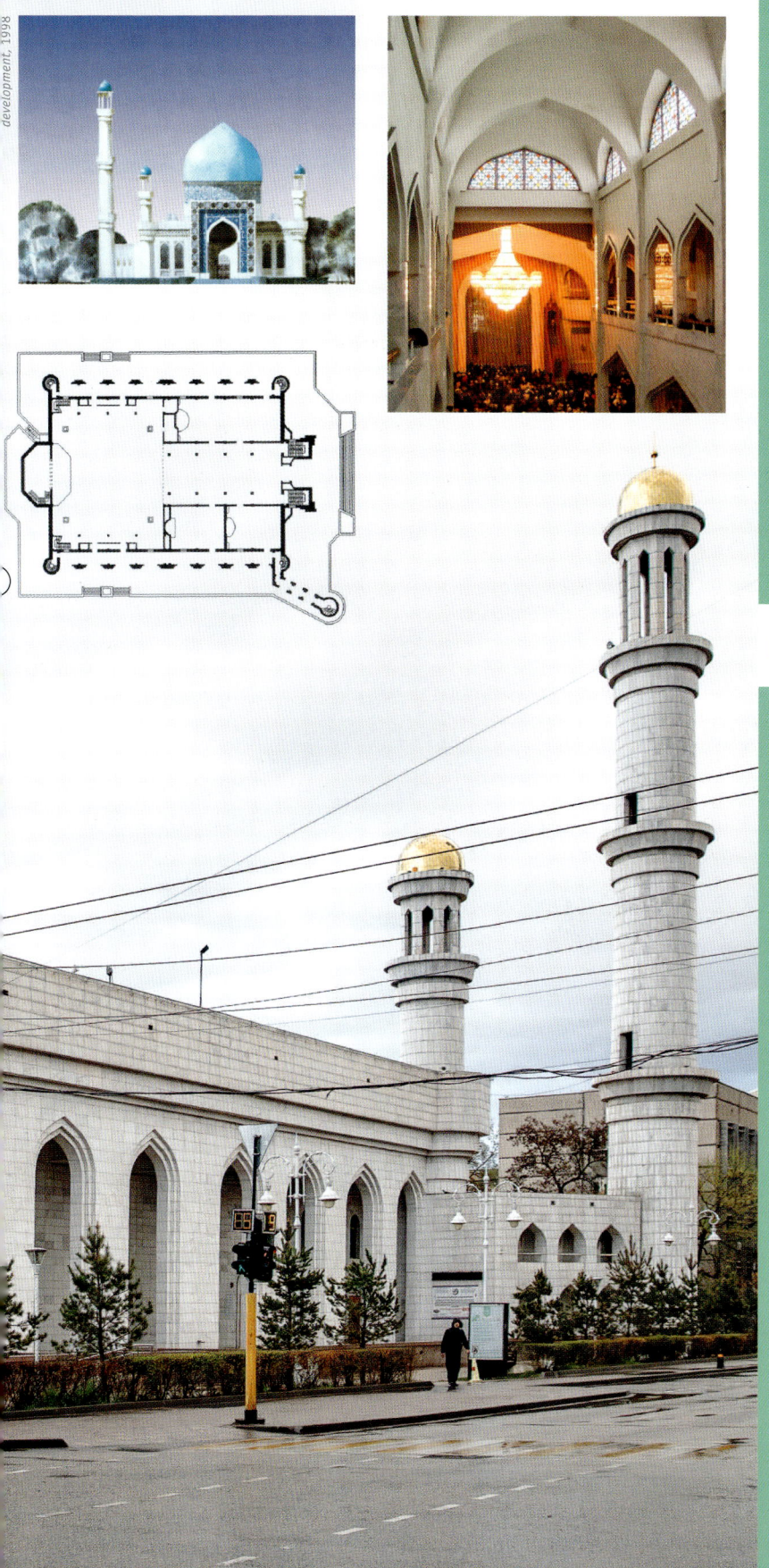

E

Esentai Park with mall (left), Esentai Tower (middle), and Esentai Residences
(right and behind the tower)

SOM

Esentai Park

092 E

77/1-3, 77/7, 77/8 Al-Farabi Ave
SOM / M.K. Abadan
2006–2014

On the south edge of the city, up the slope towards the Alatau Mountains, many exclusive developments have been built in recent years. The record for height and exclusivity is undoubtedly held by the Esentai Park complex, designed by the Chicago architects Skidmore, Owings & Merill (SOM). In addition to a luxury residential complex with apartments offering panoramic views of the mountain peaks, this $300-million ensemble includes an exclusive shopping mall and a 160-metre-high office and hotel tower, by far the tallest in the city.

SOM

E

SOM

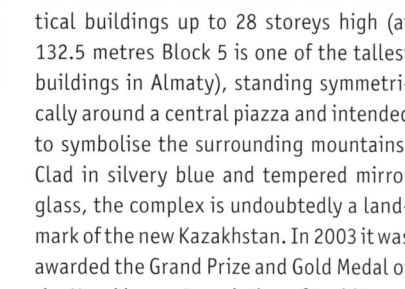

Nurly Tau office and residential complex

093 E

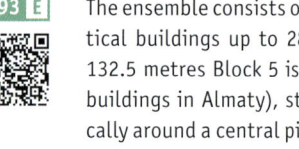

5, 7, 17, 19 Al-Farabi Ave
S.K. Baimagambetov,
T.Y. Yeraliyev, A.S. Tatygulov
2006 M.K. Abadan
2006–2015

Driving along Al-Farabi Avenue, you see from afar a building that rises out of the urban landscape like a crystal mountain massif: the Nurly Tau (Kazakh for 'shining mountain') office and residential complex. The ensemble consists of four almost identical buildings up to 28 storeys high (at 132.5 metres Block 5 is one of the tallest buildings in Almaty), standing symmetrically around a central piazza and intended to symbolise the surrounding mountains. Clad in silvery blue and tempered mirror glass, the complex is undoubtedly a landmark of the new Kazakhstan. In 2003 it was awarded the Grand Prize and Gold Medal of the Kazakhstan Association of Architects. Regrettably, however, it lacks architectural beauty and quality.

Basis Group

Almaty Financial District 094 E

34, 36, 48, 40 Al-Farabi Ave
Skidmore, Owings & Merrill
2005–2010

2010 saw the completion of another project by Chicago-based Skidmore, Owings & Merrill (SOM). This modern office complex, consisting of four blocks, was intended to be the first stage in a planned financial district, but construction was halted by the financial crisis of 2008–2009. The opening of Astana International Financial Centre (AIFC), a new Kazakh financial marketplace built to boost the

E

Kazakh capital's economy, in 2018 removed any motivation for further development of Almaty's financial district. The original plans involved construction of an entire banking and financial centre on the site of a former suburban area. As a result, the huge complex is somewhat off the beaten track, standing in isolation among the remnants of an older settlement of dachas and family houses south of Al-Farabi Avenue. To the north of the planned financial district, other residential and commercial buildings have been constructed. Go south, however, and you still find a vast wasteland.

Hotel Novotel Almaty City Center

104a Dostyk Ave
M. Dzhakipbayev,
A.I. Rustembekov
2015

095 E

The only hotel of the French Novotel chain in Kazakhstan is located on Abai Square in the centre of Almaty. In this prominent location between Cinema Arman (052) and the Palace of the Republic (053), opposite Hotel Kazakhstan (054), the designers had a choice: either to try to outdo these existing icons of Soviet Modernism, which would have been detrimental to the architectural ensemble on the square, or to take a step back and close off the south side of the square with a more modest building. Unlike so often in Kazakhstan, they chose the latter. Although the ten-storey hotel block makes the neighbouring cinema look rather puny in direct comparison, this is not apparent when entering the square from Abai Avenue. The new building is discreetly modern: the glass façade with its subtle splashes of colour is surrounded by an elegantly rounded concrete frame that is open on one side, imparting a degree of movement to the simple block shape. Next door is the valley station of the Koktobe Hill cable car with the television tower (076) – a favourite spot with locals and tourists.

E

Monuments of history and culture of Almaty, 2008

The first airport building, which later served as VIP terminal, was torn down in 2022.

Almaty International Airport   096 E

2 Mailina St
K.D. Montakhayev,
M.F. Zhaksylykov,
S.K. Baimagambetov et al.
2001–2004, 2022–2024

The first aerodrome, which opened in 1923, was built on the site of the old hippodrome, near the present Central Stadium (078). In 1935 work began on building the airport in the city's north-east outskirts, where it is still located today.

The VIP terminal (1935–1947)

The first airport building was designed by B. Zavarzin, G. Yelkin, and Toleu Basenov. Due to the intervention of the Second World War, it was built over a time span of more than ten years. In 1957 Adambek Kapanov redesigned it to give it its distinctive Stalinist appearance. The main entrance on the west façade, facing Mailin Street, featured a *pishtaq* (a rectangular portal), above an *iwan* (the tall portal arch typical of Central Asia), ogival windows, and a high cornice consisting of two rows of stylised stalactites. Facing the tarmac, the building had an oval loggia with Corinthian columns. The central part was crowned by a belvedere with a spire. In 1975 this building was redesigned by the artist V. Senchenko, the interior was rearranged, the east façade facing the runway was covered with marble, the *pishtaq* received stained-glass windows, and the windows on both main façades were doubled in height. A major renovation in the 2000s removed many of the decorative elements. The building was used as a VIP terminal until the 2020s.

Modernist lightness (1971–1973)

In the early 1970s a much larger, sleek Modernist terminal was built next to the old airport building, designed by the architects Vladimir Ishchenko, Olga Naumova, Yury Litvinenko, and Yury Sharapov. This strictly rectangular building has a continuous glass façade, *panjaras* (patterned window lattices) over the main entrances, and a 'curtain' of narrow pylons

Current main terminal of the airport

VIP

Almaty: Architecture and urban development, 1998

The Modernist airport building in the early 1990s

in front of the façade, which both shades the building and gives it a light, airy appearance. Almaty-1 Railway Station (075), built just three years later, is a blunt echo of this building's design. The Modernist airport building burnt down in 1999.

Symbol of independence (2004)

A new multifunctional terminal, designed by Kaldybai Montakhayev, Marat Zhaksylykov, and Sultan Baimagambetov, was built on the foundations of the burnt-down building between 2001 and 2004. Still in use today, the two-storey, fully

TAV Airports

Design study for the new international terminal with the currently used building, which was built in 2004, in the background

E

INTERNATIONAL AIRPORT

Design study for the integration of the historical VIP terminal into the new terminal (not realis

glazed building is covered by an undulating roof with skylights, the ends of which extend well beyond the gable ends. The large, semicircular, transparent canopy over the entrance on the west side is a steel-lattice construction supported by columns that widen in the region of their capitals. The gentle curve of the ramp to and from the first floor emphasises the building's flowing lines. The terminal resembles a giant flying bird with outstretched wings but is also reminiscent of a *kalpak*, the Kazakh headdress – a piece of literal symbolism that is typical of the architecture of Kazakhstan's early independence.

New international terminal and a replica (2024)

In 2021 the Turkish airport operator TAV Airports took over Almaty Airport and announced plans to build a new international terminal at a cost of around US$ 200 million. The new terminal is functionally simple and plays with references to early-1970s Soviet Modernism; the cantilevered, sloping canopy on the west side refers to the Palace of the Republic (053). The structure of the glass façade, with the protruding frames of the entrance areas extending over two storeys, is reminiscent of the airy design of its Modernist

predecessor. There were plans to retain the listed VIP terminal; the architect Aidyn Akbai submitted a design study integrating it structurally into the new terminal. However, according to the airport operator, this was not feasible for structural and logistical reasons. As a result, the historical building was demolished in 2022 – despite public protests in favour of preserving it. A replica of the former VIP terminal is now being built about 300 metres south of the existing terminal and will be used to receive government delegations in the future.

TAV Airports

The design study for the new international terminal, view from Mailin Street

TAV Airports

Stolichny Tsentr residential complex and Hotel Almaty (O63)

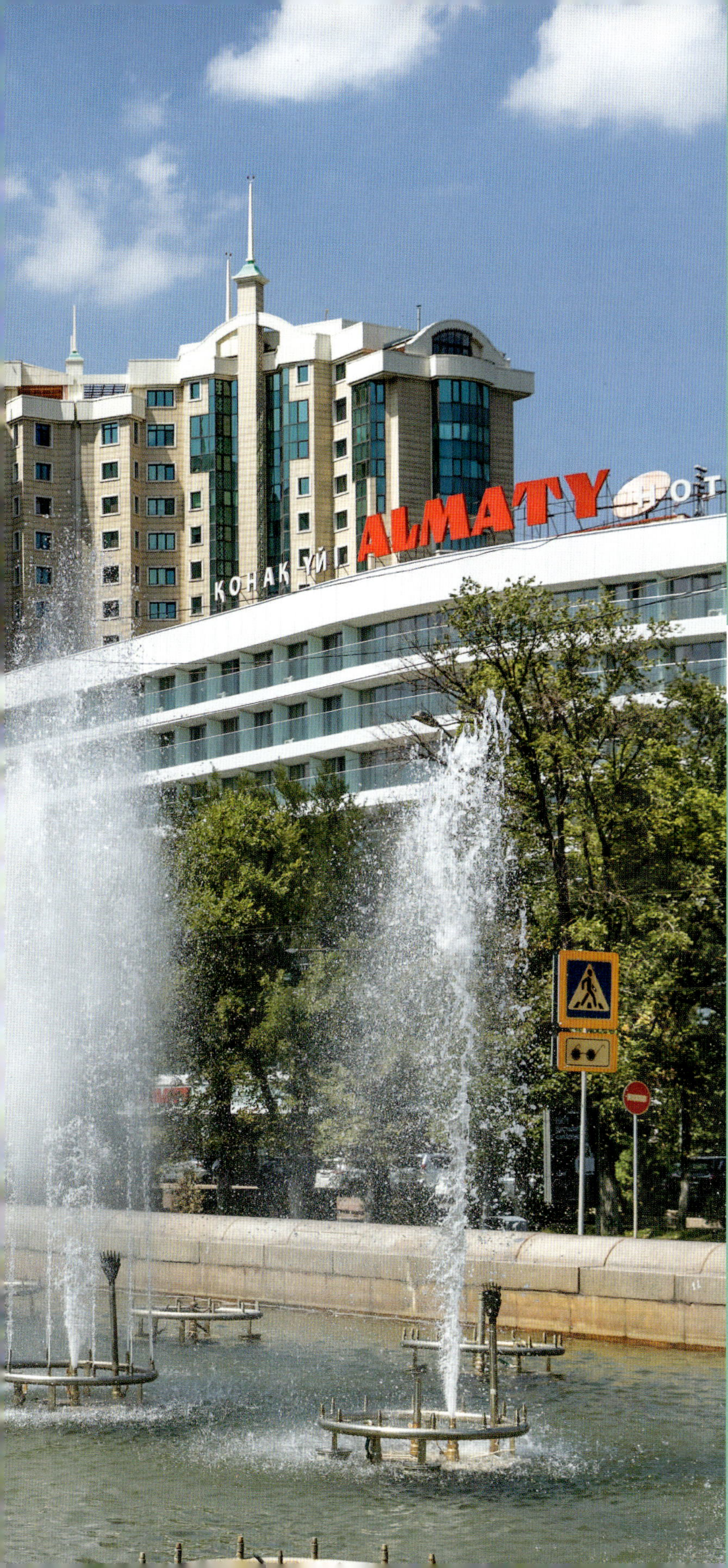
ҚОНАҚ ҮЙ
ALMATY

Stolichny Tsentr ⌃ residential complex

92 Abylai Khan Ave
Bazis-A
2004

The 160-apartment Stolichny Tsentr residential complex was one of the first massive residential towers to be built in Almaty following Kazakhstan's acquisition of independence and has long been one of the most prestigious addresses in the city centre. It is located between Abylai Khan Avenue and Baiseitova Street on what was once the city's main axis, not far from prominent buildings such as the House of Government

Archive of Vlast.kz

The Theatre of Young Spectators at the intersection of today's Abylai Khan Avenue and Kabanbai Batyr Street in 1959

(020), Abai Opera House (031), and Hotel Almaty (063). The site was previously occupied by the Theatre of Young Spectators (TYuZ), which was built between 1933 and 1936 and burnt down in 1988. Stolichny Tsentr consists of three interconnected building sections, is 23 storeys high, and has a monolithic frame with walls of reinforced concrete. The façade, which has a base faced in granite and upper storeys clad with ceramic panels, is given rhythm by vertical risalites and projecting bays, as well as vertical window ribbons on the upper floors. The building is crowned by tall spurs protruding from small hipped roofs, designed to give this complex an air of grandeur and elitism. Stolichny Tsentr is now somewhat dated and no longer offers the very highest standard of comfort provided by later residential complexes.

Almaty Towers ⌐

280 Baizakov St
Kazgor
2004–2008

These two hexagonal office towers, 100 metres tall and 25 storeys high, are a prominent landmark near the Circus (057). They are connected on the lower floors by a low, platform-like building that surrounds both towers and is also connected to the Rahat Palace Hotel to the east, which was built in 1996. The hotel was renovated during the construction of the twin towers. They are of monolithic frame construction and clad in grey

porcelain stoneware combined with windows of tinted glass. The two skyscrapers were originally named 'Rakhat Towers' after the late Rakhat Aliyev, the son-in-law of the then president, Nursultan Nazarbayev. When Aliyev fell from grace in 2007 due to overly brazen machinations, the towers were renamed.

Arkhitektura i stroityestvo Almaty, 2

Nazarbayev Foundation ≽
10 Gandhi St
Kazgor
2007

099 **E**

This building with its dome, Doric columns, and three-sided portico under a cantilevered flat roof was for a long time the headquarters of the foundation of the former president, Nursultan Nazarbayev. Combining the monumentality of oriental and Stalinist architecture and just steps away from the now demolished presidential residence, it was designed to enhance Nazarbayev's image as a philanthropist. In 2024 the foundation handed the building over to the presidential administration, another step in what the public sees as 'de-Nazarbayevisation'.

E

The former headquarters buolding of the Nursultan Nazarbayev Foundation. The helipad in the foreground belonged to the presidential residence, which was demolished in 2022.

Phil Inglis

Zhailjau golf resort

188 Mikrorayon Miras
Arnold Palmer Design Co.
2006

100 E

In the south-west outskirts of the city, where until the early 2000s gardens, orchards, and dachas still lined the streets, exclusive neighbourhoods such as the Miras micro-district have sprung up.

Miras is home to Zhailjau Golf Resort, one of Almaty's most expensive and exclusive golf clubs. In its grounds 50 almost identical, rather boring, 'classic' villas differing only in colour scheme have been built. Their interiors, however, have been designed to satisfy the unconstrainedly extravagant wishes of Almaty's moneyed elite, often in the style of modern European luxury design. In addition to

Philipp Meuser

Philipp Meuser

the villas, Zhailjau Golf Resort includes a clubhouse and hotel complex, whose fairytale castle turrets cannot disguise the extremely simple, banal design of this box-shaped building.

Hotel Rixos Almaty ⌃
106 Seyfullin Ave
Sembol Construction
2009

101 E

Hotel Rixos Almaty replicates the architecture of nineteenth-century European cities in a kitschy yet simplified way – a style which is popular in Almaty for commercial buildings and newer residential complexes when what is required is a dignified yet urban feel. Inside, the hotel has an atrium. Despite widespread protests, the Palace of Students and Pioneers, built in the early 1960s, was pulled down to make way for the hotel.

Nur-Mubarak Egypt University ⌄
73 Al-Farabi Ave
unknown
1993–2000

102 E

When the then president of Kazakhstan, Nursultan Nazarbayev, travelled to Egypt in 1993, he made an agreement with the Egyptian government to build Kazakhstan's first Islamic university with Egypt's support. In the same year the foundation stone was laid on a six-hectare plot south east of Al-Farabi Kazakh National University (090). The mosque, designed in the traditional style, was built first, followed by buildings for administration and teaching, a library, and student accommodation. To meet growing demand, the university is currently constructing a new nine-storey building on the south-west side of the site.

E

The city's first ski jumping hill was built in 1956 on the east slope of Remizovka, a foothill consisting of loess tens of metres deep, south of Al-Farabi Avenue. In 1959 the first international ski jumping and Nordic combined competitions were held here on a K-55 hill. The facility fell into disrepair during the Soviet era and was demolished in preparation for the 2011 Asian Winter Games in Almaty. The new complex with a K-125 and a K-95 hill and a 5200-seat stadium opened in 2010. In 2013 K-20 and K-40 hills and a K-60 sports hill were added. Now the complex, which is also used for festivals, houses a sports school. On the tower of the highest hill is a restaurant with a glass and steel structure with a panoramic view of the city. Above the whole complex there is a viewing platform.

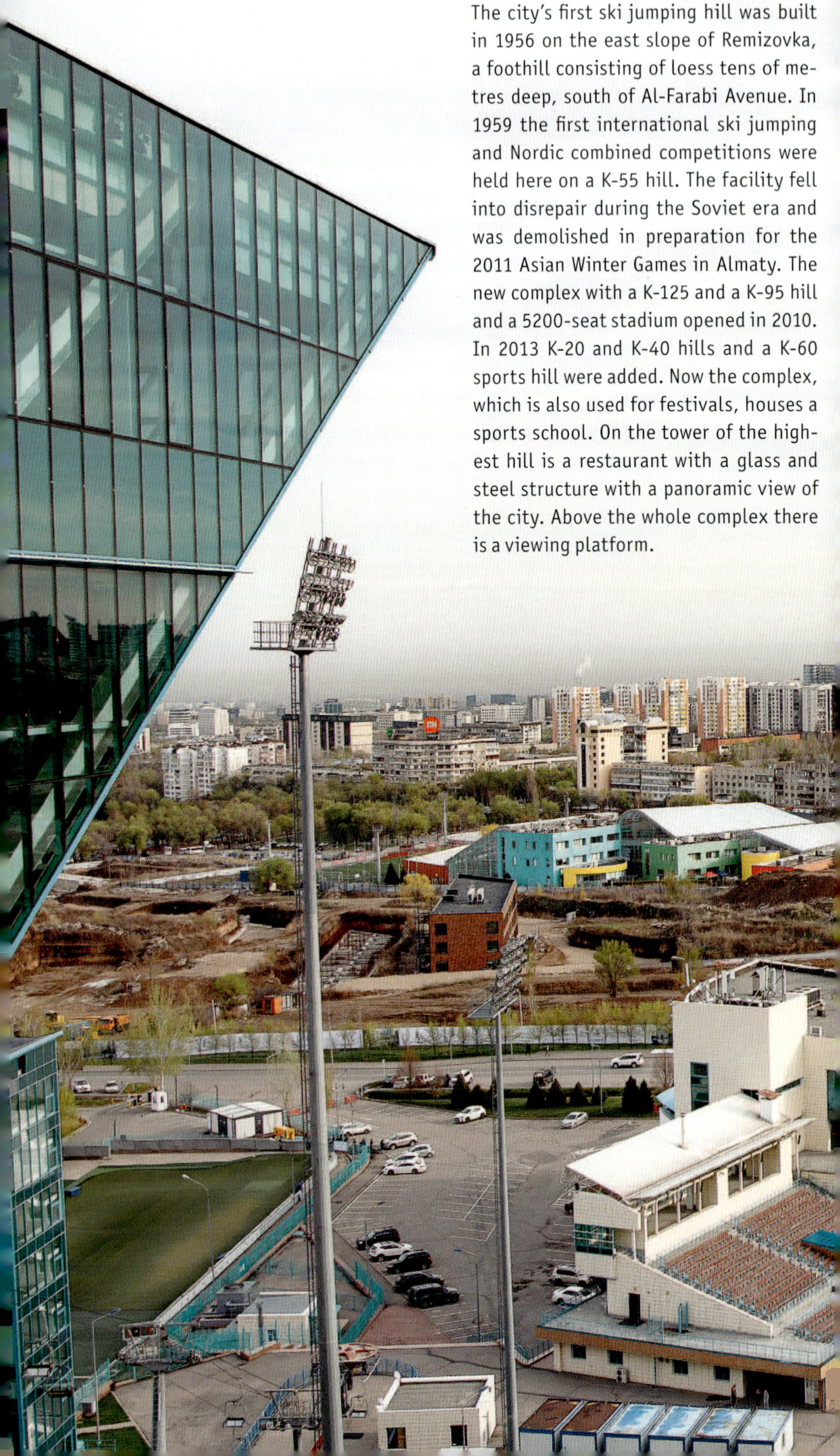

ҚАЗАҚСТАН
KAZAKHSTAN
190
2011 жылғы 7- қысқы
Азия ойындары
2010
Astana - Almaty
7 ASIAN WINTER GAMES
2011

ҚАЗАҚСТАН
KAZAKHSTAN
240
2011 жылғы 7- қысқы
Азия ойындары
2010
Трамплиннен секіру

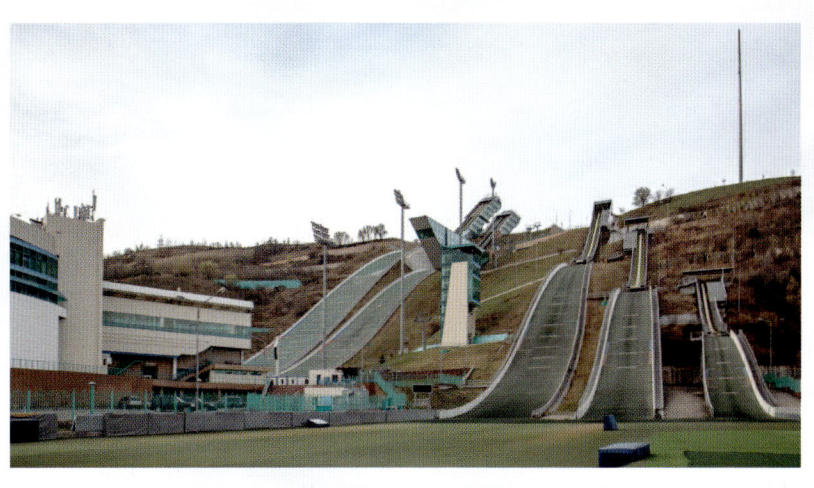

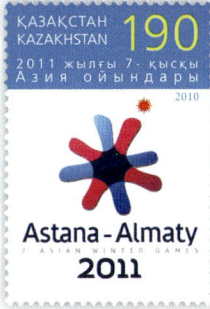

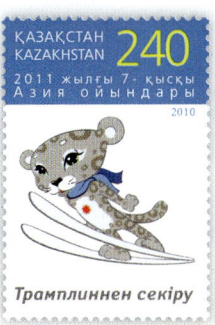

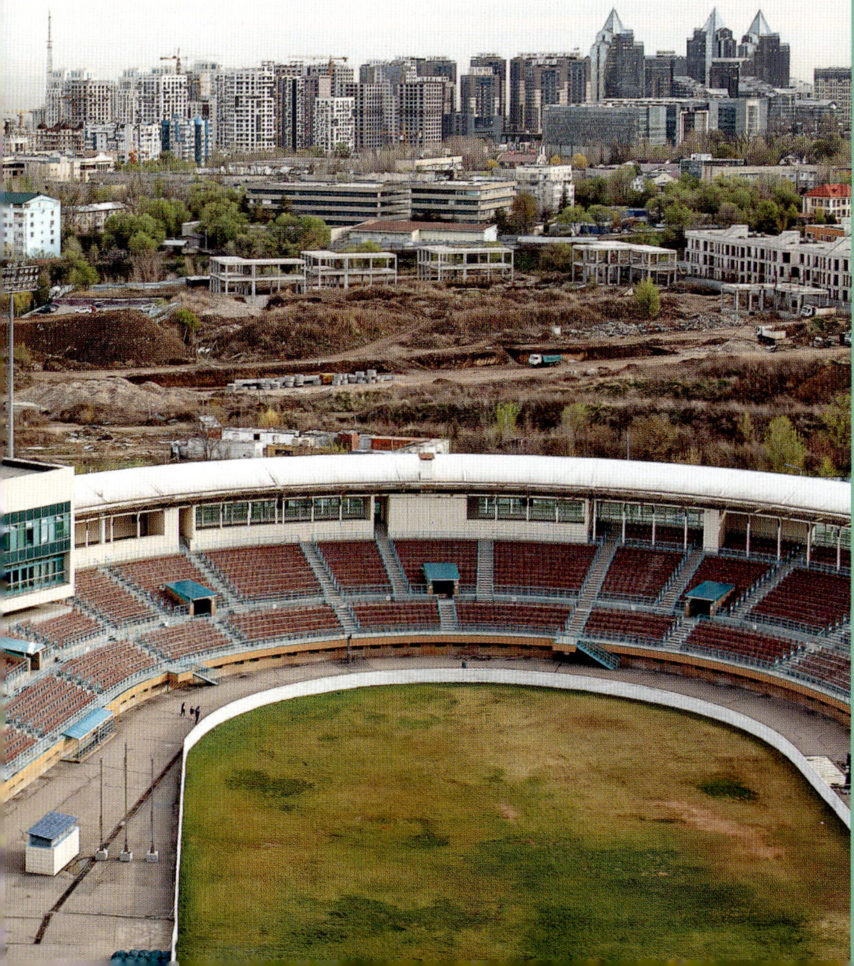

Halyk Arena

2 Kuldzhinsky trakt
Y.A. Mamanov
2016

Halyk Arena was built for the 2017 Winter Universiade, after Almaty won the event in 2011 and submitted a bid for the 2022 Winter Olympics, although the latter bid was unsuccessful. The complex was designed for all ice sports. The two larger blocks are elliptical structures, reminiscent of ice hockey helmets with their circular shape, light-coloured cladding, hinged skylights, and curved glass fronts. The larger block houses a 61-by-30-metre ice hockey arena with capacity for around 3000 spectators; the smaller, a practice rink. The two parts are connected by an administrative wing. This is the first sports facility in Almaty to be named after a sponsor, Kazakhstan's Halyk Bank. It is also used for concerts.

Aidyn Akbai

Aidyn Akbai

Aidyn Akbai

Almaty Arena

7 Nurkent Mikrorayon
Aidyn Akbai
2016

105 E

Almaty Arena was planned as the main venue of the 2017 Winter Universiade. With its two elliptical structures and a connecting wing, it is similar to Halyk Arena (104). The larger structure, the Ice Palace, in the north seats 12,000, while the smaller, the Training Arena, in the south seats 3000. The rectangular connecting wing between the two structures houses a swimming pool. The original plan was to build Almaty Arena south of Raiymbek Avenue, when Bauyrzhan Momyshuly Street was extended south from there. However, as there was insufficient space for both the arena and Alatau Theatre (106) on that site and because the current site is considered more earthquake-proof, the latter was chosen.

Aidyn Akbai

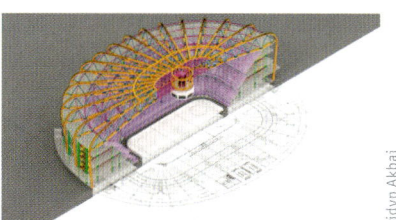

Aidyn Akbai

Aidyn Akbai

E

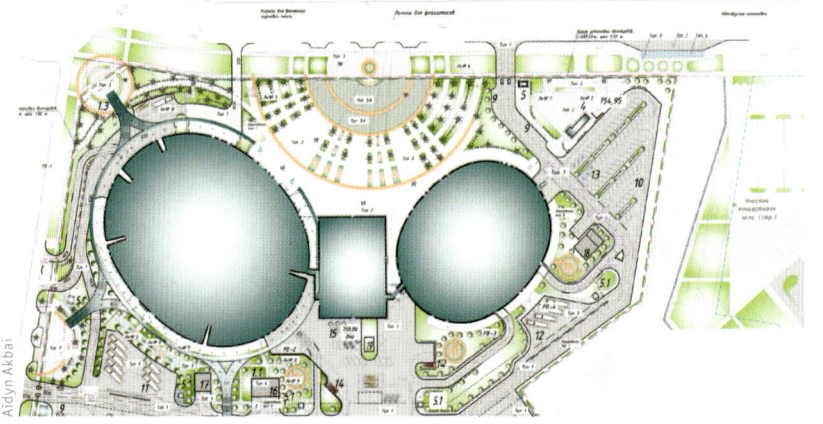

Aidyn Akbai

Alatau Theatre of Traditional Art ≪

6 Nurkent Mikrorayon

T.Y. Yeraliyev

2014

106 E

Like Almaty Arena and Halyk Arena, Alatau Theatre of Traditional Art is one of the large buildings constructed for the 2017 Winter Universiade. It is located next to Almaty Arena on Bauyrzhan Momyhuly Street, north of Raiymbek Avenue. The development of this formerly rural area was an important impetus for the further development of the new Alatau District in the north-west of Almaty, created in 2008 as one of the first examples of the implementation of the multi-centre city concept that is the aim of Almaty's urban planning today. The layout of Alatau Theatre is reminiscent of a grand piano. On the curved main façade narrow, triangular, protruding vertical bands of windows rise like organ pipes. The combination of blue glass and cladding consisting of aluminium composite panels is a trademark of Kazakhstan's fast and cheap construction of public buildings for special occasions. It is not long, however, before such buildings begin to look worn and cheap due to the poor quality of the materials used. Inside the theatre are two cinemas and a 750-seat concert hall. Here too the design is unambitious and, according to visitors, rather reminds them of a 'village club from the Soviet era'.

E

New Mosque ⌄

10 Bauyrzhan Momyshuly Street
unknown
since 2016

107 E

Since 2016 a mosque has been under construction in the north-west district of Alatau. It will have space for 7000 people at a time, making it the largest mosque in Almaty. The total area of the site is 6.3 hectares, and the building itself will cover 16,000 square metres, housing an Islamic library, workshops, and an administrative wing in addition to prayer halls. Of the six minarets originally planned, with a maximum height of 75 metres, only four have been built; they are significantly lower. The foundation stone was laid by the former president, Nursultan Nazarbayev. Little else is known about this project, other than that it is backed by private investors.

Tenir Eco Hotel
640 Kerey-Zhanibek Khandar
Bekzat Amanjol, Levelstudio
2020

108 **E**

Tenir Eco Hotel represents young, urban Kazakhstan – even though it is located in the least urban setting imaginable, at an altitude of 3200 metres, about ten minutes from the top station of Combi-2, the third and highest section of the cableway in Shymbulak ski resort. The city centre is a good 20 kilometres away. With its ten bungalows attached to metal structures in the mountain, this is one of the most exclusive glamping addresses in Almaty – glamorous camping for those who don't want to do without luxuries such as their own sauna, even in such inhospitable mountain surroundings. The design and construction of the hotel is the work of Levelstudio, an Almaty-based architecture firm founded by Bekzat Amanjol in 2006. The project was designed and built in less than five months. Each of the 30-square-metre bungalows consists of three 4.5-by-2.7-by-3.15-metre modules prefabricated in Almaty. The modules consist of a steel frame and aluminium sandwich panels with sustainable rock wool insulation. This makes them both rigid and well insulated – a must in this high mountain location, which is at risk from both soil erosion and earthquakes and where the extreme climatic and weather conditions place the highest demands on materials. To transport the modules to the remote location, large sledges were custom-built, and a bulldozer was used to pull the modules up the slope, which has a gradient of up to 45 degrees. As the hotel is located in Ile-Alatau National Park, environmental considerations were a key part of the project. The modules were installed on steel supports instead of heavy concrete foundations to prevent snow from getting under the buildings. The façades are clad in natural wood shingles and painted aluminium sheeting, which helps manage the wind and snow loads on the buildings. The modules can be disassembled and moved to a new location without the need for demolition.

Damir Otegen

Damir Otegen

Damir Otegen

E

Almaty Theatre

30 Al-Farabi Ave
Bazis-A
2022

109 E

The land south of Al-Farabi Avenue, not far from the glass towers of Nurly-Tau business centre (093) and the banking centre, which was originally planned as the core of a financial district (094), is among the most expensive in Almaty. Whoever builds here has political influence. And so, from the outset, myths have swirled about who was behind Almaty Theatre, built on a site formerly owned by Halyk Bank. With the eye-catching theatre building at its centre, this complex covers some 14,000 square metres. The theatre building itself has an austere, cubic rear section with a towering stage structure protruding at the back and a front that is given dynamism by undulating volumes of varying heights. The two-part curved portico rests on three pairs of columns that are probably intended to convey lightness but look strangely fragile. The foyer behind the portico is framed by a façade of structural glazing, which rises over three storeys, following the wavy shape of the building and contrasting with pale façades of natural stone. The curved forms are intended to create a link with the surrounding park. However, this whole area on the main highway, which is dominated by car traffic, seems strangely lifeless and inaccessible and has not yet become a new centre for theatrical art, especially ballet, as was announced when the theatre opened. In 2024 there were rumours that the $50-million property, allegedly financed by the Central Asian Fund for Cultural Promotion, was up for sale. The fund is directly linked to former president Nursultan Nazarbayev, who is said to have given the theatre to his second wife as a gift. The fact that interest in the theatre now seems to have waned is probably due to the shift in political power that has occurred since 2022.

Chapman Taylor

E

Almaty Museum of Arts

Al-Farabi Ave / Nazarbayev Ave
Chapman Taylor
2024

`110` `E`

One of the city's most recent architecturally significant additions is Almaty Museum of Arts. The area to the south of Al-Farabi Avenue and to the west of Nazarbayev Avenue had lain fallow since the expansion of this intersection at the end of the 2000s and was made available by the city's *akimat* to the museum's financier, Nurlan Smagulov, a Kazakh oligarch whose holdings include Almaty Hotel (063) and who has made a significant contribution to the preservation of Kazakh art and architecture. This building, which is said to have cost around US$100 million, was designed by the British architects Chapman Taylor, who have worked with Smagulov on several occasions. When built, it will be easily recognisable by its slanted walls that form two distorted, interlocking L-shaped volumes, symbolising the city and the mountains. Some 10,000 square metres will house contemporary art galleries, a library, restaurants, and boutiques.

Chapman Taylor

Aigerim
residential complex ⌃

111 E

289 Rozybakiyeva St
Astana-Stroyinvest
2012

Built in the aftermath of the financial crisis of 2007–2008, this apartment block reflects the eclecticism of the high-rise construction boom that has followed. Built in monolithic frame construction, it consists of an 18-storey cylindrical central volume with two attached 16-storey wings spiralling in opposite directions. All three structures have cupolas, a rather clumsy nod to oriental architecture. Otherwise, the design of the bays and balconies is openly modelled on the Modernist Auyl apartment complex (087)

from the late Soviet era. The apartments were sold as elite class, but the shoddy construction led to protests from residents shortly after moving in, who had to deal with loose façade panels, water damage, and other construction defects.

Metropole
residential complex ⌄»

112 E

41 Al-Farabi Ave
Bazis-A
2023

In promoting this street block at one of the city's busiest intersections the developer Bazis-A is using the vertical garden concept as a unique selling point – a first in Almaty. The 12-, 17-, and 19-storey buildings are an exclusive address. However,

the air pollution directly on Seyfullin Avenue and Al-Farabi Avenue is likely to be particularly high, with constant car traffic day and night. Even the small trees planted on the balconies are of little use here; many of them look withered soon after being planted. Otherwise, the façades provide an interesting break from the often monotonous surfaces of the apartment blocks. Staggered balconies and irregular vertical and horizontal and large and small window areas play with geometry, giving the blocks an overall airy appearance.

E

E

4You residential complex – one of the dozens of new middle-class apartment blocks currently under construction

4you residential complex ⪢ ⪢
30 Al-Farabi Ave
INK Architects
2022

**President's Park
residential complex** »
115 Mikrorayon Miras
INK Architects
2024

Designed by Kazakh INK Architects for developer BI Group, Quartal 4You covers 7.5 hectares between Rosybakiyev Street and Gagarin Avenue. The architects wanted to combine high-quality living with a city centre feel. The lower level of the complex, with 4.5-metre-high ceilings, is accordingly given over to shops and restaurants. A pedestrian zone has been created on Radovtsov Street, which runs through the quarter. The courtyards between the four clinker-clad, high-rise blocks have green areas and playgrounds.

This exclusive complex of modern townhouses and apartment blocks borders the First President's Park (115) to the west and was named after the park to emphasise its elitist aspirations; it could not have been foreseen at the planning stage that this first president would soon fall out of favour and be erased from the cityscape as far as possible. A total of 31 blocks of houses in three quarters, with different exterior designs, cover an area of 4.3 hectares on a site that rises from

INK Architects

INK Architects

E

north to south, offering some 70,000 square metres of usable space. The houses are three-storey with basements. Some are townhouses. Others contain apartments with between one and four bedrooms with up to 300 square metres of living space. All homes have roof terraces, balconies, or patios. 15,000 square metres are reserved for underground parking. The courtyards have sculptures, fountains, green spaces, sports facilities, and playgrounds to give this neighbourhood an urban feeling. Natural stone, brick, and artistically designed metal and mosaic panels have been used for the façades.

N

A8.1 32
1 эт

A8
3 эт

8

A5
3 эт
5

A9
3 эт
9

A3
3 эт
3

2

6

A6
3 эт

10

A2
3 эт

A
22

A10
3 эт

A1
3 эт
1

4

A4
3 эт

A7
3 эт
7

33

34

34

3

31

16

B5
3 эт

17

B6
3 эт

15

B4
3 эт

22

18

B7
3 эт

33

30

B

B3
3 эт
14

B10
3 эт.
21

B2
3 эт
13

12

B1
3 эт

20

B9
3 эт

19

B8
3 эт

C5
3 эт
27

C1
3 эт
23

22

C

30

28

C6
3 эт

C2
3 эт
24

26

C4
3 эт

33

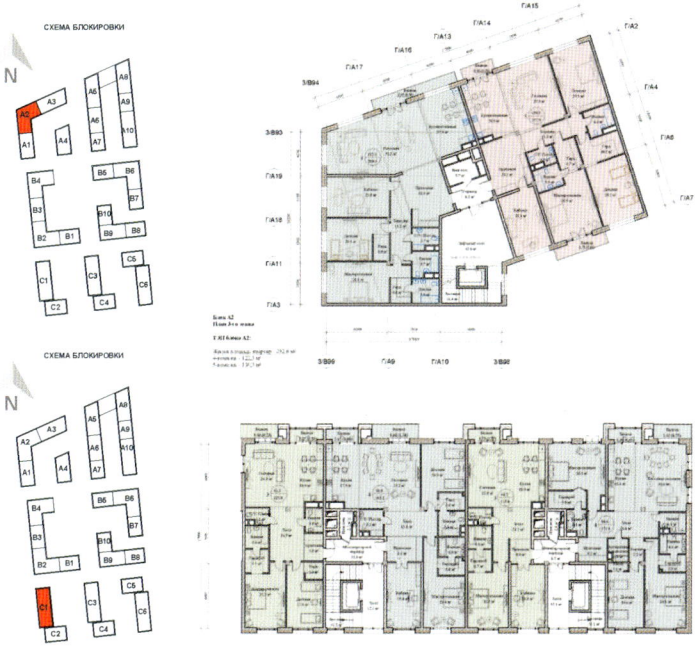

Visualisations and floor plans for the President's Park residential complex

First President's Park

Al-Farabi Ave / Nazarbayev Ave
unknown
2001

115 **E**

In Almaty the green city, parks, and green spaces have always played an important role for residents – as recreational areas, green lungs to aerate the city, and a source of identity for long-time residents who are proud of the charm of their hometown. The largest recent addition is the 60-hectare First President's Park, named after Nursultan Nazarbayev, president of Kazakhstan until 2019. Until the 1990s this area was dominated by apple orchards and fields managed by Soviet collective farms called 'sovkhozes'. After the collapse of the Soviet Union, the state farms were dismantled and the land taken out of state ownership and sold off for what now seem ridiculously low sums of money for development purposes. The new owners are now some of the richest people in the country. The family of the park's namesake also owns a lavish estate, hidden from view and well guarded, just south of the park. Construction of the park, designed as an arboretum, began in 2001. However, it did not open to the public until 2010. It is divided into dendrological plots with different species of trees, such as elms, oaks, and chestnuts, with avenues and footpaths between them. There is also a small Japanese garden and a waterfall. The main entrance, on the narrow north side, is marked by propylaea and a fountain. The latter consists of five stacked bowls with a sculpture in the centre. In the south part of the park a 12-metre-high artificial mound has been created; the pavilion on top is a popular vantage point. Since opening, the park has undergone several repairs. A major redesign could be on the cards in the future – as well as a change of name, so as to disassociate the park from the legacy of the former president.

E

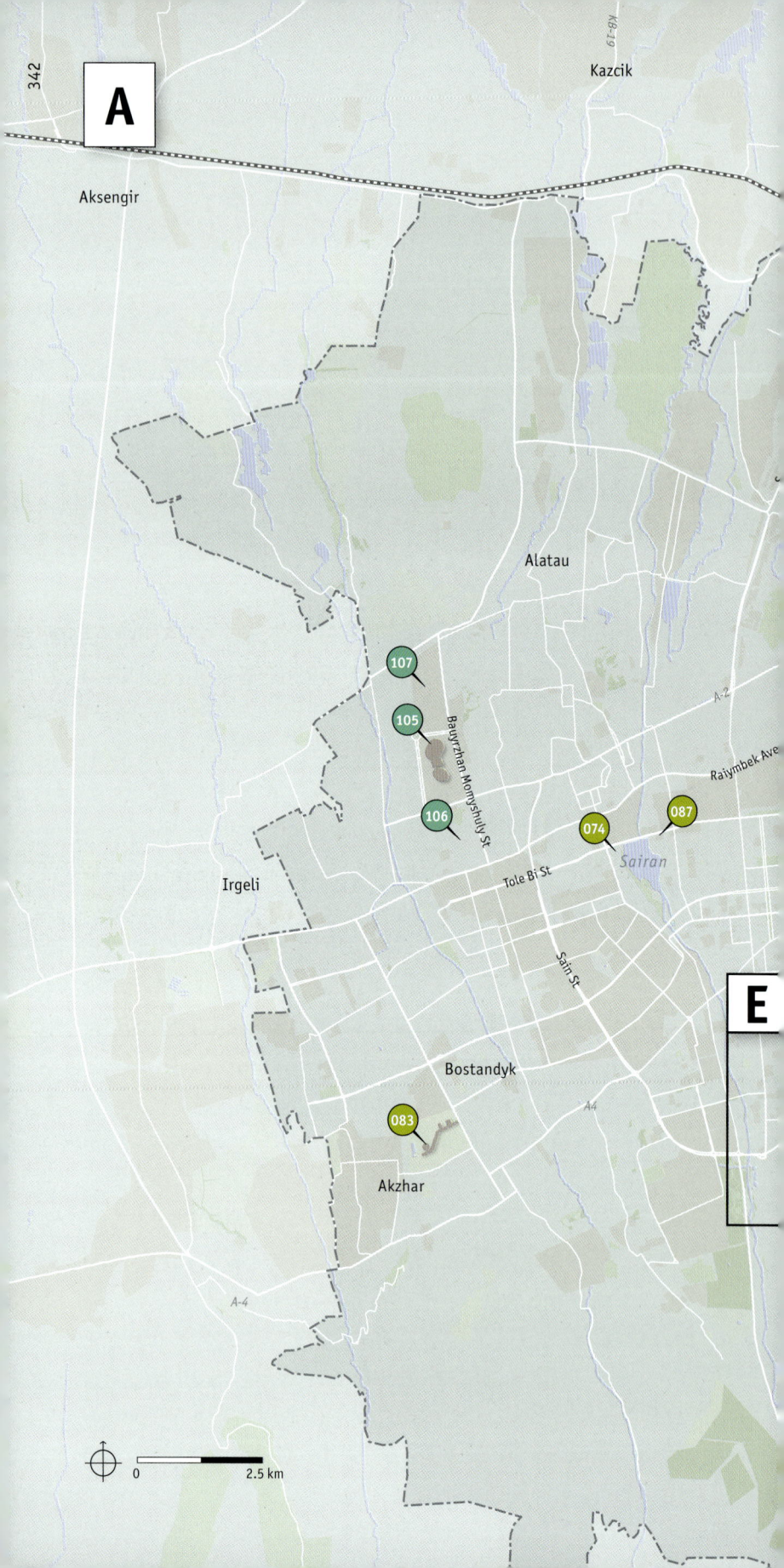

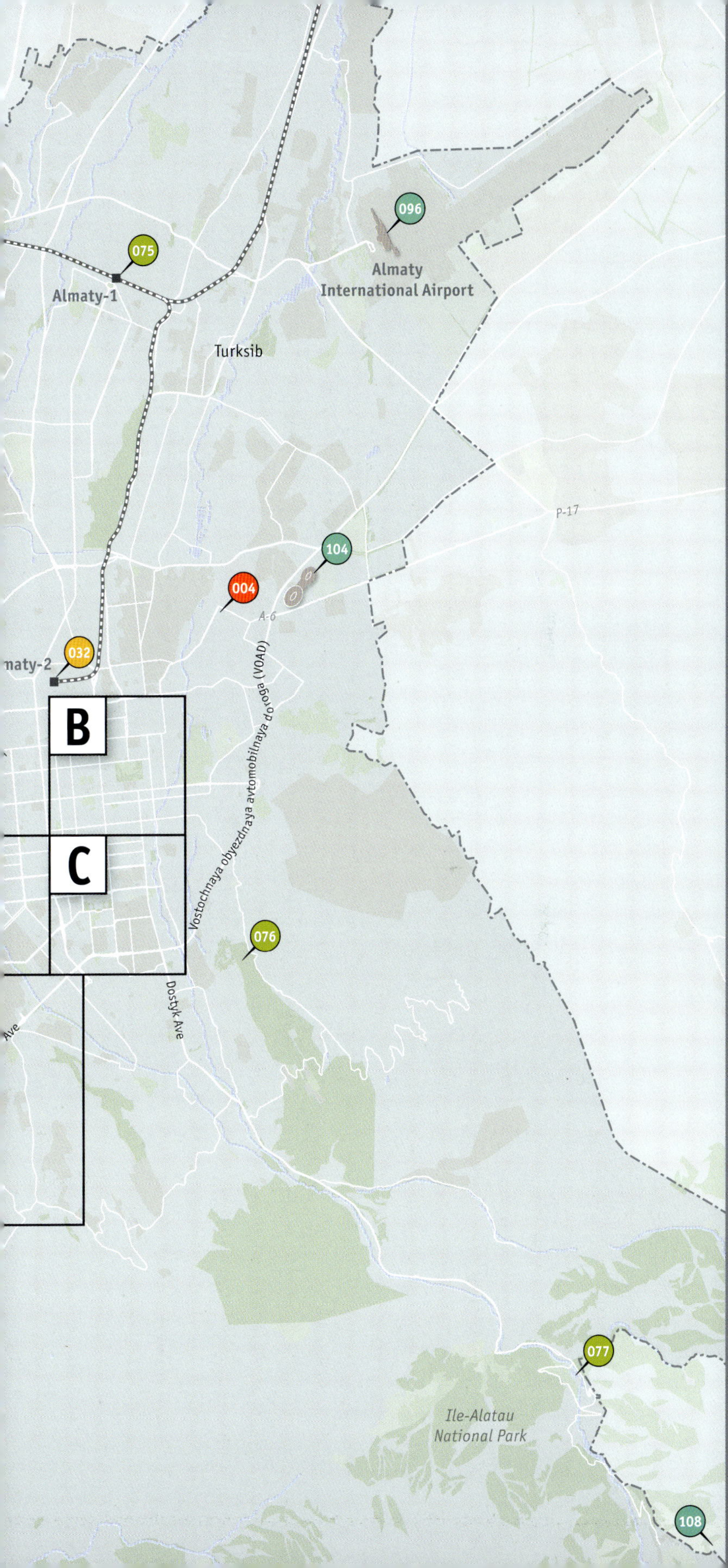

075

Almaty-1

Turksib

096

**Almaty
International Airport**

P-17

104

004

A-6

032

maty-2

B

C

Vostochnaya obyezdnaya avtomobilnaya doroga (VOAD)

076

Dostyk Ave

Ave

077

*Ile-Alatau
National Park*

108

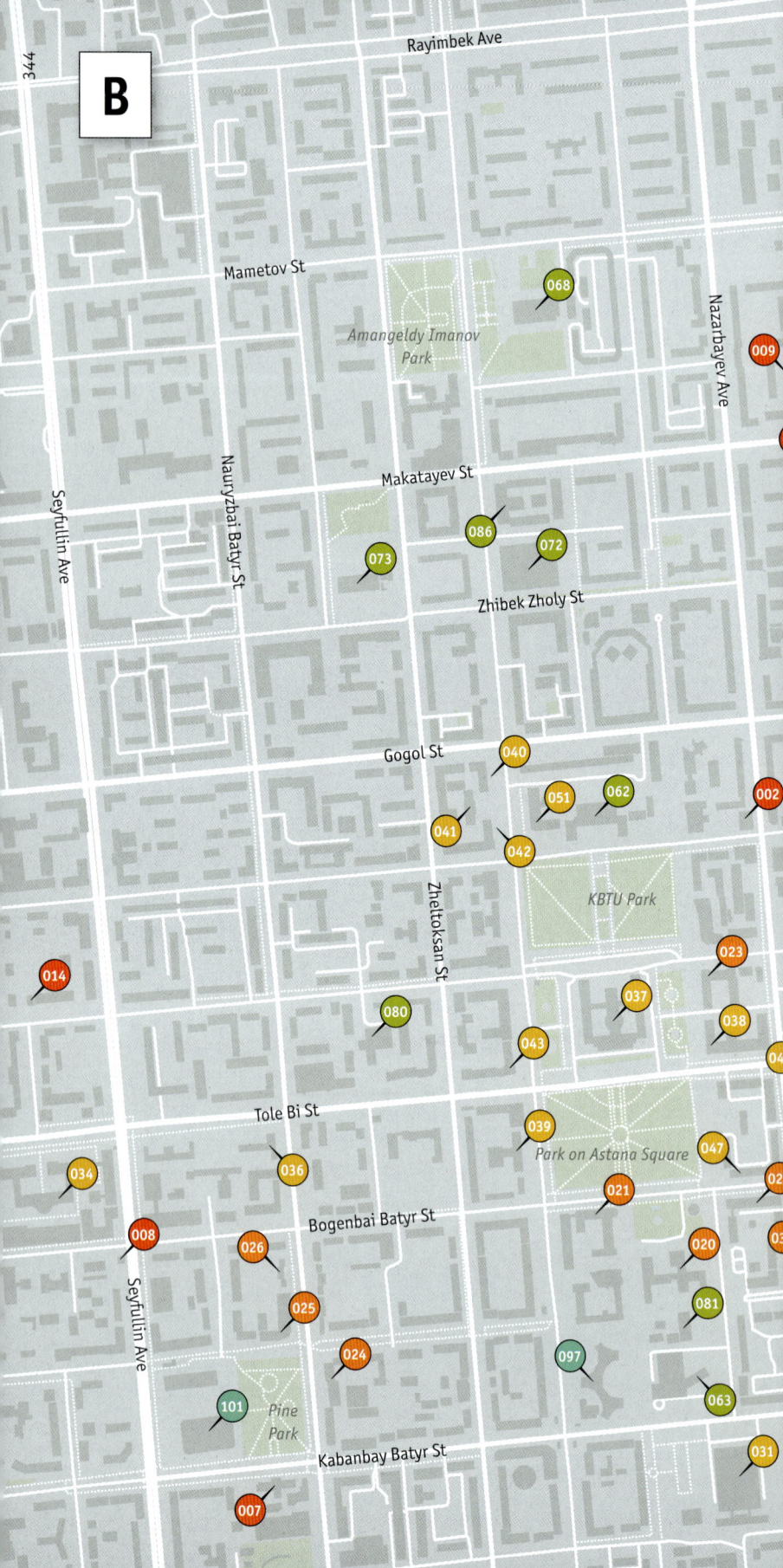

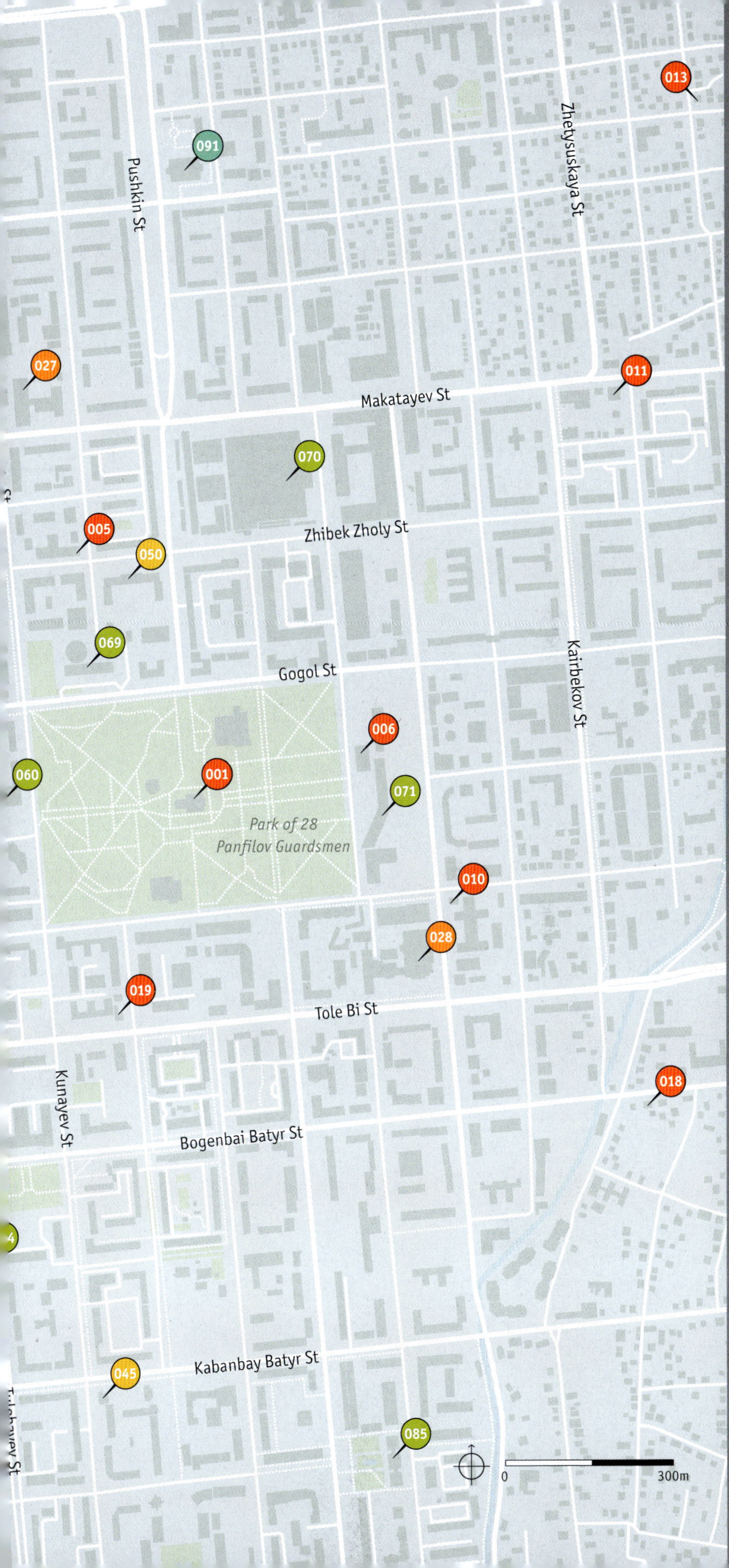

013

Zhetysuskaya St

Pushkin St

091

027

011

Makatayev St

070

Zhibek Zholy St

005

050

069

Gogol St

Kairbekov St

006

060

001

071

Park of 28
Panfilov Guardsmen

010

028

019

Tole Bi St

018

Kunayev St

Bogenbai Batyr St

4

045

Kabanbay Batyr St

085

0   300m

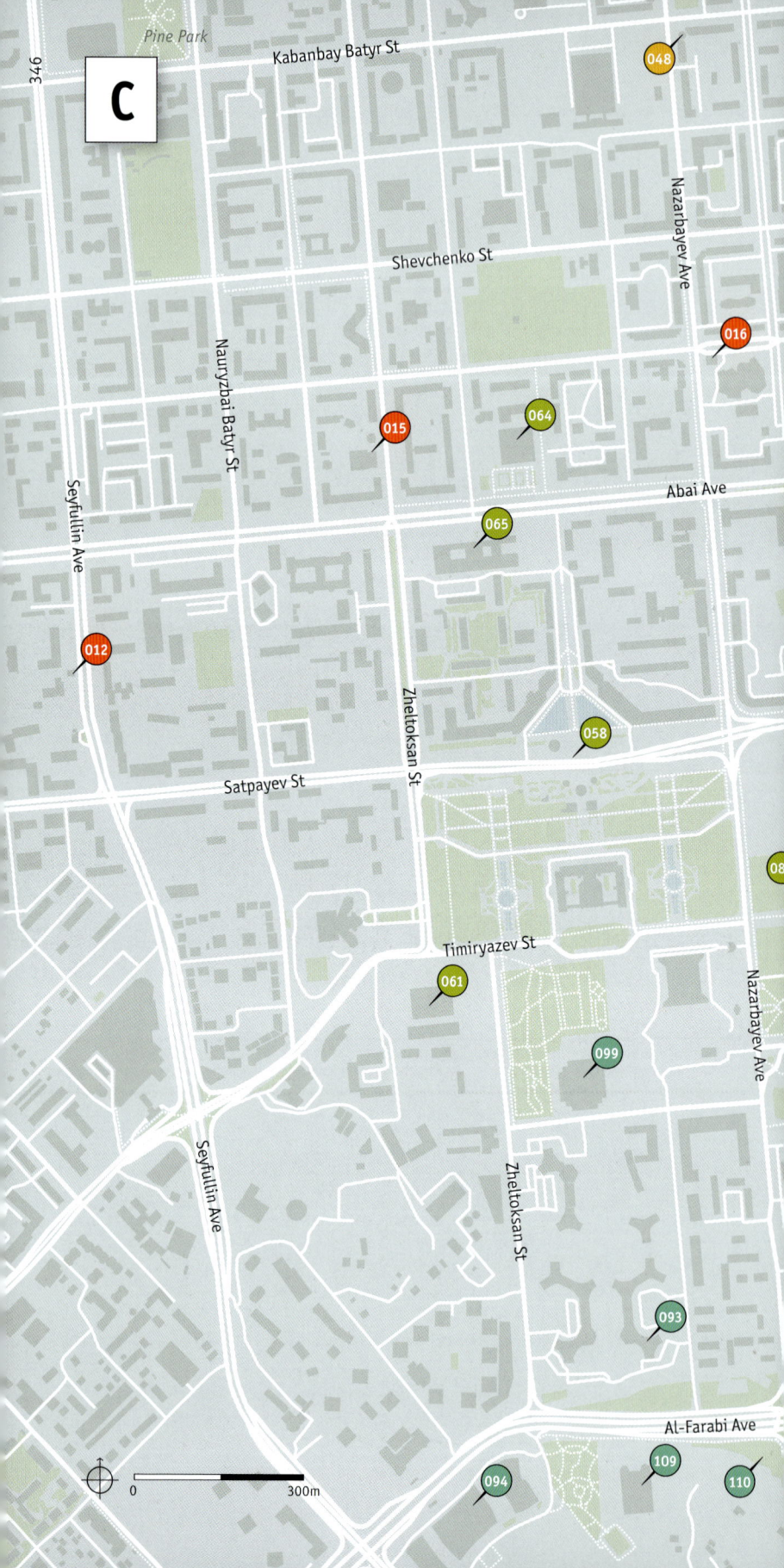

C

Pine Park

Kabanbay Batyr St

Shevchenko St

Nazarbayev Ave

048

016

Nauryzbai Batyr St

015

064

Abai Ave

Seyfullin Ave

065

012

Zheltoksan St

058

Satpayev St

08

Timiryazev St

061

099

Seyfullin Ave

Zheltoksan St

Nazarbayev Ave

093

Al-Farabi Ave

109

094

110

0   300m

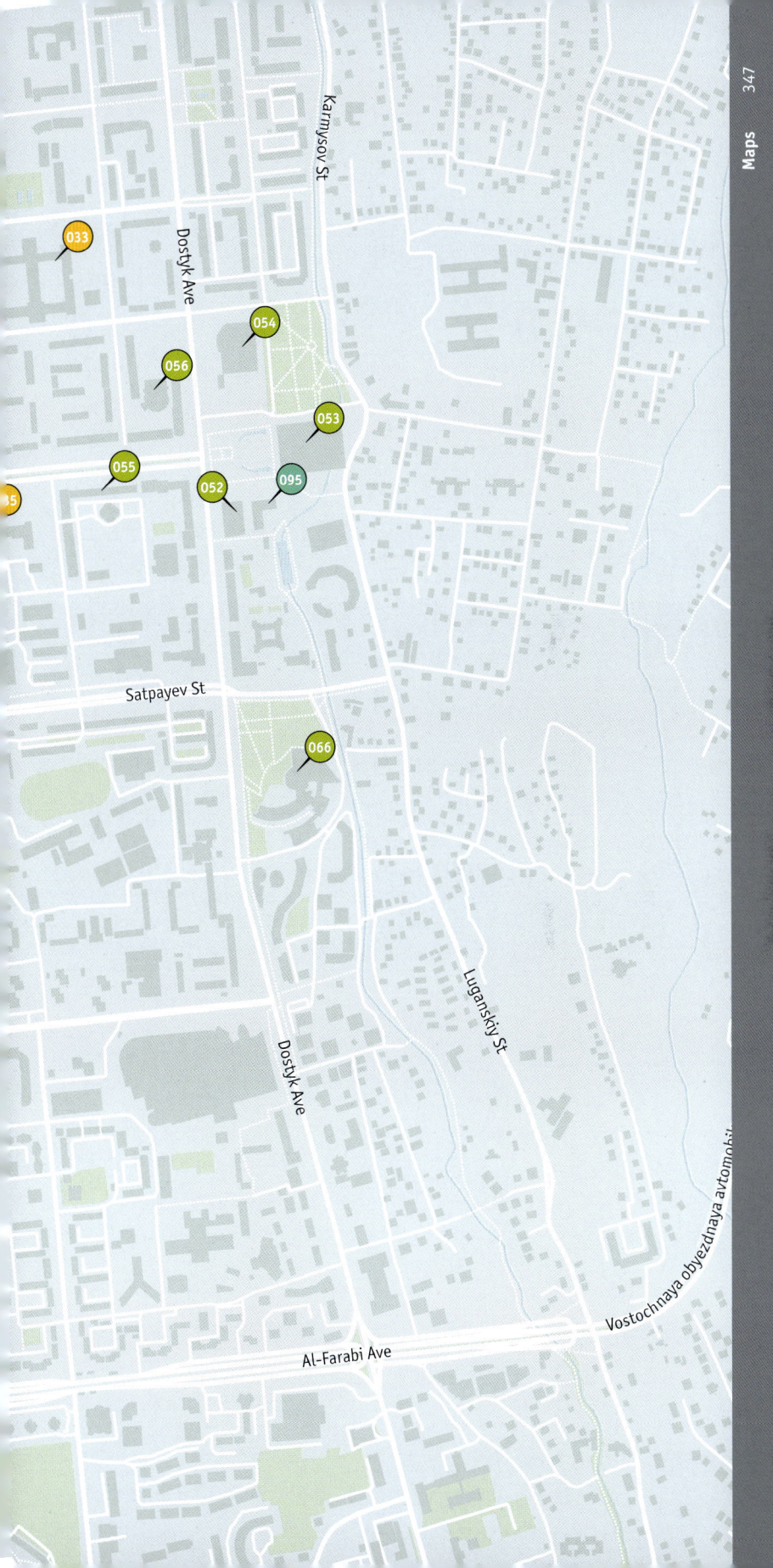

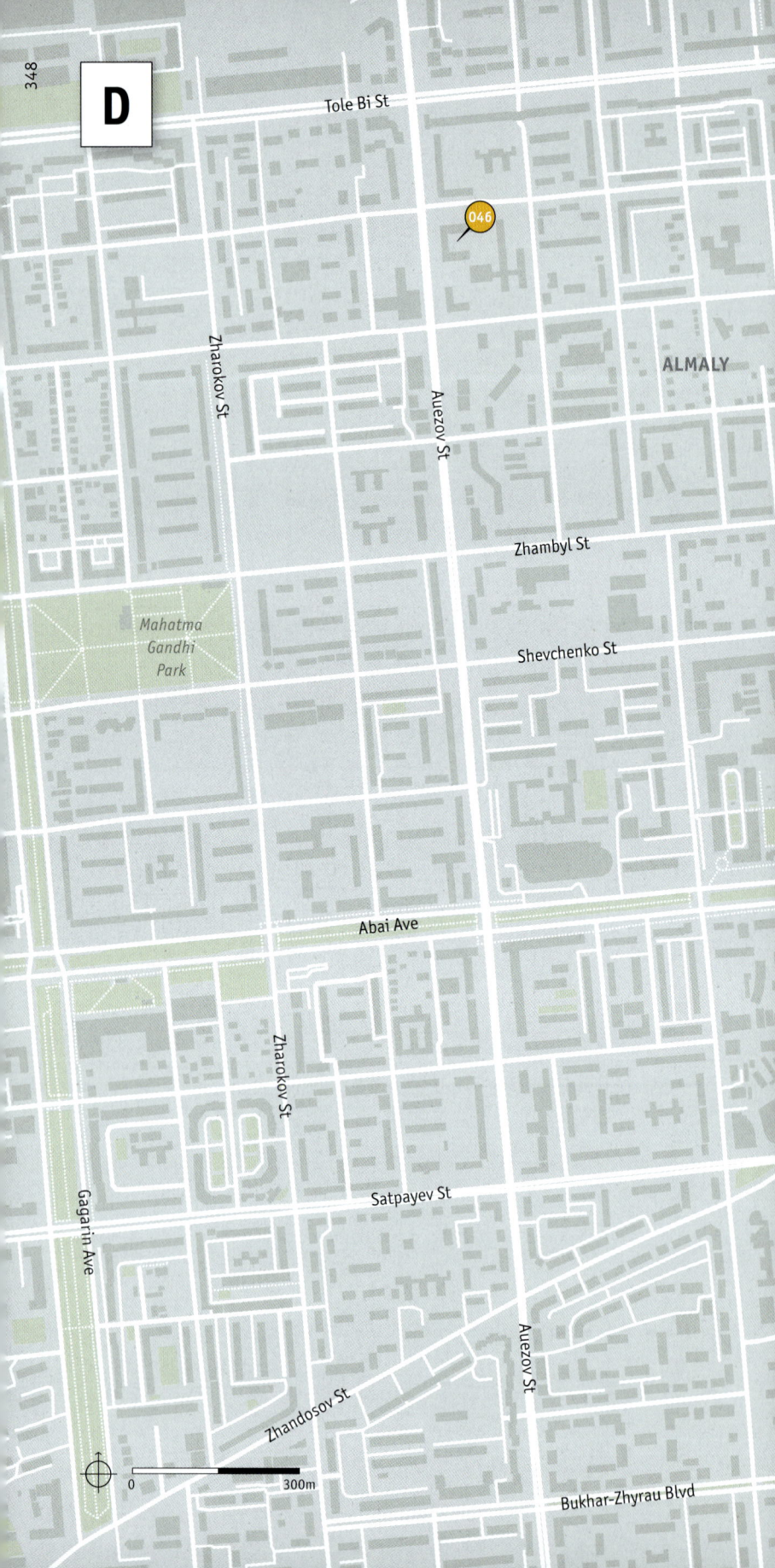

D

Tole Bi St

046

ALMALY

Zharokov St

Auezov St

Zhambyl St

Mahatma
Gandhi
Park

Shevchenko St

Abai Ave

Zharokov St

Satpayev St

Gagarin Ave

Auezov St

Zhandosov St

0   300m

Bukhar-Zhyrau Blvd

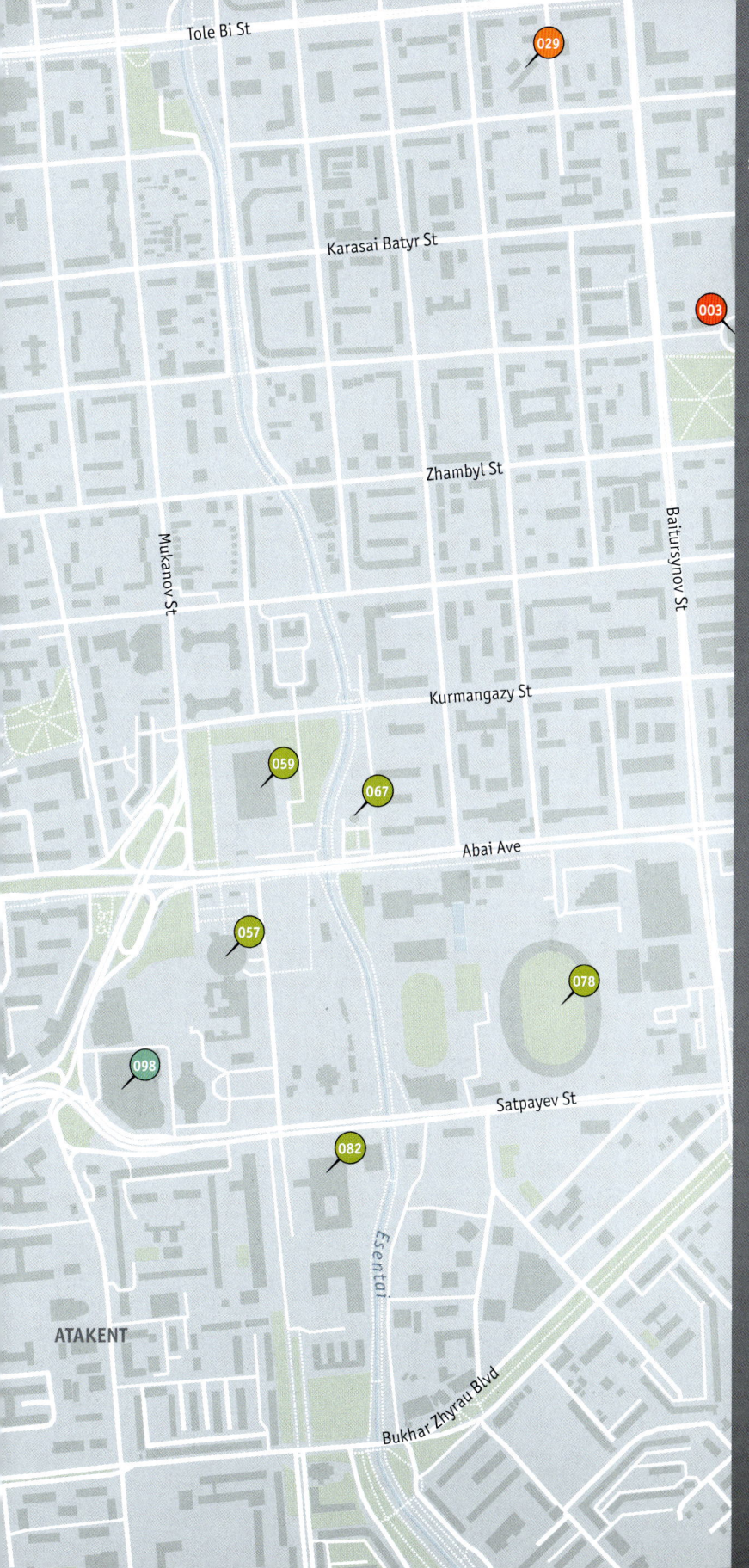

Tole Bi St

029

Karasai Batyr St

003

Zhambyl St

Mukanov St

Baitursynov St

Kurmangazy St

059

067

Abai Ave

057

078

098

Satpayev St

082

Esentai

ATAKENT

Bukhar Zhyrau Blvd

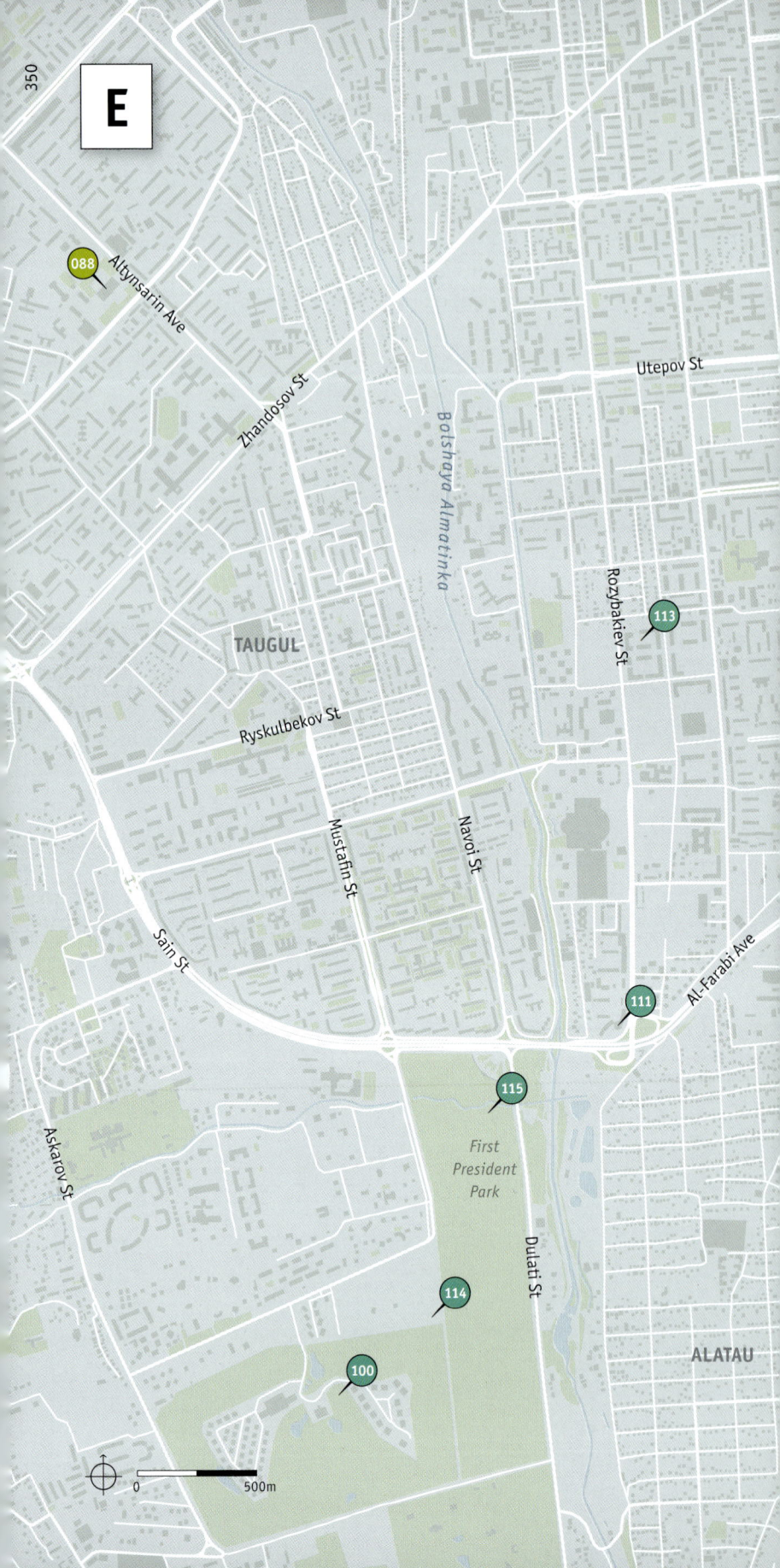

E

088 Altynsarin Ave

Zhandosov St

Utepov St

Bołshaya Almatinka

Rozybakiev St

113

TAUGUL

Ryskulbekov St

Mustafin St

Navoi St

Sain St

111

Al-Farabi Ave

115

First President Park

Askarov St

Dulati St

114

ALATAU

100

0   500m

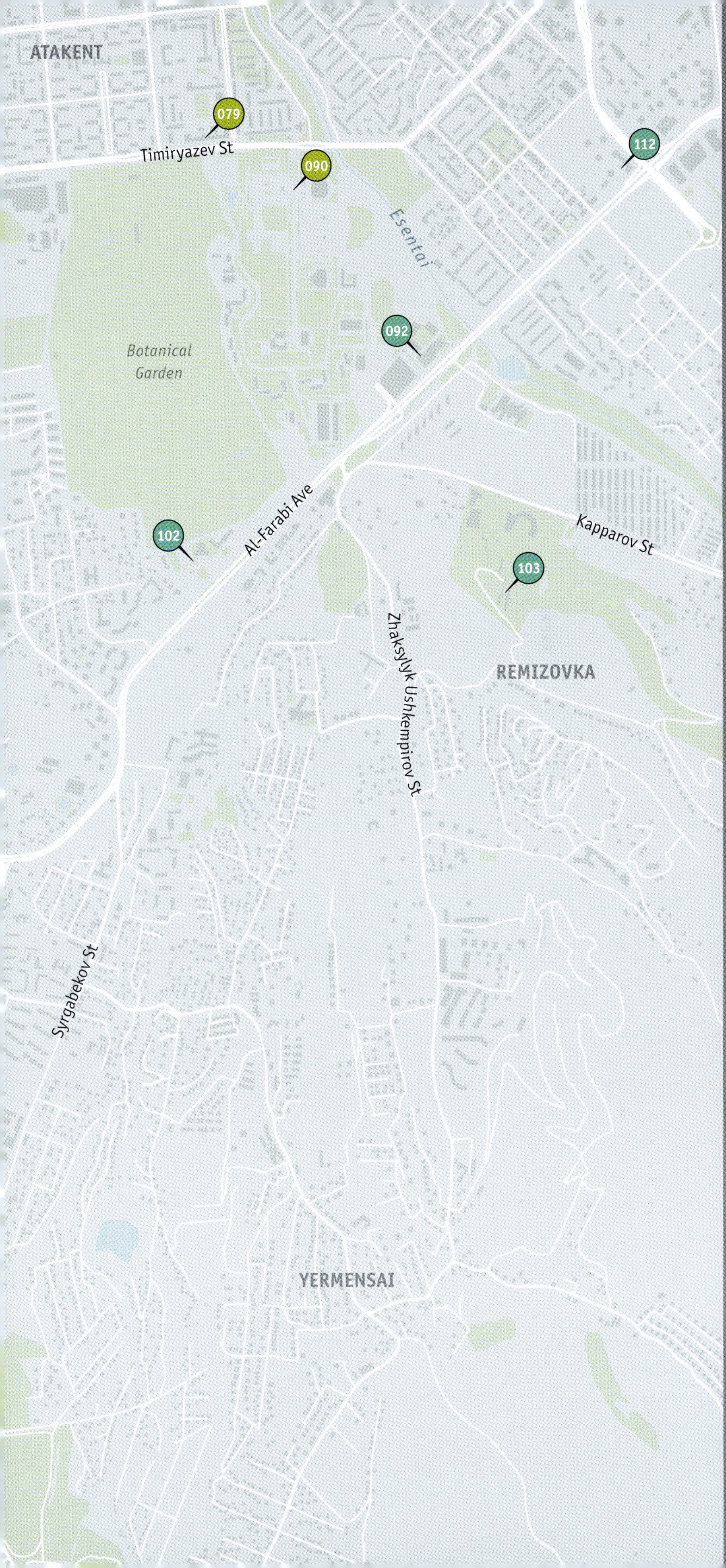

ATAKENT

079

Timiryazev St

090

Esentai

092

Botanical
Garden

112

Al-Farabi Ave

102

Kapparov St

103

Zhaksylyk Ushkempirov St

REMIZOVKA

Syrgabekov St

YERMENSAI

Index of Architects and Artists

By building number

Index of Buildings and Projects

By project number

Bibliography

Books

Airikh, Y.E. et al., *Arkhitektura i stroitel-stvo Almaty* (Redaktsiya Zolotaya Kniga, 2007).

Bronovitskaya, A., Malinin, N., Palmin, Y., *Alma-Ata: Arkhitektura sovietskovo modernizma 1955–1991 (*Garage, 2018).

Duysenov, Y. D., *Alma-Ata* (Izdatelstvo Kazakhstan, 1968).

Glaudinov, B. A., Seydalin, M. G., Kapanov, A. K., Baimagambetov, S. K., *Almaty: Architecture and urban development* (Didar Publishing, 1998).

Karpikov, A. S., *Architecture of Soviet Kazakhstan* (Stroyizdat, 1987).

Kun, A. L., *Turkestanskiy albom po rasporyazhenyu turkestanskogo general gubernatora general adyutanta K. P. von Kaufmana 1-go, 1871–1872.*

Matveyeva, L. A., *Monuments of history and culture of Almaty* (2008).

Mendikulov, M.M, *Arkhitektura goroda Alma-Aty* (Izdateltstvo Akademii nauk Kazakhskoy SSR, 1953).

Meuser, P., *Architekturführer Kazakhstan* (DOM publishers, 2014).

Samoilov, K. I., *Architecture of Kazakhstan of the 20th century* (2004).

Tuyakbayeva, B.T., *Almaty: Drevniy srednyevekovyy kolonyalnyy sovietskiy. Etapy urbanizatsiy* (Izdatelstvo World Discovery, NPTs Istoriko-kulturnnogo naslediya, 2008).

Internet sources

https://archcode.kz/
http://www.monumentalalmaty.com/
https://starinariy.kz
http://theconstructivistproject.com/ru/tag/20/almaty
https://vernoye-almaty.kz

www.instagram.com/
zveryagina_almaty/
almaty.memories/
gorod_verniy/
almaty.tourstudio/

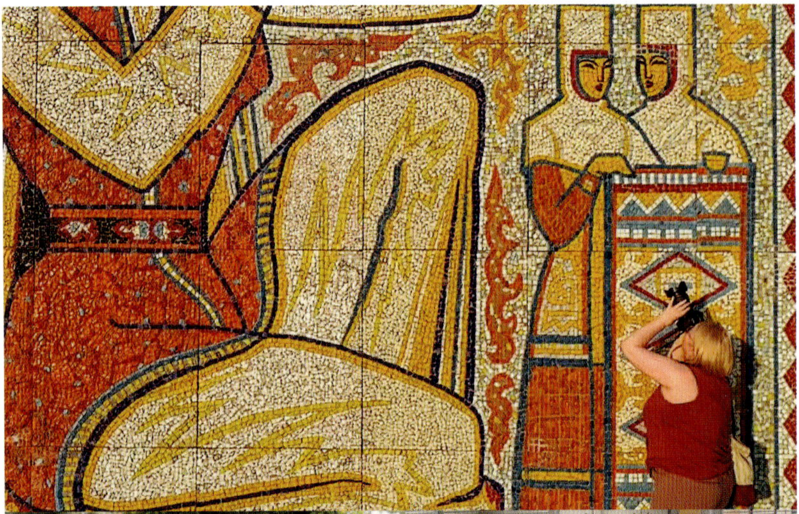

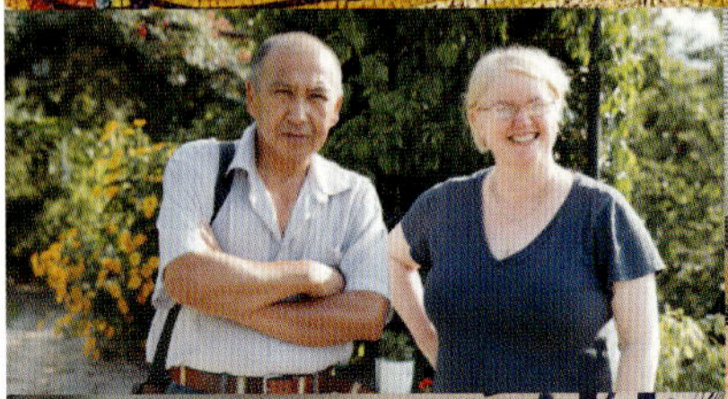

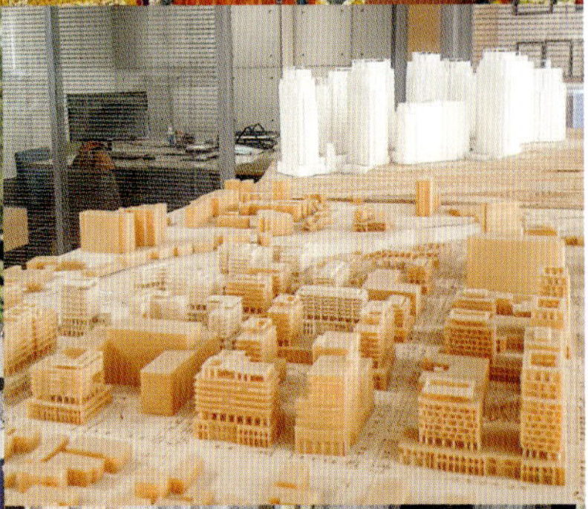

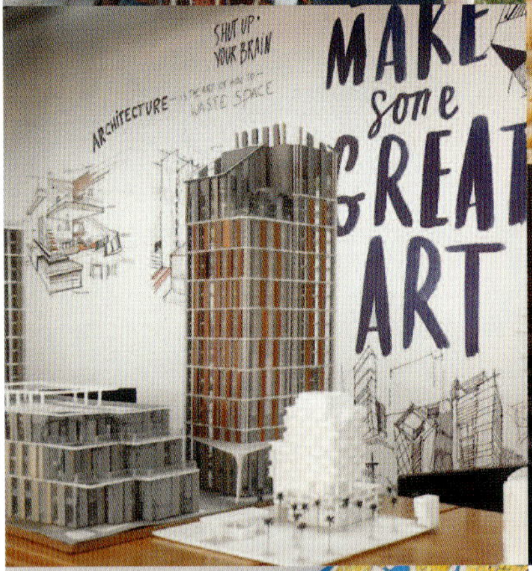

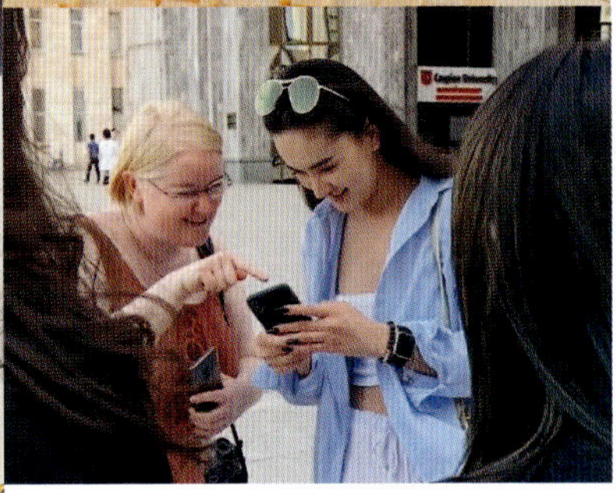

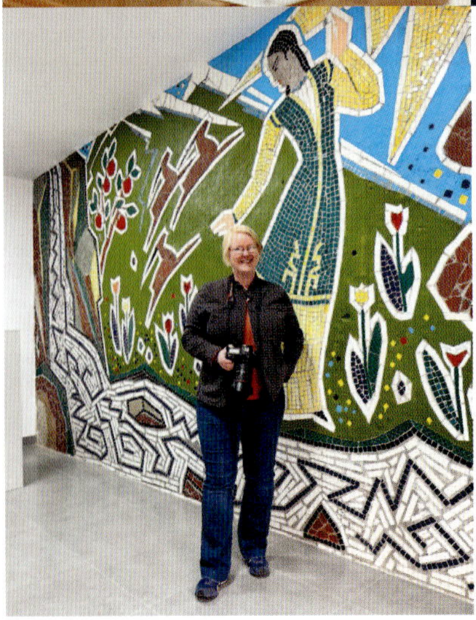

Acknowledgements

The book has been supported by Malene Hein, Monika Hollacher, Maya Kristin Schönfelder, Philipp Meuser, and Franz Müller and funded by a grant from VG Wort. Many thanks to everyone else who was involved in this project, especially to my family and friends who held my hand during the entire process of making the book.

Authors

Edda Schlager (1972)

Journalist and photographer. Lived in Almaty from 2005 to 2023, reporting on Central Asia for German and international newspapers, magazines, radio, and TV stations. Has a MA in geography. Author of *Architekturführer Duschanbe*, published (in German) by DOM publishers in 2017.

Gulnara Abdrasilova

Gulnara Abdrasilova (1958)

Doctor of architecture, professor, researcher. Member of the Union of Architects and of the Union of Town Planners of Kazakhstan. Works at the Kazakh Academy of Architecture and Construction (KasGASA) in Almaty. Author of monographs and articles published in international academic journals on the subject of teaching methods of architecture, as well as on problems of regionalism in modern architecture in Kazakhstan.

Khalima Truspekova (1953)

Doctor of art history, an associate professor at Kazakh National Zhurgenov Academy of Arts, and a senior researcher at Auezov Institute of Literature and Art in Almaty. Member of the International Association of Art Critics (AICA). Until 2013 taught at the Kazakh Academy of Architecture and Construction (KazGASA). Author of numerous monographs and articles in scientific publications in Kazakhstan and abroad.

Svetlana Romashkina (1980)

Journalist. Editor-in-chief of *voxpopuli.kz* from 2012 to 2014 and of the online magazine *vlast.kz* since 2018. Founded the architecture and urbanism sections of both these media. Has conducted courses for architects on writing to improve coverage of architecture and urbanism. Takes a keen interest in the architectural history of Almaty. Co-author of the book *Excuse me, Fuck Off* and author of a forthcoming book on Almaty's Tselinny Cinema.

The *Deutsche Nationalbibliothek* lists this publication in the *Deutsche Nationalbibliografie*; detailed bibliographic data are available online at http://dnb.d-nb.de.

ISBN 978-3-86922-727-6

2025 by DOM publishers, Berlin
www.dom-publishers.com

Photo credits
Pictures without listed credits have been provided by Edda Schlager or are from her archives.

Proofreading
John Nicolson

Graphic design
Edda Schlager

Maps
Ariel Chen

Printing
Tiger Printing (Hong Kong) Co., Ltd.
www.tigerprinting.hk